NOT FOR TOURISTS
ILLUSTRATED GUIDE TO

NEW YORK CITY

GET MORE ON
WWW.NOTFORTOURISTS.COM

STAY CONNECTED WITH:

TWITTER: @NOTFORTOURISTS
FACEBOOK: NOTFORTOURISTS
IPHONE APPS: AVAILABLE ON ITUNES

NOT FOR TOURISTS, INC.

SKYHORSE PUBLISHING

DESIGNED BY:

NOT FOR TOURISTS, INC
NFT™ NOT FOR TOURISTS™ GUIDE TO NEW YORK CITY
WWW.NOTFORTOURISTS.COM

PUBLISHER

SKYHORSE PUBLISHING

CREATIVE DIRECTION & INFORMATION DESIGN

JANE PIRONE

DIRECTOR

STUART FARR

MANAGING EDITORS

CRAIG NELSON
SCOTT SENDROW
ROB TALLIA

GRAPHIC DESIGN & PRODUCTION MANAGER

JOHN BERGDAHL

ILLUSTRATORS

LUISITO NAZARIO
ELLEN LINDNER

INFORMATION SYSTEMS MANAGER

JUAN MOLINARI

PRINTED IN CHINA

PRINT ISBN: 978-1-63450-086-9 $12.99

EBOOK ISBN: 978-1-63450-087-6

ISSN 2376-5682

COPYRIGHT ©2015 BY NOT FOR TOURISTS, INC.

1ST EDITION

EVERY EFFORT HAS BEEN MADE TO ENSURE THAT THE INFORMATION IN THIS BOOK IS AS UP-TO-DATE AS POSSIBLE AT PRESS TIME. HOWEVER, MANY DETAILS ARE LIABLE TO CHANGE—AS WE HAVE LEARNED. NOT FOR TOURISTS CANNOT ACCEPT RESPONSIBILITY FOR ANY CONSEQUENCES ARISING FROM THE USE OF THIS BOOK.

NOT FOR TOURISTS DOES NOT SOLICIT INDIVIDUALS, ORGANIZATIONS, OR BUSINESSES FOR LISTINGS INCLUSION IN OUR GUIDES, NOR DO WE ACCEPT PAYMENT FOR INCLUSION INTO THE EDITORIAL PORTION OF OUR BOOK; THE ADVERTISING SECTIONS, HOWEVER, ARE EXEMPT FROM THIS POLICY. WE ALWAYS WELCOME COMMUNICATIONS FROM ANYONE REGARDING ANYTHING HAVING TO DO WITH OUR BOOKS; PLEASE VISIT US ON OUR WEBSITE AT WWW.NOTFORTOURISTS.COM FOR APPROPRIATE CONTACT INFORMATION.

SKYHORSE PUBLISHING BOOKS MAY BE PURCHASED IN BULK AT SPECIAL DISCOUNTS FOR SALES PROMOTION, CORPORATE GIFTS, FUND-RAISING, OR EDUCATIONAL PURPOSES. SPECIAL EDITIONS CAN ALSO BE CREATED TO SPECIFICATIONS. FOR DETAILS, CONTACT THE SPECIAL SALES DEPARTMENT, SKYHORSE PUBLISHING, 307 WEST 36TH STREET, 11TH FLOOR, NEW YORK, NY 10018 OR INFO@SKYHORSEPUBLISHING.COM.

VISIT OUR WEBSITE AT WWW.SKYHORSEPUBLISHING.COM.

10 9 8 7 6 5 4 3 2 1

"ONE BELONGS TO NEW YORK INSTANTLY, ONE BELONGS TO IT AS MUCH IN FIVE MINUTES AS IN FIVE YEARS." - TOM WOLFE

DEAR NFT USER:

ONCE UPON A TIME, WAY BACK IN THE YEAR 2000, WE RELEASED OUR VERY FIRST BOOK, THE NFT GUIDE TO MANHATTAN. TODAY THAT LITTLE BLACK BOOK HAS BECOME ONE OF THE MOST RELIED UPON RESOURCES FOR NAVIGATING NEW YORK CITY. THE FACT THAT SO MANY NEW-COMERS AND LONGTIMERS OVER THE YEARS HAVE POUNDED THE PAVEMENT WITH NFT STUCK IN THEIR BACK POCKETS IS A GREAT SOURCE OF PRIDE FOR US. PLUS, YOU CAN STILL FIND IT IN ALL OVER TOWN IN OUR FAVORITE BOOKSTORES (OR AT LEAST WHAT'S LEFT OF THEM). AND NOW WE ARE READY TO ADD A NEW PRODUCT TO THE SHELF AND OPEN A NEW CHAPTER IN THE HISTORY OF NFT.

THIS BRAND NEW GUIDE YOU'RE HOLDING IS BOLDLY REDESIGNED WHERE NO NFT HAS GONE BEFORE, OFFERING A QUICK SNAPSHOT OF EACH NEIGHBORHOOD FROM THE LOWER EAST SIDE AND GREENWICH VILLAGE TO HARLEM AND INWOOD IN A COLORFUL AND STYLISH LAYOUT. START FLIPPING THROUGH, AND YOU'LL IMMEDIATELY NOTICE SOMETHING VERY DIFFERENT FROM NFT CLASSIC. SAY HELLO TO BEAUTIFUL CITY PHOTOS AND ORIGINAL ILLUSTRATIONS THAT HAVE BEEN HANDCRAFTED IN THE SAME TRADITION OF THE FINEST HOUSE-CURED MEATS IN BROOKLYN OR THE CHEWIEST COALFIRED PIZZA CRUST IN MANHATTAN.

BECAUSE REMEMBER, THIS ILLUSTRATED GUIDE IS, AT ITS CORE, AN ARTISANAL PRODUCT. WITH NFT, THE BLURBS YOU GET ARE ALL HOUSE MADE, NEVER PROCESSED, ESPECIALLY VIA SOME FACELESS ALGORITHM—BECAUSE, LET'S FACE IT, OUR SERVERS COULD NEVER HANDLE IT ANY-WAY. LIKE THAT ROOMY BOUTIQUE ON THAT SKETCHY BLOCK DOWN BY THE WATERFRONT, NFT IS CAREFULLY CURATED TO OFFER YOU THE BEST OF WHAT A NEIGHBORHOOD HAS TO OFFER.

HAVE SOME FEEDBACK? PLEASE, DON'T BE SHY, BECAUSE WE CERTAINLY ARE NOT. PLEASE SEND US A NOTE AT WWW.NOTFORTOURISTS.COM OR ON TWITTER @NOTFORTOURISTS, BE-CAUSE IN THE END, NFT IS A FAMILY, AND WE WOULDN'T BE WHO WE ARE WITHOUT YOU. SO IF YOU'RE NEW TO US AND THE CITY, WELCOME! AND IF YOU'VE BEEN WITH NFT FOR THE LONG HAUL, THANKS FOR PICKING UP OUR NEWEST ADVENTURE IN CITY GUIDES.

CHEERS,

JANE, ROB, SCOTT, CRAIG, ET AL.

TABLE OF CONTENTS

NEIGHBORHOODS

PARKS & PLACES

TRANSIT

SPORTS

GENERAL INFORMATION

ARTS & ENTERTAINMENT

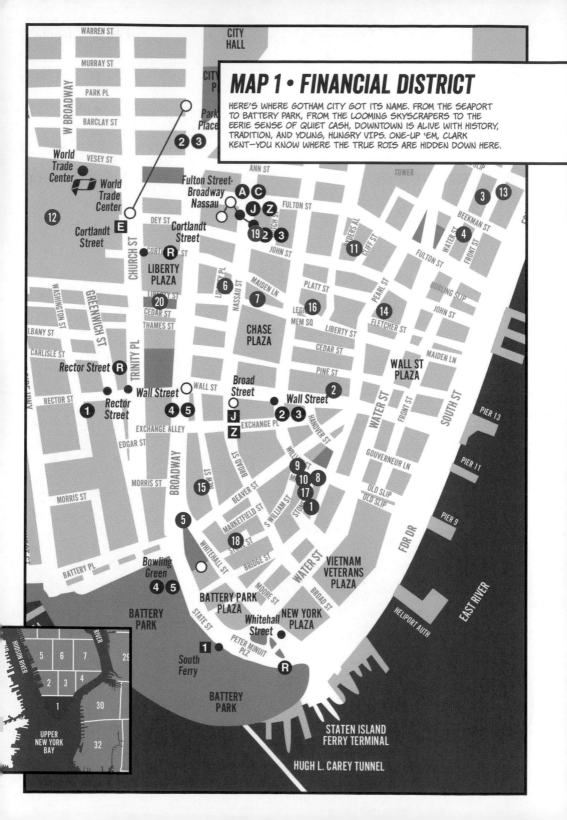

MAP 1 • FINANCIAL DISTRICT

HERE'S WHERE GOTHAM CITY GOT ITS NAME. FROM THE SEAPORT TO BATTERY PARK, FROM THE LOOMING SKYSCRAPERS TO THE EERIE SENSE OF QUIET CASH, DOWNTOWN IS ALIVE WITH HISTORY, TRADITION, AND YOUNG, HUNGRY VIPS. ONE-UP 'EM, CLARK KENT—YOU KNOW WHERE THE TRUE ROIS ARE HIDDEN DOWN HERE.

1 ADRIENNE'S PIZZA BAR
54 STONE STREET
DELECTABLE RECTANGULAR PIES FROM A NYC PIZZA MASTER.

2 AMERICAN INTERNATIONAL BUILDING
70 PINE STREET
GREAT ART DECO SKYSCRAPER.

3 BIN 220
220 FRONT STREET
ESCAPE THE TOURISTS AT THIS EXCELLENT LITTLE WINE BAR.

4 BOWNE & CO STATIONERS
211 WATER STREET
OLD FASHIONED PRESSES MAKE PRINTS, MAPS & CARDS.

5 CHARGING BULL
BOWLING GREEN PARK
RUB HIS COJONES FOR LUCK.

6 DOWNTOWN CELLARS
55 LIBERTY STREET
FANTASTIC EVERYTHING—SMALL LABEL WINES, CHAMPAGNES, AND SPIRITS.

7 FEDERAL RESERVE BANK OF NEW YORK
33 LIBERTY STREET.
WHERE "DIE HARD 3" TOOK PLACE.

8 FINANCIER PATISSERIE
62 STONE STREET
HAVE YOUR CAKE AND A LIGHT MEAL, TOO.

9 HARRY'S CAFE & STEAK
1 HANOVER SQUARE
THE VINTAGE FRENCH WINE FLOWS LIKE A RIVER. OR AT LEAST IT USED TO.

10 INDIA HOUSE CLUB
1 HANOVER SQUARE
SECRET BAR TO THE LEFT UP THE STAIRS. YOU'RE WELCOME.

11 JUBILEE MARKETPLACE
99 JOHN STREET
GODSEND FOR FINANCIAL DISTRICT DWELLERS.

12 NATIONAL SEPTEMBER 11 MEMORIAL & MUSEUM
GREENWICH STREET
AWE-INSPIRING TRIBUTE TO THOSE LOST, SURROUNDED BY REBIRTH.

13 NELSON BLUE
233 FRONT STREET
NEW ZEALAND LOLLICHOP LOLLICHOP, WHOAH LOLLICHOP...

14 PEARL STREET DINER
212 PEARL STREET
GREASY SPOON HIDDEN AMONG THE SKYSCRAPERS.

15 SOPHIE'S CUBAN
73 NEW STREET
GREAT CHEAP CUBAN/CARIBBEAN.

16 TOLOACHE
83 MAIDEN LANE
UPSCALE MEXICAN AND A GIGANTIC TEQUILA SELECTION.

17 ULYSSES FOLK HOUSE
95 PEARL STREET
SLIGHTLY HIPPER DOWNTOWN BAR.

18 WHITEHORSE TAVERN
25 BRIDGE STREET
DOWNTOWN DIVE. NOT TO BE CONFUSED WITH THE ONE IN THE WEST VILLAGE.

19 ZAITZEFF
72 NASSAU STREET
QUICK AND ORGANIC BURGERS FOR LUNCH.

20 ZUCCOTTI PARK
TRINITY PLACE & CEDAR STREET
BIRTHPLACE OF OCCUPY WALL STREET, CA. 2011.

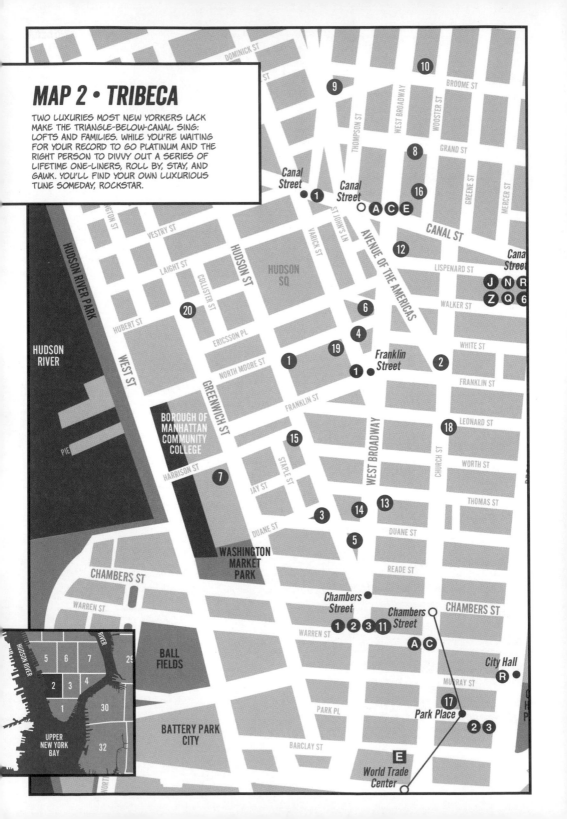

MAP 2 · TRIBECA

TWO LUXURIES MOST NEW YORKERS LACK
MAKE THE TRIANGLE-BELOW-CANAL SING:
LOFTS AND FAMILIES. WHILE YOU'RE WAITING
FOR YOUR RECORD TO GO PLATINUM AND THE
RIGHT PERSON TO DIVVY OUT A SERIES OF
LIFETIME ONE-LINERS, ROLL BY, STAY, AND
GAWK. YOU'LL FIND YOUR OWN LUXURIOUS
TUNE SOMEDAY, ROCKSTAR.

1 BUBBY'S
120 HUDSON STREET
GREAT ATMOSPHERE – GOOD HOME-STYLE EATS AND
HOMEMADE PIES.

2 DREAM HOUSE

275 CHURCH STREET
COOL SOUND + LIGHT INSTALLATION BY LA MONTE
YOUNG AND MARIAN ZAZEELA. CLOSED DURING
SUMMER.

3 DUANE PARK
DUANE STREET & HUDSON STREET
ONE OF THE NICEST SPOTS IN ALL OF NEW YORK.

4 GHOSTBUSTERS FIREHOUSE
14 NORTH MOORE STREET
ARE YOU THE GATEKEEPER?

5 GOTHAM BIKES
112 WEST BROADWAY
SUPER HELPFUL STAFF, GOOD STUFF.

6 GRANDAISY BAKERY

250 WEST BROADWAY
BREAD AND PIZZAS BY THE ONE AND ONLY.

7 HARRISON STREET ROW HOUSES
HARRISON STREET & GREENWICH STREET
UNIQUE COLLECTION OF PRESERVED FEDERALIST
ARCHITECTURE.

8 LUCKY STRIKE
59 GRAND STREET
HIPSTERS, LOCALS, EX-SMOKY. RECOMMENDED.

9 LUPE'S EAST LA KITCHEN

110 SIXTH AVENUE
TEX-MEX. QUAINT. EAT HERE.

**10 MARIEBELLE'S FINE TREATS &
CHOCOLATES**
484 BROOME STREET
TOP NYC CHOCOLATIER. KILLER HOT CHOCOLATE.

11 THE MYSTERIOUS BOOKSHOP
58 WARREN STREET
CHANNELING YOUR INNER AGATHA.

12 NANCY WHISKEY PUB
1 LISPENARD STREET
GOOD DIVE. AS IF THERE WERE ANY OTHER KIND.

13 THE ODEON
145 WEST BROADWAY
WE CAN'T AGREE ABOUT THIS ONE, SO GO AND MAKE
YOUR OWN DECISION.

14 PETITE ABEILLE
134 WEST BROADWAY
BELGIAN WAFFLE CHAIN, GREAT BEER SELECTION.
TRY THE STOEMP.

15 PUFFY'S TAVERN

81 HUDSON STREET
SUITS, OLD TIMERS, AND HIPSTERS. TOP TRIBECA
WATERING HOLE.

16 SOHO ART MATERIALS
7 WOOSTER STREET
A PAINTER'S CANDY STORE.

17 TENT & TRAILS
21 PARK PLACE
TOP OUTFITTER FOR GEARHEADS.

18 TEXTILE BUILDING
66 LEONARD STREET
HENRY J HARDENBERGH GOODNESS IN TRIBECA.

19 WALKER'S

16 NORTH MOORE STREET
SURPRISINGLY GOOD FOOD FOR A PUB!

20 'WICHCRAFT
397 GREENWICH STREET
SANDWICHES, SOUPS, AND SWEETS FROM ONE OF
THOSE TV CHEFS.

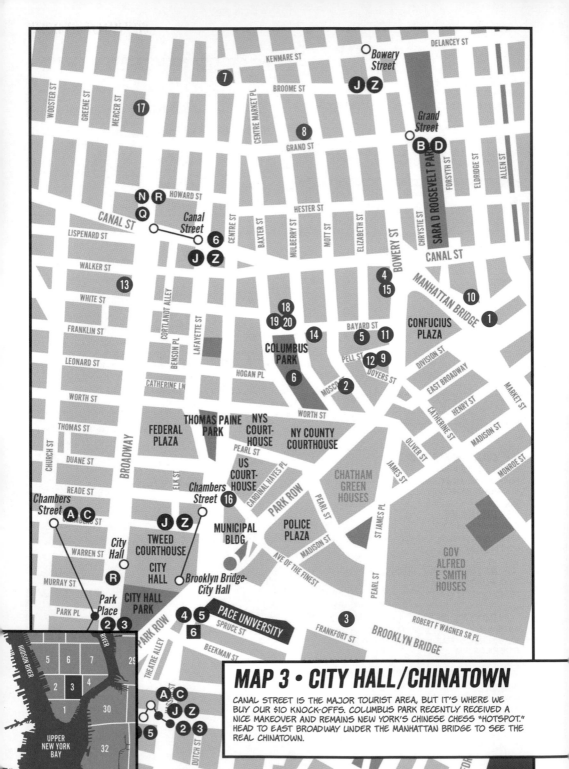

MAP 3 · CITY HALL/CHINATOWN

CANAL STREET IS THE MAJOR TOURIST AREA, BUT IT'S WHERE WE BUY OUR $10 KNOCK-OFFS. COLUMBUS PARK RECENTLY RECEIVED A NICE MAKEOVER AND REMAINS NEW YORK'S CHINESE CHESS "HOTSPOT." HEAD TO EAST BROADWAY UNDER THE MANHATTAN BRIDGE TO SEE THE REAL CHINATOWN.

1 **88 PALACE**
88 EAST BROADWAY
DIM SUM MADNESS UNDER THE MANHATTAN BRIDGE.

2 **APOTHEKE**
9 DOYERS STREET
FLAMING EXPENSIVE EURO-COCKTAILS IN A
(SUPPOSEDLY) FORMER OPIUM DEN.

3 **BROOKLYN BRIDGE**
ENTRANCE ON CENTRE STREET & PARK ROW
THE GRANDDADDY OF THEM ALL. WALKING TOWARDS
MANHATTAN AT SUNSET IS AS GOOD AS IT GETS.

4 **CHINATOWN ARCADE**
48 BOWERY
BIZARRE INDOOR MALL/PASSAGEWAY. CHECK IT OUT.

5 **CHINATOWN ICE CREAM FACTORY**
65 BAYARD STREET
THE BEST ICE CREAM (GINGER, BLACK SESAME,
MANGO, RED BEAN, ET AL.), EVER.

6 **COLUMBUS PARK**
67 MULBERRY STREET
FORMER FIVE POINTS HUB NOW OPERATES AS PRIME
CHINATOWN HANGOUT.

7 **DESPANA**
408 BROOME STREET
EXCELLENT SPANISH TAKE-OUT/GOURMET GROCERY,
COMPLETE W/ BULL.

8 **DI PALO FINE FOODS**
200 GRAND STREET
DELICACIES FROM ACROSS ITALY. EXCELLENT CHEESE.

9 **DOYERS STREET**
ENTRANCES ON PELL AND BOWERY
RARE CURVY STREET IN MANHATTAN. HAS A DECIDEDLY
OTHERWORLDLY FEEL.

10 **FORSYTH OUTDOOR PRODUCE MARKET**
FORSYTH STREET & DIVISION STREET
CHEAPEST VEGGIES AND FRUIT IN MANHATTAN. LONG
LINES.

11 **GREAT NY NOODLETOWN**
28 BOWERY
CHEAP CHINESE SOUPS AND BBQ AND DEEP-FRIED
SQUID. AT 2 AM.

12 **JOE'S SHANGHAI**
9 PELL STREET
CRAB SOUP DUMPLING MECCA. WORTH THE WAIT.

13 **K & M CAMERA**
385 BROADWAY
GOOD ALL-AROUND CAMERA STORE; OPEN SATURDAYS!

14 **NEW BEEF KING**
89 BAYARD STREET
SERIOUS JERKY FOR SERIOUS JERKS.

15 **NEW MALAYSIA**
46 BOWERY
A HIDDEN GEM THAT'S LITERALLY HIDDEN. TRY THE
SPECIALS.

16 **NEW YORK CITY STORE**
1 CENTRE STREET
GREAT NYC BOOKS AND SCHWAG YOU CAN'T GET
ANYWHERE ELSE.

17 **PEARL RIVER MART**
477 BROADWAY
CHINESE HOUSEWARES AND MORE. ALMOST
MIND-NUMBING.

18 **PHO VIET HUONG**
73 MULBERRY STREET
VERY GOOD VIETNAMESE—GET THE SALT AND PEPPER
SQUID.

19 **PONGSRI THAI**
106 BAYARD STREET
EVER WONDER WHERE DISTRICT ATTORNEYS GO FOR
CHEAP, TASTY THAI?

20 **WINNIE'S**
104 BAYARD STREET
CHINESE GANGSTER KARAOKE. WE KID YOU NOT.

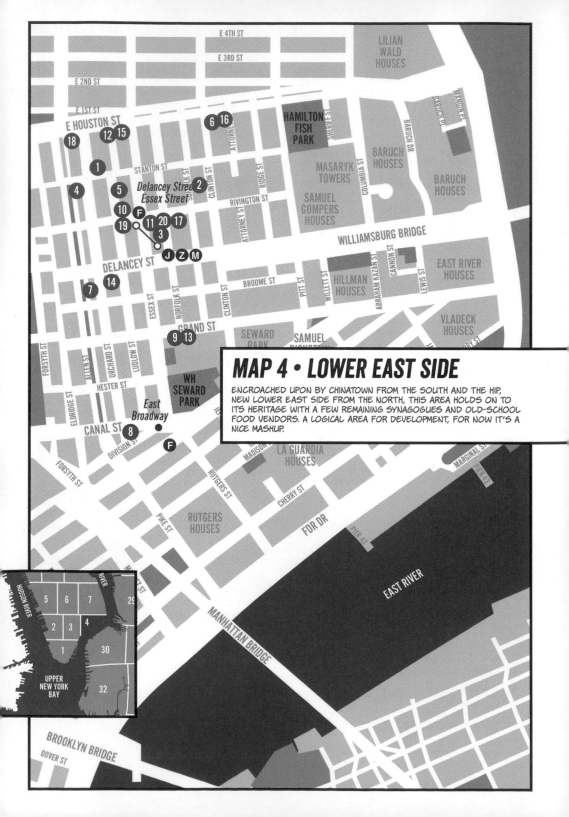

MAP 4 • LOWER EAST SIDE

ENCROACHED UPON BY CHINATOWN FROM THE SOUTH AND THE HIP, NEW LOWER EAST SIDE FROM THE NORTH, THIS AREA HOLDS ON TO ITS HERITAGE WITH A FEW REMAINING SYNAGOGUES AND OLD-SCHOOL FOOD VENDORS. A LOGICAL AREA FOR DEVELOPMENT, FOR NOW IT'S A NICE MASHUP.

1 ANGEL ORENSANZ FOUNDATION FOR THE ARTS
172 NORFOLK STREET
PERFORMANCE SPACE IN EX-SYNAGOGUE. AMAZING.

2 BARRAMUNDI
67 CLINTON STREET
GOOD COCKTAILS IN A LOW-KEY SETTING.

3 BLUE CONDO
105 NORFOLK STREET
BERNARD TSCHUMI'S ODD MASTERPIECE.

4 BLUESTOCKINGS
172 ALLEN STREET
EXCELLENT POLITICAL/LEFT WING BOOKSHOP.

5 CAKE SHOP
152 LUDLOW STREET
COFFEE, RECORDS, BEER, ROCK SHOWS, AND A "MOST RADICAL JUKEBOX."

6 CLINTON STREET BAKING CO.
4 CLINTON STREET
HOMEMADE BUTTERMILK EVERYTHING. LES LAID BACK. TOP 5 BACON.

7 CONGEE VILLAGE
100 ALLEN STREET
PORRIDGE NEVER TASTED SO GOOD.

8 DAH BIKE SHOP
134 DIVISION STREET
BMX EXPERTS. TOTALLY RAD!

9 DOUGHNUT PLANT
379 GRAND STREET
GREAT, WEIRD, RECOMMENDED.

10 ECONOMY CANDY
108 RIVINGTON STREET
FLOOR-TO-CEILING CANDY MADNESS.

11 ESSEX STREET MARKET
120 ESSEX STREET
CLASSIC PUBLIC MARKET WITH A GREAT COMBO OF OLD-SCHOOL AND FRESH-FACED VENDORS.

12 KATZ'S DELICATESSEN
205 EAST HOUSTON STREET
CLASSIC NY DELI, INTERIOR HASN'T CHANGED IN DECADES.

13 KOSSAR'S BIALYS
367 GRAND STREET
OLDEST BIALY BAKERY IN THE US. THE ABSOLUTE SH**.

14 LOWER EAST SIDE TENEMENT MUSEUM
108 ORCHARD STREET
GREAT ILLUSTRATION OF TURN-OF-THE-CENTURY (20TH, THAT IS) LIFE.

15 MERCURY LOUNGE
217 EAST HOUSTON STREET
ROCK VENUE WITH OCCASIONAL TOP-NOTCH ACTS.

16 PARKSIDE LOUNGE
317 EAST HOUSTON STREET
GOOD BASIC BAR, LIVE ACTS IN THE BACK.

17 POK POK PHAT THAI
137 RIVINGTON STREET
TINY THAI WITH BIG FLAVORS.

18 RUSS & DAUGHTERS
179 EAST HOUSTON STREET
FAB JEWISH SOUL FOOD—LOX, HERRING, SABLE, ETC.

19 SPITZER'S CORNER
101 RIVINGTON STREET
40 BEERS ON TAP BEST ENJOYED SUNDAY THROUGH WEDNESDAY.

20 WELCOME TO THE JOHNSON'S
123 RIVINGTON STREET
GREAT DÉCOR, BUT TOO CROWDED MOSTLY.

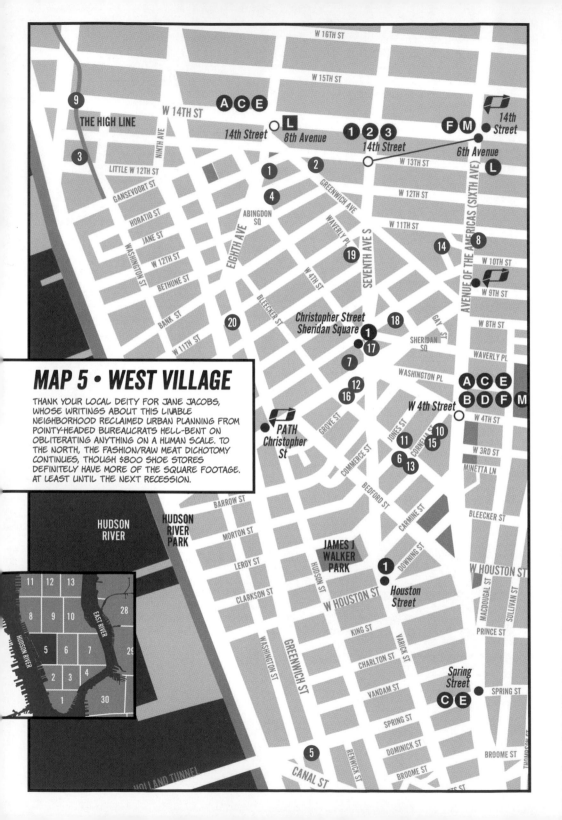

MAP 5 · WEST VILLAGE

THANK YOUR LOCAL DEITY FOR JANE JACOBS, WHOSE WRITINGS ABOUT THIS LIVABLE NEIGHBORHOOD RECLAIMED URBAN PLANNING FROM POINTY-HEADED BUREAUCRATS HELL-BENT ON OBLITERATING ANYTHING ON A HUMAN SCALE. TO THE NORTH, THE FASHION/RAW MEAT DICHOTOMY CONTINUES, THOUGH $800 SHOE STORES DEFINITELY HAVE MORE OF THE SQUARE FOOTAGE. AT LEAST UNTIL THE NEXT RECESSION.

1 ART BAR
52 EIGHTH AVENUE
GREAT SPACES, COOL CROWD.

2 A SALT & BATTERY
112 GREENWICH AVENUE
IF YOU CAN EAT IT, THEY CAN FRY IT.

3 BRASS MONKEY
55 LITTLE WEST 12TH STREET
LOTS OF BEERS, BIG WOOD TABLES, LOW LIGHT, AND
MULTIPLE LEVELS.

4 CORNER BISTRO
331 WEST 4TH STREET
TOP NYC BURGERS. PERFECT AT 3 AM.

5 THE EAR INN
326 SPRING STREET
SECOND-OLDEST BAR IN NEW YORK; GREAT SPACE.

6 FAICCO'S ITALIAN SPECIALITIES
260 BLEECKER STREET
PROSCUITTO BREAD, HOMEMADE SAUSAGE, HUGE
HEROS, PORK HEAVEN.

7 FAT CAT
75 CHRISTOPHER STREET
LAID BACK VIBE; POOL, PING PONG AND JAZZ!

8 FRENCH ROAST
78 WEST 11TH STREET
OPEN 24 HOURS. FRENCH COMFORT FOOD.

9 THE HIGH LINE
GANSEVOORT TO 34TH ST B/N 10TH & 11TH AVE
STUNNING ELEVATED PARK; A TESTAMENT TO HUMAN
CREATIVITY.

10 HOME
20 CORNELIA STREET
THERE'S NO PLACE LIKE IT.

11 KESTÉ PIZZA & VINO
271 BLEECKER STREET
SO AUTHENTIC, IT'S THE HEADQUARTERS FOR THE APN
(LOOK IT UP).

12 MARIE'S CRISIS
59 GROVE STREET
SHOWTUNES ONLY! AND NO, BILLY JOEL DOESN'T
COUNT.

13 MURRAY'S CHEESE
254 BLEECKER STREET
WE LOVE CHEESE, AND SO DOES MURRAY'S.

14 PATCHIN PLACE
W 10TH ST B/N 6TH AVE & GREENWICH AVE
TINY GATED ENCLAVE, ONCE HOME TO E.E. CUMMINGS.

15 PEARL OYSTER BAR
18 CORNELIA STREET
FOR ALL YOUR LOBSTER ROLL CRAVINGS. NFT FAVE.

16 REBEL REBEL RECORDS
319 BLEECKER STREET
SMALL CD AND LP SHOP WITH KNOWLEDGEABLE STAFF.

17 STONEWALL INN
53 CHRISTOPHER STREET
FROM THE L TO THE GB AND T, THIS IS WHERE IT
ALL BEGAN.

18 THREE LIVES & COMPANY
154 WEST 10TH STREET
CLASSIC VILLAGE BOOKSHOP. THANK GOD.

19 VILLAGE VANGUARD
178 7TH AVENUE SOUTH
CLASSIC NYC JAZZ VENUE. NOT TO BE MISSED.

20 WHITE HORSE TAVERN
567 HUDSON STREET
ANOTHER OLD, COOL BAR. DYLAN THOMAS DRANK HERE
(TOO MUCH).

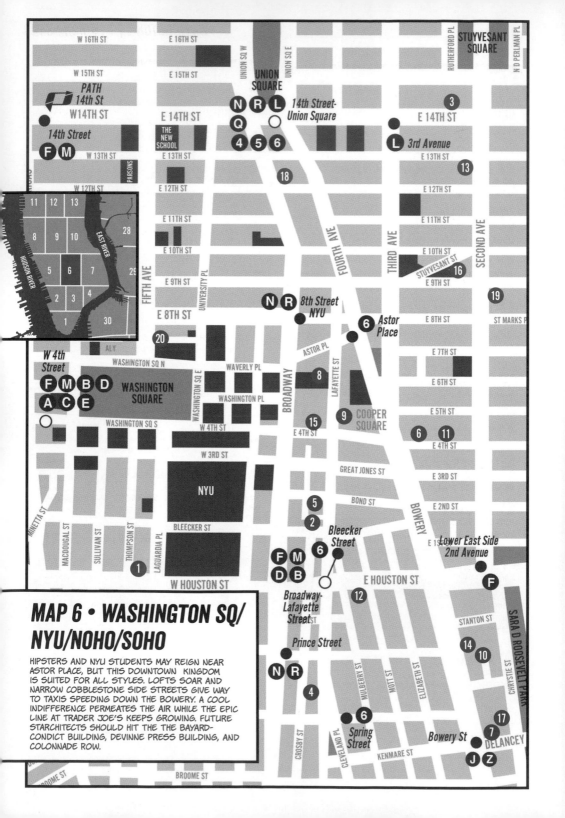

MAP 6 • WASHINGTON SQ/
NYU/NOHO/SOHO

HIPSTERS AND NYU STUDENTS MAY REIGN NEAR
ASTOR PLACE, BUT THIS DOWNTOWN KINGDOM
IS SUITED FOR ALL STYLES. LOFTS SOAR AND
NARROW COBBLESTONE SIDE STREETS GIVE WAY
TO TAXIS SPEEDING DOWN THE BOWERY. A COOL
INDIFFERENCE PERMEATES THE AIR WHILE THE EPIC
LINE AT TRADER JOE'S KEEPS GROWING. FUTURE
STARCHITECTS SHOULD HIT THE THE BAYARD-
CONDICT BUILDING, DEVINNE PRESS BUILDING, AND
COLONNADE ROW.

① ARTURO'S PIZZA
106 WEST HOUSTON STREET
CLASSIC NYC PIZZA JOINT WITH LIVE JAZZ. NFT FAVORITE.

② BAYARD-CONDICT BUILDING
65 BLEECKER STREET
LOUIS SULLIVAN'S ONLY NEW YORK BUILDING.

③ BEAUTY BAR
231 EAST 14TH STREET
JUST A LITTLE OFF THE TOP, DAHLING?

④ BICYCLE HABITAT
244 LAFAYETTE STREET
FULL-TIME MECHANICS AND SALES, TOO.

⑤ BLICK ART MATERIALS
1 BOND STREET
HUGE, SUPER ORGANIZED, RECOMMENDED.

⑥ BOND STREET CHOCOLATE
63 EAST 4TH STREET
THE HIPPEST CHOCOLATE THIS SIDE OF BELGIUM. GET THE SKULLS.

⑦ BOWERY BALLROOM
6 DELANCEY STREET
GREAT SPACE THAT ATTRACTS GREAT BANDS.

⑧ COLONNADE ROW
428 LAFAYETTE STREET
REMAINS OF A VERY DIFFERENT ERA.

⑨ DEVINNE PRESS BUILDING
399 LAFAYETTE STREET
KILLER 1885 BRICK-AND-GLASS MASTERPIECE BY BABB, COOK & WILLARD.

⑩ FREEMANS
FREEMAN ALLEY
TAXIDERMY-FILLED HIDEAWAY WITH FAB COCKTAILS AND DELICIOUS, RUSTIC FARE.

⑪ KGB BAR
85 EAST 4TH STREET
FORMER CP HQ. MEET YOUR COMRADES. READINGS, TOO.

⑫ MILANO'S
51 EAST HOUSTON STREET
GRUNGY, NARROW, AWESOME, NARROW, GRUNGY.

⑬ MOMOFUKU SSAM BAR
207 2ND AVENUE
PORK. PORK. OTHER STUFF. PORK. YUM.

⑭ NEW MUSEUM
235 BOWERY
BRILLIANT WHITE STACKED CUBES HOUSES CONTEMPORARY ART AND KILLER BOOKSTORE. YAH.

⑮ OTHER MUSIC
15 EAST 4TH STREET
UNDERGROUND, EXPERIMENTAL CD'S, LP'S, IMPORTS, AND OUT-OF-PRINT OBSCURITIES.

⑯ ROBOTAYA
231 EAST 9TH STREET
SIT AT THE COUNTER AND WATCH THEM GRILL.

⑰ SAMMY'S ROUMANIAN
157 CHRYSTIE STREET
AN EXPERIENCE NOT TO BE MISSED. CHOPPED LIVER WHICH WILL INSTANTLY KILL YOU.

⑱ STRAND BOOKSTORE
828 BROADWAY
USED MECCA; WORLD'S MESSIEST AND BEST BOOKSTORE.

⑲ UKRAINIAN EAST VILLAGE RESTAURANT
140 2ND AVENUE
PIEROGIS, BORSCHT, BLINTZES, GOULASH. COMFORT FOOD.

⑳ WASHINGTON MEWS
ENTRANCES ON 5TH AVENUE AND UNIVERSITY PLACE WHERE HORSES AND SERVANTS USED TO LIVE. NOW COVETED NYU SPACE.

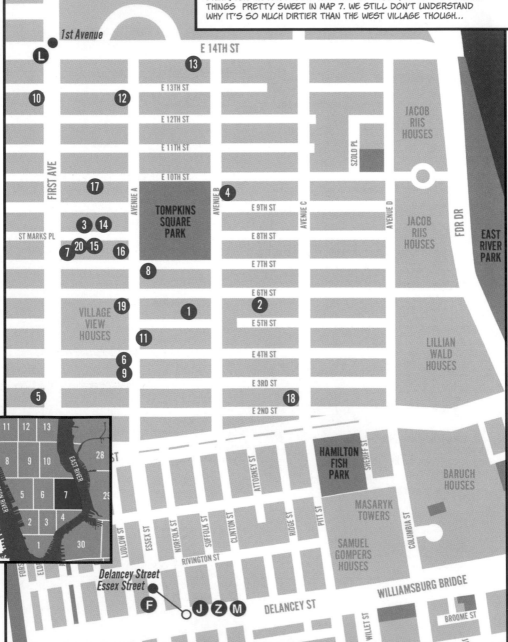

MAP 7 • EAST VILLAGE

THOUGH OLD-TIMERS SAY THIS AREA IS IRREVOCABLY WRECKED, WE'RE STILL PARTIAL TO THE EAST VILLAGE...AFTER ALL, IT WAS THE BIRTHPLACE OF NFT. THE SMALL-SCALE FEEL, EXCELLENT FOOD AND DRINK, AND NEVER-ENDING RESERVE OF SMALL, COOL SHOPS MAKE THINGS PRETTY SWEET IN MAP 7. WE STILL DON'T UNDERSTAND WHY IT'S SO MUCH DIRTIER THAN THE WEST VILLAGE THOUGH...

1 ACE BAR
531 EAST 5TH STREET
DARTS, PINBALL, POOL, AND EVEN SKEE-BALL!

2 6BC COMMUNITY GARDEN
624 EAST 6TH STREET
EARLY ALPHABET CITY COMMUNITY GARDEN, NOW
PERMANENT PARK.

3 CAFÉ MOGADOR
101 ST. MARK'S PLACE
PERFECT PLACE FOR HUMMUS AND A LATTE.

4 CHARLIE PARKER RESIDENCE
151 AVENUE B
THE BIRD LIVED HERE. GREAT FESTIVAL EVERY SUMMER
IN TOMPKINS SQUARE.

5 D.B.A.
41 FIRST AVENUE
AWESOME BEER LIST AND OUTDOOR PATIO. NFT FAVE.

6 EXIT 9
51 AVENUE A
ALWAYS FUN AND CHANGEABLE HIPSTER GIFTS. FIRST
PLACE TO SELL NFT!

7 INTERNATIONAL BAR
120 FIRST AVENUE
A BEER & A SHOT FOR $4? LIFE IS GOOD.

8 JOE STRUMMER MURAL
112 AVENUE A
HA, YOU THINK IT'S FUNNY... TURNING REBELLION
INTO MONEY?

9 LANDMARK BICYCLES
43 AVENUE A
SCHWINN LOVERS UNITE: NICE COLLECTION OF VINTAGE
BIKES AND PARTS.

10 LUZZO'S
211 FIRST AVENUE
REAL COAL OVEN. TOP TEN WORTHY.

11 MAST BOOKS
66 AVENUE A
SMALL BUT EXCELLENT SELECTION.

12 OBSCURA ANTIQUES & ODDITIES
207 AVENUE A
KITSCHY & ARBITRARY AMERICANA. PRICEY, BUT
SOCIOLOGICALLY FASCINATING.

13 OTTO'S SHRUNKEN HEAD
538 EAST 14TH STREET
NOT YOUR GRANDMA'S TIKI BAR.

14 PDT
113 ST. MARK'S PLACE
ENTER THROUGH A PHONE BOOTH IN A HOT DOG JOINT.
NO JOKE.

15 PORCHETTA
110 EAST 7TH STREET
BEST ITALIAN PORK SANDWICHES. EVER.

16 RAY'S CANDY STORE
113 AVENUE A
AVENUE A'S BELGIAN FRIES-AND-ICE CREAM
INSTITUTION.

17 RUSSIAN AND TURKISH BATHS
268 EAST 10TH STREET
SWEAT AWAY ALL YOUR URBAN STRESS.

18 THE STONE
69 AVENUE C
ALL PROCEEDS GO TO THE AVANT-GARDE JAZZ
ARTISTS. GO NOW.

19 TAKAHACHI
85 AVENUE A
SUPER-GOOD JAPANESE AND SUSHI. A MAINSTAY.

20 XE MAY
96 ST. MARK'S PLACE
KILLER BANH MI SERVED WITH A SMILE.

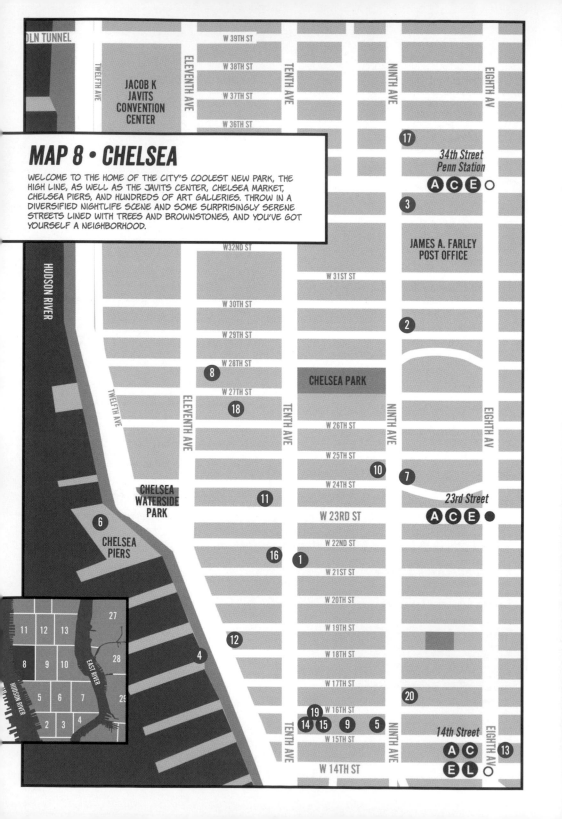

MAP 8 • CHELSEA

WELCOME TO THE HOME OF THE CITY'S COOLEST NEW PARK, THE HIGH LINE, AS WELL AS THE JAVITS CENTER, CHELSEA MARKET, CHELSEA PIERS, AND HUNDREDS OF ART GALLERIES. THROW IN A DIVERSIFIED NIGHTLIFE SCENE AND SOME SURPRISINGLY SERENE STREETS LINED WITH TREES AND BROWNSTONES, AND YOU'VE GOT YOURSELF A NEIGHBORHOOD.

1 **192 BOOKS**
192 10TH AVENUE
READS LIKE A LIBRARY—WITH A PREMIUM ON ART
BOOKS AND LITERATURE.

2 **BILLYMARK'S WEST**
332 9TH AVENUE
DOWN AND DIRTY DIVE.

3 **B & H PHOTO**
420 9TH AVENUE
WHERE EVERYONE IN NORTH AMERICA BUYS THEIR
CAMERAS AND FILM. CLOSED SATURDAYS.

4 **CHELSEA BREWING COMPANY**
CHELSEA PIERS
WHEN YOU'RE DONE PLAYING BASKETBALL.

5 **CHELSEA MARKET**
75 9TH AVENUE
FOODIES FLOCK HERE. SO SHOULD YOU.

6 **CHELSEA PIERS**
WEST 23RD STREET & HUDSON RIVER PARK
28-ACRE WATERFRONT SPORTS MECCA.

7 **CO.**
230 9TH AVENUE
PIZZA OF THE GODS.

8 **THE EAGLE**
554 WEST 28TH STREET
GET YOUR LEATHER ON (OR OFF).

9 **FRIEDMAN'S LUNCH**
75 9TH AVENUE
SUPER-DELISH BRUNCH/LUNCH SPOT INSIDE BUSTLING
CHELSEA MARKET.

10 **GRAND SICHUAN**
229 9TH AVENUE
SOME OF THE BEST CHINESE IN NYC. RECOMMENDED.

11 **THE HALF KING**
505 WEST 23RD STREET
ALWAYS THE PERFECT DRINKING CHOICE IN CHELSEA.
AMAZING BRUNCH.

12 **IAC BUILDING**
555 WEST 18TH STREET
GEHRY FINALLY COMES TO NYC. AND KICKS ASS.

13 **LA TAZA DE ORO**
96 8TH AVENUE
SIT AT THE COUNTER WITH THE LOCALS FOR GREAT
PUERTO RICAN.

14 **L'ARTE DEL GELATO**
75 9TH AVENUE
GELATO TO MAKE YOU SING AN ARIA. OR JUST PIG OUT.

15 **THE LOBSTER PLACE**
75 9TH AVENUE
FRESH FISH AND MAINE LOBSTER, IF YOU CAN
AFFORD IT.

16 **PRINTED MATTER**
195 10TH AVENUE
ASTOUNDING SELECTION OF ARTIST'S BOOKS; HIGHLY
RECOMMENDED.

17 **SERGIMMO SALUMERIA**
456 9TH AVENUE
SERIOUS SANDWICHES STUFFED WITH MOUTHWATER-
ING ITALIAN MEATS.

18 **STARRETT-LEHIGH BUILDING**
601 WEST 26TH STREET
ONE OF THE COOLEST FACTORIES/WAREHOUSES
EVER BUILT.

19 **TIPPLER**
425 WEST 15TH STREET
PERFECTLY MIXED COCKTAILS IN A DARK ROOM UNDER
CHELSEA MARKET.

20 **THE MARITIME HOTEL**
363 WEST 16TH STREET
AHOY! PORTHOLE OFFICE BUILDING NOW UBER-COOL
HOTEL.

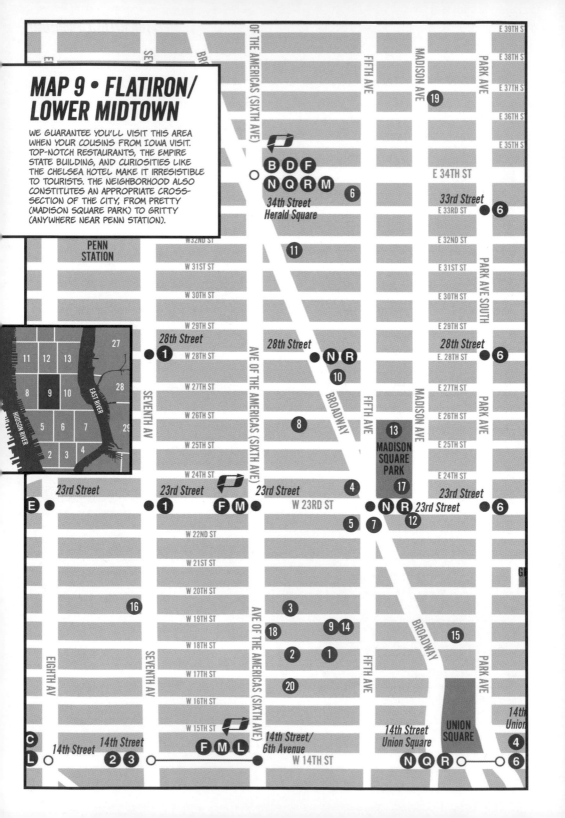

MAP 9 • FLATIRON/ LOWER MIDTOWN

WE GUARANTEE YOU'LL VISIT THIS AREA WHEN YOUR COUSINS FROM IOWA VISIT. TOP-NOTCH RESTAURANTS, THE EMPIRE STATE BUILDING, AND CURIOSITIES LIKE THE CHELSEA HOTEL MAKE IT IRRESISTIBLE TO TOURISTS. THE NEIGHBORHOOD ALSO CONSTITUTES AN APPROPRIATE CROSS-SECTION OF THE CITY, FROM PRETTY (MADISON SQUARE PARK) TO GRITTY (ANYWHERE NEAR PENN STATION).

1 ACADEMY RECORDS
12 WEST 18TH STREET
TOP JAZZ/CLASSICAL MECCA.

2 ADORAMA
42 WEST 18TH STREET
GOOD CAMERA ALTERNATIVE TO B&H. STILL CLOSED SATURDAYS, THOUGH.

3 BOQUERIA
53 WEST 19TH STREET
CHEESE STUFFED DATES WRAPPED IN BACON? WE'RE THERE.

4 EATALY
200 5TH AVENUE
OVER THE TOP (IN A GOOD WAY) ITALIAN CULINARY SUPERSTORE.

5 EISENBERG'S SANDWICH SHOP
174 5TH AVENUE
OLD-SCHOOL CORNED BEEF AND PASTRAMI.

6 EMPIRE STATE BUILDING
350 5TH AVENUE
VIEW UNLIKE ANY OTHER (EXCEPT MAYBE TOP OF THE ROCK).

7 FLATIRON BUILDING
175 5TH AVENUE
A LESSON FOR ALL ARCHITECTS: DESIGN FOR THE ACTUAL SPACE.

8 HILL COUNTRY
30 WEST 26TH STREET
GOOD OL' TEXAS 'CUE; GO FOR THE WET BRISKET.

9 IDLEWILD BOOKS
12 WEST 19TH STREET
ONE OF THE BEST TRAVEL + LITERATURE BOOK-STORES ON THE PLANET.

10 THE JAZZ GALLERY
1160 BROADWAY
NOT-FOR-PROFIT JAZZ VENUE.

11 KANG SUH
1250 BROADWAY
LATE-NIGHT KOREAN. GO FOR THE PRIVATE ROOMS.

12 LIVE BAIT
14 EAST 23RD STREET
STILL A GREAT FEEL. A MAINSTAY.

13 MADISON SQUARE PARK
EAST 23RD STREET & BROADWAY
ONE OF THE MOST UNDERRATED PARKS IN THE CITY. LOTS OF GREAT WEIRD SCULPTURE.

14 MUJI CHELSEA
16 WEST 19TH STREET
BEAUTIFUL JAPANESE AESTHETIC APPLIED TO DAILY LIVING.

15 OLD TOWN BAR
45 EAST 18TH STREET
CLASSIC NY PUB HOUSED IN FORMER SPEAK-EASY.

16 PETER MCMANUS
152 7TH AVENUE
REFRESHINGLY BASIC. GORGEOUS OLD PHONE BOOTHS.

17 SHAKE SHACK
MADISON SQUARE PARK
ENJOY HOMEMADE SHAKES 'N BURGERS IN THE PARK. ON A 2-HOUR LINE.

18 SIEGEL-COOPER CO. DEPARTMENT STORE
616 6TH AVENUE
BEAUX-ARTS RETAIL MADNESS. NOW A F***IN' BED, BATH & BEYOND.

19 THE MORGAN LIBRARY & MUSEUM
225 MADISON AVENUE
SEE COOL STUFF THE DEAD RICH DUDE COLLECTED.

20 THE RAINES LAW ROOM
48 WEST 17TH STREET
COCKTAILS WORTH YOUR TIME. AND MONEY.

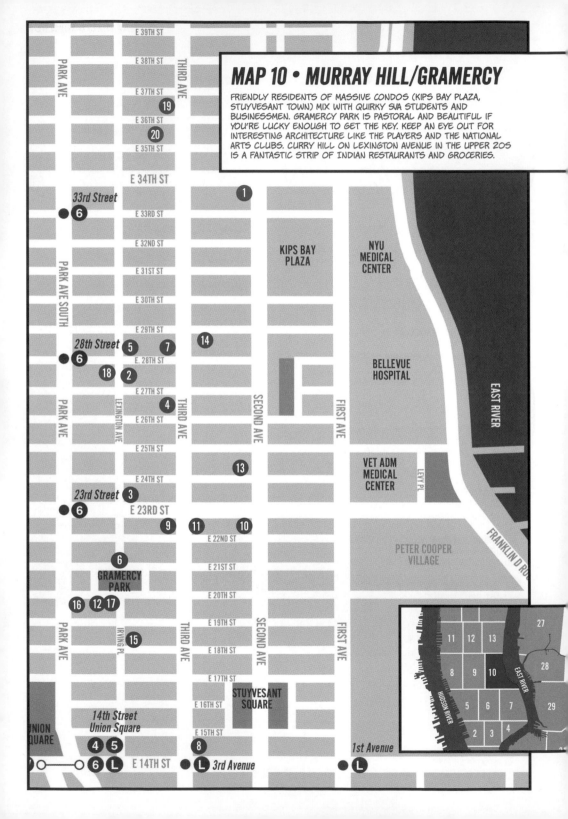

MAP 10 • MURRAY HILL/GRAMERCY

FRIENDLY RESIDENTS OF MASSIVE CONDOS (KIPS BAY PLAZA, STUYVESANT TOWN) MIX WITH QUIRKY SVA STUDENTS AND BUSINESSMEN. GRAMERCY PARK IS PASTORAL AND BEAUTIFUL IF YOU'RE LUCKY ENOUGH TO GET THE KEY. KEEP AN EYE OUT FOR INTERESTING ARCHITECTURE LIKE THE PLAYERS AND THE NATIONAL ARTS CLUBS. CURRY HILL ON LEXINGTON AVENUE IN THE UPPER 20S IS A FANTASTIC STRIP OF INDIAN RESTAURANTS AND GROCERIES.

1 CLOVER DELICATESSEN
621 2ND AVENUE
THIS STELLAR DELI HAS ONE OF THE BEST SIGNS IN NYC.

2 CURRY HILL
LEXINGTON AVENUE & EAST 28TH STREET
EAT YOUR WAY DOWN LEXINGTON IN THE 20S!

3 DAVINCI ARTIST SUPPLY
137 EAST 23RD STREET
DISCOUNTS TO STUDENT, TEACHERS, AND ART PROFESSIONALS.

4 EAST JAPANESE
366 3RD AVENUE
SUSHI COMES BY ON A CONVEYOR BELT, SO ACT FAST.

5 FOODS OF INDIA
121 LEXINGTON AVENUE
HUGE SELECTION INCLUDING HARDER TO FIND SPICES.

6 GRAMERCY PARK
EAST 20TH STREET AND IRVING PLACE
NEW YORK'S ONLY KEYED PARK. THIS IS WHERE THE REVOLUTION WILL DOUBTLESSLY START.

7 JAIYA
396 3RD AVENUE
INVENTIVE, SPICY THAI.

8 JAM PAPER AND ENVELOPE
135 THIRD AVENUE
AND...THE ENVELOPE, PLEASE.

9 LAMARCA CHEESE SHOP
161 EAST 22ND STREET
ITALIAN CULINARY GOODIES.

10 McSWIGGAN'S
393 2ND AVENUE
ONE OF THE BEST DIVE BARS ON THE ISLAND.

11 MOLLY'S
287 3RD AVENUE
GREAT IRISH PUB WITH A FIREPLACE.

12 THE NATIONAL ARTS CLUB
15 GRAMERCY PARK SOUTH
ONE OF TWO BEAUTIFUL BUILDINGS ON GRAMERCY PARK SOUTH.

13 NEW YORK COMEDY CLUB
241 EAST 24TH STREET
...AND THE BARTENDER ASKS, "WHERE DID YOU GET THAT?"

14 NUTHOUSE HARDWARE
202 EAST 29TH STREET
OPEN 24-HOURS; EQUIPMENT RENTALS, TOO.

15 PETE'S TAVERN
129 EAST 18TH STREET
WHERE O. HENRY HUNG OUT. AND SO SHOULD YOU, AT LEAST ONCE.

16 L'EXPRESS
249 PARK AVENUE SOUTH
ALWAYS-OPEN FRENCH DINER.

17 THE PLAYERS CLUB
16 GRAMERCY PARK SOUTH
THE OTHER COOL BUILDING ON GRAMERCY PARK SOUTH.

18 PONGAL
110 LEXINGTON AVENUE
POSSIBLY NY'S BEST VEGETARIAN INDIAN. SADA DOSA...MMMM.

19 SARGE'S
548 3RD AVENUE
24-HOUR-A-DAY PASTRAMI, CONVENIENT TO GCT.

20 SNIFFEN COURT
3RD AVENUE AND EAST 36TH STREET
GREAT LITTLE SPACE.

MAP 11 • HELL'S KITCHEN

HELL'S KITCHEN IS STILL REALLY MOSTLY JUST THAT—EXCEPT FOR THE GREAT RESTAURANT SCENE ON NINTH AVE. OTHERWISE, LOTS OF TRAFFIC, ALHAMBRA-LIKE CAR REPAIR/CAR DEALERS ON 11TH AVE, AND HORDES OF TOURISTS WANDERING AROUND. JOIN US IN REFUSING TO CALL THE AREA "CLINTON," AS REAL ESTATE BROKERS AND TAXI MAPS DO.

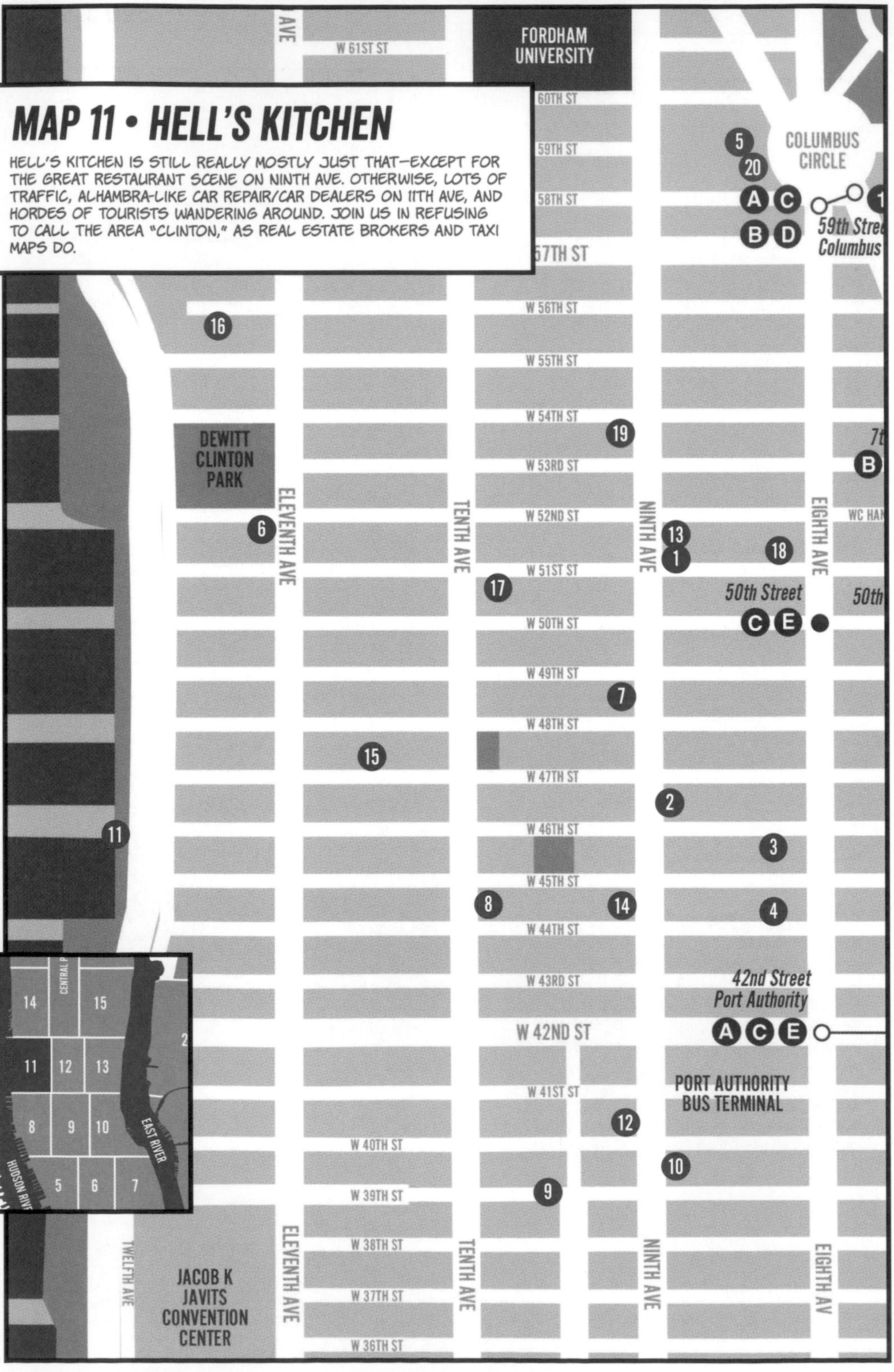

AVE
W 61ST ST
FORDHAM UNIVERSITY
60TH ST
59TH ST
58TH ST
57TH ST

COLUMBUS CIRCLE

5
20
Ⓐ Ⓒ
Ⓑ Ⓓ
59th Stree
Columbus
1

W 56TH ST
W 55TH ST
W 54TH ST
W 53RD ST

7t
Ⓑ

16

DEWITT CLINTON PARK

ELEVENTH AVE
TENTH AVE
NINTH AVE
EIGHTH AVE

19

W 52ND ST
W 51ST ST
W 50TH ST
W 49TH ST
W 48TH ST
W 47TH ST
W 46TH ST
W 45TH ST
W 44TH ST
W 43RD ST

6
13
1
18
WC HAN

17

50th Street
Ⓒ Ⓔ
50th

7

15

2

3

8
14
4

11

42nd Street
Port Authority
Ⓐ Ⓒ Ⓔ

W 42ND ST

W 41ST ST

PORT AUTHORITY BUS TERMINAL

12

10

9

W 40TH ST
W 39TH ST
W 38TH ST
W 37TH ST
W 36TH ST

ELEVENTH AVE
TENTH AVE
NINTH AVE
EIGHTH AV

TWELFTH AVE

JACOB K JAVITS CONVENTION CENTER

CENTRAL P
HUDSON RIVER
EAST RIVER

14 15
11 12 13
8 9 10
5 6 7

2

1 AFGHAN KEBAB HOUSE
764 9TH AVENUE
ADDICTIVE SKEWERS OF MEAT, FRIENDLY AND BYOB.

2 AMY'S BREAD
672 9TH AVENUE
PROVIDING THE HEAVENLY SMELLS THAT WAKE UP
HELL'S KITCHEN.

3 BAR CENTRALE
324 WEST 46TH STREET
MAKE RESERVATIONS TO SEE BROADWAY STARS RE-
LAXING AFTER THE SHOW.

4 BIRDLAND
314 WEST 44TH STREET
TOP-NOTCH JAZZ SHOWS.

5 BOUCHON BAKERY
10 COLUMBUS CIRCLE
HEAVENLY PASTRIES IN A GIGANTIC MALL.

6 DAILY SHOW STUDIO
733 11TH AVENUE
HOME OF OUR FAVORITE TV SHOW. THANK YOU
JON STEWART.

7 GAZALA PLACE
709 9TH AVENUE
BRILLIANT MIDDLE EASTERN FOOD & BREADS WITH A
BYOB BONUS.

8 HALLO BERLIN
626 10TH AVENUE
BEST WURST IN THE CITY. PLUS BIER!

9 HELL'S KITCHEN FLEA MARKET
WEST 39TH STREET B/W 9TH & 10TH AVENUES
VINTAGE TREASURES ABOUND EVERY SATURDAY &
SUNDAY.

10 HOLLAND BAR
532 9TH AVENUE
ONE OF THE LAST REAL DIVES OF NEW YORK.

11 INTREPID, SEA, AIR & SPACE MUSEUM
12TH AVENUE & WEST 46TH STREET
HOLY CRAP! AN AIRCRAFT CARRIER IN THE MIDDLE OF
THE HUDSON RIVER!

12 NINTH AVENUE INTERNATIONAL GROCERY
543 9TH AVENUE
EXCELLENT MEDITERRANEAN AND GREEK SPECIALTY
FOOD STORE.

13 PURE THAI COOKHOUSE
766 9TH AVENUE
TASTY, AFFORDABLE GRUB IN A CLASSY LITTLE DINING
ROOM.

14 RUDY'S BAR & GRILL
627 9TH AVENUE
DIVEY, DIRTY AND DEFINITELY NOT FOR TOURISTS.
PLUS FREE HOT DOGS!

15 SULLIVAN STREET BAKERY
533 WEST 47TH STREET
FOODIE-APPROVED BREADS, FOCCACIA AND SWEETS.

16 TERMINAL 5
610 WEST 56TH STREET
MID-SIZE VENUE FOR INDIE ROCK GODS.

17 TOTTO RAMEN
366 WEST 52ND STREET
FOR TASTY BOWLS AT THIS FRIENDLY COUNTER, BE
PREPARED TO LINE UP.

18 TOUT VA BIEN
311 WEST 51ST STREET
OLD-SCHOOL, PRE-THEATER FRENCH CLASSIC.

19 VALHALLA
815 9TH AVENUE
GOOD AFTER-WORK HANG OUT WITH STAGGERING
BEER SELECTION.

20 WHOLE FOODS
10 COLUMBUS CIRCLE
GRAB SOME FANCY FEASTS FOR A CENTRAL PARK
PICNIC.

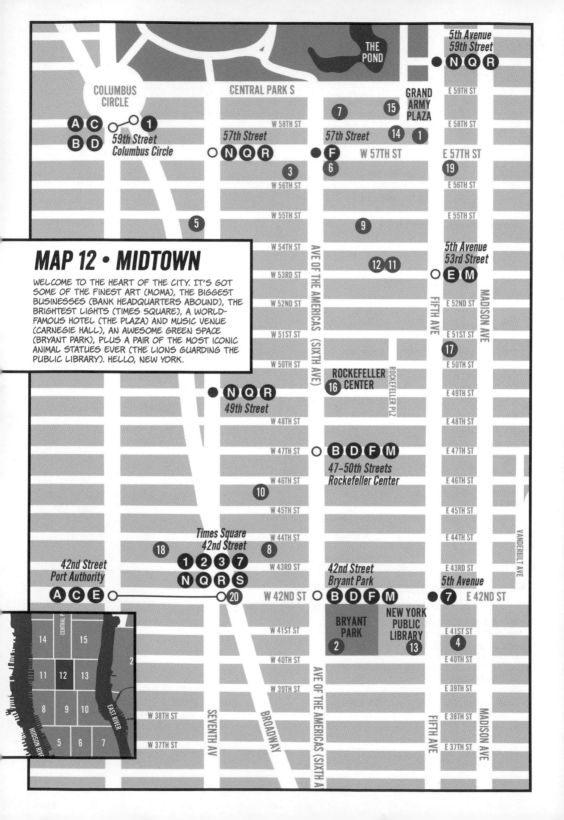

MAP 12 • MIDTOWN

WELCOME TO THE HEART OF THE CITY. IT'S GOT SOME OF THE FINEST ART (MOMA), THE BIGGEST BUSINESSES (BANK HEADQUARTERS ABOUND), THE BRIGHTEST LIGHTS (TIMES SQUARE), A WORLD-FAMOUS HOTEL (THE PLAZA) AND MUSIC VENUE (CARNEGIE HALL), AN AWESOME GREEN SPACE (BRYANT PARK), PLUS A PAIR OF THE MOST ICONIC ANIMAL STATUES EVER (THE LIONS GUARDING THE PUBLIC LIBRARY). HELLO, NEW YORK.

① BERGDORF GOODMAN
754 5TH AVENUE
HANDS DOWN, THE BEST DEPARTMENT STORE
WINDOWS IN THE BUSINESS.

② BRYANT PARK
6TH AVENUE & 42ND STREET
GRAB A CHAIR AND RELAX ON MIDTOWN'S COMMUNAL
LAWN. ICE SKATE IN THE WINTER.

③ BURGER JOINT
119 WEST 56TH STREET
FANCY HOTEL LOBBY LEADS TO AN UNEXPECTED
BURGER DIVE. AWESOME.

④ CAFE ZAIYA
18 EAST 41ST STREET
JAPANESE FOOD COURT THAT'S CHEAP AND FAST.

⑤ CARNEGIE DELI
854 7TH AVENUE
SERVING GREAT PASTRAMI SINCE 1937.

⑥ CARNEGIE HALL
881 7TH AVENUE
CLASSIC AND CLASSY MUSIC VENUE.

⑦ FIKA
41 WEST 58TH STREET
SWEDISH OASIS: STRONG COFFEE AND HOMEMADE
PASTRIES.

⑧ JIMMY'S CORNER
140 WEST 44TH STREET
THIS COZY JOINT IS THE BEST BAR AROUND HERE,
TRUST US.

⑨ LA BONNE SOUPE
48 WEST 55TH STREET
OOH LA LA, THE BEST SALAD DRESSING ACCOMPANIES
SOUPE A L'OIGNON.

⑩ MARGON
136 WEST 46TH STREET
GREAT CUBAN SANDWICHES BUT THE COFFEE IS THE
REAL HIT.

⑪ THE MODERN
9 WEST 53RD STREET
WITH GNOCCHI TO DIE FOR, SPEND A LOT AND THEN
STILL SPLURGE ON DESSERT.

**⑫ MUSEUM OF MODERN ART
(MOMA)**
11 WEST 53RD STREET
BLOCKBUSTER EXHIBITS PLUS A COOL GIFT SHOP,
CINEMA, SCULPTURE GARDEN, AND BIG CROWDS.

⑬ NEW YORK PUBLIC LIBRARY
5TH AVENUE & 42ND STREET
A WONDERFUL BEAUX ARTS BUILDING. THE MAP AND
ROSE READING ROOMS RULE.

⑭ PARIS THEATER
4 WEST 58TH STREET
CLASSIC ART HOUSE CINEMA WITH A BALCONY.

⑮ THE PLAZA HOTEL
768 5TH AVENUE
ANYONE CAN CHECK OUT THE LOBBY SPACES, BUT
GOOD LUCK AFFORDING A ROOM.

⑯ ROCKEFELLER CENTER
45 ROCKEFELLER PLAZA
ART DECO ARCHITECTURE, ICE SKATING, AND A MALL!

⑰ ST. PATRICK'S CATHEDRAL
5TH AVENUE & 50TH STREET
HEAVENLY REFUGE IN THE HEART OF MIDTOWN.

⑱ SARDI'S
234 WEST 44TH STREET
CLASSIC BROADWAY DINING & DRINKING WITH AL
HIRSCHFELD SKETCHES ON THE WALLS.

⑲ TIFFANY & CO.
727 5TH AVENUE
GRANDE DAME OF THE LITTLE BLUE BOX.

⑳ TIMES SQUARE
7TH AVE & WEST 42ND STREET
IT LOOKS EVEN COOLER THAN IT DOES ON TV!

QR
5th Avenue
59th Street

NQR

15

18

4 5 6
59th Street

E 60TH ST

E 59TH ST

E 58TH ST

E 57TH ST

LEXINGTON AVE

E 56TH ST

1

12

E 55TH ST

Lexington Avenue
53rd Street

E 54TH ST

5th Avenue
53rd Street

M

E V

14

6
51st Street

6

THIRD AVE

E 53RD ST

E 52ND ST

8

E 51ST ST

4

10

SECOND AVE

FIRST AVE

9

SUTTON SQ

17

SUTTON PL

PARK AVE

MADISON AVE

E 50TH ST

20

E 49TH ST

E 48TH ST

LEXINGTON AVE

E 47TH ST

E 46TH ST

E 45TH ST

11

GRAND
CENTRAL
STATION

E 44TH ST

DAG
HAMMARSKJOLD
PLAZA

PEACE
GARDENS

BEEKMAN PL

EAST RIVER

VANDERBILT AVE

Grand Central
42nd Street

2 5
6 7

4

5 7 3

13

E 43RD ST

16

UNITED
NATIONS

19

6 S

E 42ND ST

E 41ST ST

QUEENS-MIDT

E 40TH ST

MAP 13 • EAST MIDTOWN

EAST MIDTOWN HAS A LOT GOING ON—IN A GOOD WAY. IT'S GOT
THE TRANQUILITY OF ELEGANT SUTTON PLACE, THE ROWDY
NIGHTLIFE ALONG SECOND AVENUE, THE COMMUTER BUSTLE OF
GRAND CENTRAL TERMINAL, AND THE INTERNATIONAL CROWD AROUND
THE U.N. NOT TO MENTION THE LEGENDARY ARCHITECTURE. YOU
MIGHT HAVE HEARD OF A LITTLE SKYSCRAPER CALLED THE CHRYSLER
BUILDING, PERHAPS.

E 39TH ST

E 38TH ST

E 37TH ST

E 36TH ST

14 CENTRAL P 15

11 12 13

2

8 9 10

EAST RIVER

5 6 7

HUDSON RIV

1 AQUAVIT
65 EAST 55TH STREET
STELLAR DINING EXPERIENCE: TOP-DRAWER
SCANDINAVIAN.

2 THE CAMPBELL APARTMENT
15 VANDERBILT AVENUE
AWESOME SPACE, AWESOMELY SNOOTY!

3 CHRYSLER BUILDING
405 LEXINGTON AVENUE
THE STUFF OF ART DECO DREAMS. WISH THE CLOUD
CLUB WAS STILL THERE.

4 ESS-A-BAGEL
831 3RD AVENUE
BAGELS WITH ATTITUDE AND FLAVOR.

5 GRAND CENTRAL MARKET
87 EAST 42ND STREET
PICK UP FIXINGS FOR A GOURMET DINNER BEFORE
JUMPING ON THE TRAIN.

6 GRAND CENTRAL OYSTER BAR
89 EAST 42ND STREET
CLASSIC NEW YORK SEAFOOD JOINT. GRAB A SEAT
AT THE COUNTER OR IN THE SALOON.

7 GRAND CENTRAL TERMINAL
89 EAST 42ND STREET
ANOTHER BEAUX ARTS MASTERPIECE. CEILING, STAIR-
CASES, TILES, CLOCK, ALL GREAT.

8 HIDE-CHAN RAMEN
248 EAST 52ND STREET
THIS BROTH IS PORKTASTIC.

9 IDEAL CHEESE
942 1ST AVENUE
SMALL SPOT PACKED WITH OVER 250 TYPES.

10 LE BATEAU IVRE
230 EAST 151 STREET
FRENCH WINE BAR OPEN 'TIL 4 AM.

11 MACCHIATO ESPRESSO BAR
141 EAST 44TH STREET
NICE COFFEE SHOP FOR THIS PART OF TOWN.

12 P.J. CLARKE'S
915 3RD AVENUE
OLD-TIMEY MIDTOWN PUB WITH BURGERS, BEERS AND
BANKERS.

13 SAKAGURA
211 EAST 43RD STREET
MIDTOWNERS ARE VERY HAPPY TO HAVE THIS
EXCELLENT IZAKAYA.

14 SEAGRAM BUILDING
375 PARK AVENUE
OR, "HOW TO BE A MODERNIST IN 3 EASY STEPS!"

15 SHERRY-LEHMANN WINE & SPIRITS
505 PARK AVENUE
FINE BOOZE SELECTION FOR THE CONNOISSEUR AND
THE RICH.

16 SUSHI YASUDA
204 EAST 43RD STREET
BEST SUSHI IN NYC. LET THE DEBATE BEGIN...

17 SUTTON PLACE
SUTTON PLACE BETWEEN 57TH & 59TH STREET
QUIET, EXCLUSIVE LITTLE LANE FOR THE RICH AND
SOMETIMES FAMOUS.

18 YANKEES CLUBHOUSE
110 EAST 59TH STREET
A NEW YORK BASEBALL FAN'S PARADISE.

19 UNITED NATIONS
405 EAST 42ND STREET
NYC IS THE CAPITAL OF THE PLANET. JUST SAYIN'.

20 WALDORF ASTORIA
301 PARK AVENUE
CLASSIC. A WALK THROUGH THE LOBBY IS WORTH IT.

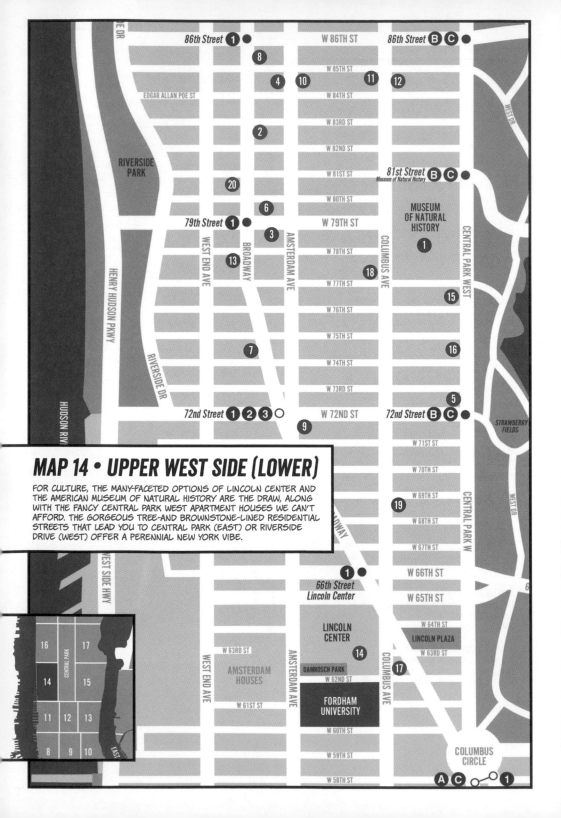

MAP 14 • UPPER WEST SIDE (LOWER)

FOR CULTURE, THE MANY-FACETED OPTIONS OF LINCOLN CENTER AND THE AMERICAN MUSEUM OF NATURAL HISTORY ARE THE DRAW, ALONG WITH THE FANCY CENTRAL PARK WEST APARTMENT HOUSES WE CAN'T AFFORD. THE GORGEOUS TREE-AND BROWNSTONE-LINED RESIDENTIAL STREETS THAT LEAD YOU TO CENTRAL PARK (EAST) OR RIVERSIDE DRIVE (WEST) OFFER A PERENNIAL NEW YORK VIBE.

① AMERICAN MUSEUM OF NATURAL HISTORY

CENTRAL PARK WEST & WEST 79TH STREET
INCLUDES AN OUTSTANDING PLANETARIUM AND LOTS
AND LOTS OF STUFFED ANIMALS.

② ARTIE'S DELICATESSEN
2290 BROADWAY
HOT PASTRAMI ON RYE NEVER GOES OUT OF STYLE.

③ BLONDIES SPORTS BAR
212 WEST 79TH STREET
WANT TO CATCH A GAME? ANY GAME? WITH SOME
WINGS? COME HERE.

④ CELESTE
502 AMSTERDAM AVENUE
CHEAP AND TASTY HOMEMADE PASTAS. A TRUE GEM
BUT THERE'S ALWAYS A LINE.

⑤ THE DAKOTA

WEST 72ND STREET & CENTRAL PARK WEST
CLASSIC APARTMENT BUILDING AND THE FORMER
HOME OF JOHN LENNON.

⑥ DUBLIN HOUSE
225 WEST 79TH STREET
GREAT DINGY IRISH TAVERN. RECOMMENDED.

⑦ FAIRWAY
2127 BROADWAY
TOP-NOTCH SUPERMARKET, BUT ALWAYS PACKED.

⑧ FRENCH ROAST
2340 BROADWAY
24-HOUR HANGOUT WITH A GOOD CROQUE-MONSIEUR.

⑨ GRANDAISY
176 WEST 72ND STREET
EXCELLENT PASTRIES, BREADS AND UNIQUE SQUARE
PIZZA SLICES.

⑩ JACOB'S PICKLES
509 AMSTERDAM AVENUE
UPMARKET SOUTHERN-STYLE MENU AND BOOZE, AND
YES, PLENTY OF PICKLES.

⑪ JOE THE ART OF COFFEE
514 COLUMBUS AVENUE
JOE REALLY KNOWS HIS JOE.

⑫ KEFI

505 COLUMBUS AVENUE
GREEK FOOD GETS AN UPGRADE AT THIS AMAZINGLY
AFFORDABLE GEM.

⑬ LA CARIDAD 78
2199 BROADWAY
CHEAP, OLD-SCHOOL CUBAN PARADISE.

⑭ LINCOLN CENTER

70 LINCOLN CENTER PLAZA
A RICH AND WONDERFUL COMPLEX. HIGHLY RECOM-
MENDED WITH MOVIES, THEATER, DANCE, MUSIC,
OPERA, AND FOUNTAIN.

⑮ NEW-YORK HISTORICAL SOCIETY
170 CENTRAL PARK WEST
OLDEST MUSEUM IN THE CITY AND RECENTLY RENO-
VATED.

⑯ SAN REMO
CENTRAL PARK WEST & WEST 74TH STREET
EMERY ROTH'S HANDSOME CONTRIBUTION TO THE
UPPER WEST SIDE SKYLINE.

⑰ ROSA MEXICANO
61 COLUMBUS AVENUE
INVENTIVE MEXICAN. GREAT GUAC.

⑱ SHAKE SHACK
366 COLUMBUS AVENUE
BURGERS, FROZEN CUSTARD AND LINES OUT THE
DOOR.

⑲ TELEPAN
72 WEST 69TH STREET
THE UPSCALE SEASONAL MENUS NEVER DISAPPOINT.

⑳ ZABAR'S

2245 BROADWAY
MANHATTAN SUPERMARKET LEGEND THAT'S ALWAYS
PACKED WITH UWS OLD TIMERS.

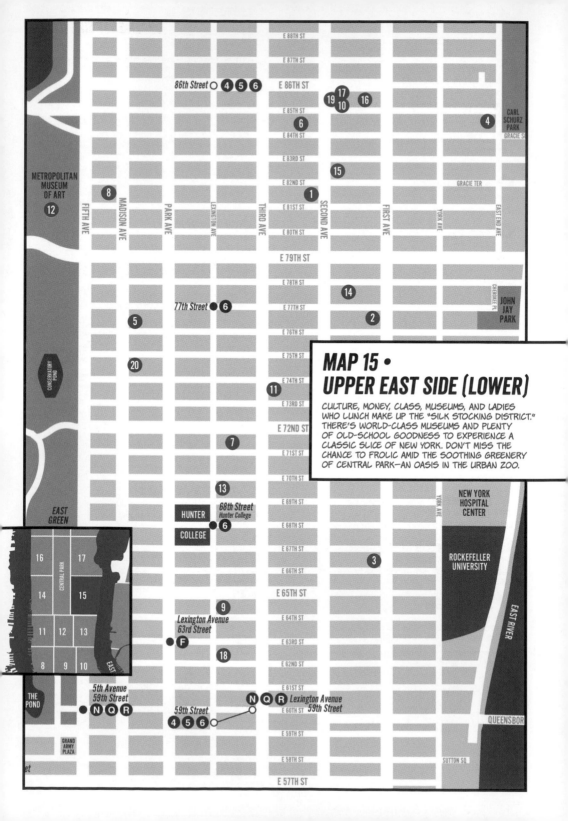

MAP 15 •
UPPER EAST SIDE (LOWER)

CULTURE, MONEY, CLASS, MUSEUMS, AND LADIES
WHO LUNCH MAKE UP THE "SILK STOCKING DISTRICT."
THERE'S WORLD-CLASS MUSEUMS AND PLENTY
OF OLD-SCHOOL GOODNESS TO EXPERIENCE A
CLASSIC SLICE OF NEW YORK. DON'T MISS THE
CHANCE TO FROLIC AMID THE SOOTHING GREENERY
OF CENTRAL PARK—AN OASIS IN THE URBAN ZOO.

1 AGORA TURKISH
1565 2ND AVENUE
BYOB FAMILY-RUN TURKISH WITH BIG FLAVORS AND A SMALL PRICE.

2 AMERICAN TRASH
1471 1ST AVENUE
PUNK ROCKIN' I-BANKERS UNITE.

3 BAGELWORKS
1229 1ST AVENUE
LOCAL SHOP WITH TRULY EXCELLENT BAGELS.

4 BAILEY'S CORNER PUB
1607 YORK AVENUE
FRIENDLY IRISH LOCAL. WATCH THE GAME OR PLAY DARTS.

5 BEMELMAN'S BAR
35 EAST 76TH STREET
CLASSIC UPPER EAST SIDE SCENE WITH A LOVELY AND FAMOUS MURAL. BRING BUCKETS OF CASH.

6 BRANDY'S PIANO BAR
235 EAST 84TH STREET
GOOD OL' ROLLICKING TIME.

7 BREAKFAST AT TIFFANY'S APARTMENT
169 EAST 71ST STREET
WHERE HOLLY GOLIGHTLY AND "FRED" LIVED IN BREAKFAST AT TIFFANY'S.

8 CRAWFORD DOYLE BOOKS
1082 MADISON AVENUE
LOVELY PLACE TO BROWSE AND FIND A CLASSIC.

9 DONOHUE'S STEAKHOUSE
845 LEXINGTON AVENUE
OLD-SCHOOL IRISH. SIT AT THE BAR AND DRINK WHISKEY.

10 HEIDELBERG
1648 2ND AVENUE
DIRNDLS AND LEDERHOSEN SERVING COLOSSAL BEERS AND SAUSAGE PLATTERS.

11 JG MELON
1291 THIRD AVENUE
TOP NYC BURGERS. ALWAYS CROWDED. GREAT VIBE WITH LONGTIME WAITSTAFF.

12 METROPOLITAN MUSEUM OF ART
1000 5TH AVENUE
THE MOTHER OF ALL ART MUSEUMS. SPEND AN AFTERNOON OR A WEEK! AND DON'T MISS THE ROOF GARDEN IN THE SUMMER.

13 NEIL'S COFFEE SHOP
961 LEXINGTON AVENUE
OLD-SCHOOL DINER.

14 ORWASHER'S
308 EAST 78TH STREET
HANDMADE WINE BREADS. BEST CHALLAH ON THE EAST SIDE.

15 THE PENROSE
1590 2ND AVENUE
TASTY COCKTAILS & PUB GRUB WITH A TOUCH OF CLASS.

16 POKE SUSHI
343 EAST 85TH STREET
GOOD SUSHI AND FAMILY-FRIENDLY CONFINES. BYO SAKE.

17 SCHALLER & WEBER
1654 2ND AVENUE
A RELIC OF OLD YORKVILLE WITH GREAT GERMAN MEATS.

18 TENDER BUTTONS
143 E 62ND STREET
ANTIQUE, RARE, AND UNUSUAL BUTTONS (NO, REALLY).

19 TWO LITTLE RED HENS
1652 2ND AVENUE
LOVELY CASES OF CAKES AND PIES FLANKED BY KITSCHY HEN MEMORABILIA.

20 WHITNEY MUSEUM OF AMERICAN ART
945 MADISON AVENUE
ALWAYS HAS SOMETHING TO TALK ABOUT, LIKE THE CONTROVERSIAL BIENNIAL.

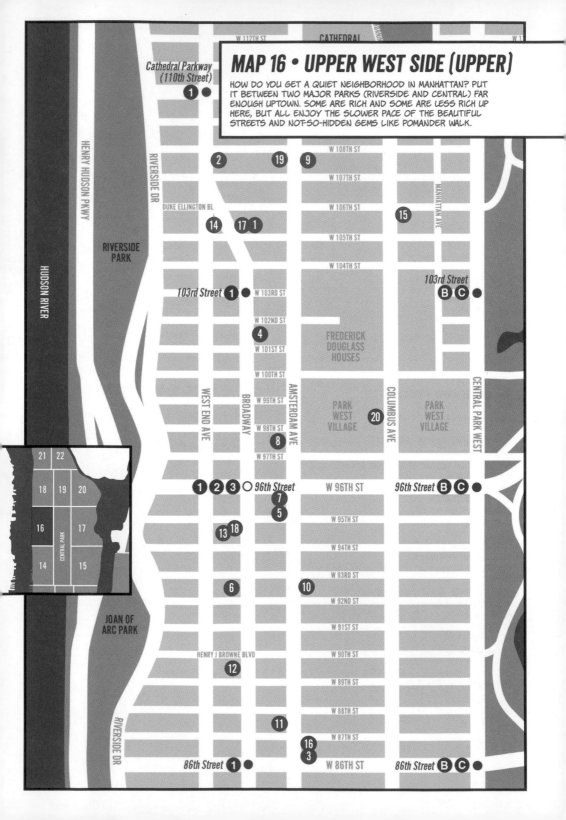

MAP 16 • UPPER WEST SIDE (UPPER)

HOW DO YOU GET A QUIET NEIGHBORHOOD IN MANHATTAN? PUT IT BETWEEN TWO MAJOR PARKS (RIVERSIDE AND CENTRAL) FAR ENOUGH UPTOWN. SOME ARE RICH AND SOME ARE LESS RICH UP HERE, BUT ALL ENJOY THE SLOWER PACE OF THE BEAUTIFUL STREETS AND NOT-SO-HIDDEN GEMS LIKE POMANDER WALK.

1 ABBEY PUB
237 WEST 105TH STREET
COZY COLUMBIA HANGOUT.

2 ABSOLUTE BAGELS
2788 BROADWAY
AMAZING? ABSOLUTELY! HOME OF THE HARD-TO-FIND PUMPERNICKEL RAISIN.

3 BARNEY GREENGRASS
541 AMSTERDAM AVENUE
CLASSIC NEW YORK EATS. STURGEON AND EGGS, BAGELS AND MORE.

4 BROADWAY RESTAURANT
2664 BROADWAY
NOTHING FANCY, JUST A GOOD PLACE TO START THE DAY.

5 CAFE CON LECHE
424 AMSTERDAM AVENUE
CUBAN-DOMINICAN HAVEN.

6 CLEOPATRA'S NEEDLE
2485 BROADWAY
SOLID MIDDLE EASTERN FOOD AND SOLID LIVE JAZZ PERFORMANCES.

7 DIVE BAR
732 AMSTERDAM AVENUE
THAT'S "DIVE" AS IN "DEEP"; COLUMBIA HANGOUT.

8 EL MALECON
764 AMSTERDAM AVENUE
ROAST CHICKEN AND A CAFE CON LECHE.

9 EL REY DE LA CARIDAD
973 AMSTERDAM AVENUE
ENJOY A DOMINICAN FEAST. BRING YOUR SPANISH DICTIONARY.

10 GENNARO
665 AMSTERDAM AVENUE
CROWDED ITALIAN. ALSO DELICIOUS AND DECENTLY PRICED.

11 MERMAID INN
568 AMSTERDAM AVENUE
SIMPLE SEAFOOD CREATIONS IN A TASTEFUL SETTING, PLUS HAPPY HOUR.

12 MURRAY'S STURGEON SHOP
2429 BROADWAY
NYC COMFORT FOOD: RUGELACH, KNISHES, AND LOTS OF SMOKED FISH.

13 POMANDER WALK
261 WEST 94TH STREET
GREAT (AND GATED) LITTLE HIDEAWAY OF SMALL TUDOR REVIVAL APARTMENT BUILDINGS.

14 SMOKE
2751 BROADWAY
LOCAL JAZZ HANGOUT. SUNDAY NIGHTS ARE FUN.

15 SAIGUETTE
935 COLUMBUS AVENUE
DAMN GOOD VIETNAMESE TAKE-OUT INCLUDING UNIQUE BANH MI SANDWICHES.

16 SCHATZIE THE BUTCHER
555 AMSTERDAM AVENUE
FULL-SERVICE MARKET WITH PRIME MEATS AND POULTRY.

17 SILVER MOON BAKERY
2740 BROADWAY
DELICIOUS MORNING PASTRIES AND BREADS.

18 SYMPHONY SPACE
2537 BROADWAY
NEIGHBORHOOD CONCERT HALL WITH ECLECTIC PROGRAMS OF THEATRE, FILM, LITERATURE, MUSIC, AND DANCE.

19 TAQUERIA Y FONDA
968 AMSTERDAM AVENUE
KILLER MEXICAN DIVE. COLUMBIA KIDS LOVE THIS PLACE.

20 WHOLE FOODS WINE
808 COLUMBUS AVENUE
FEATURING LOTS OF NY STATE WINES.

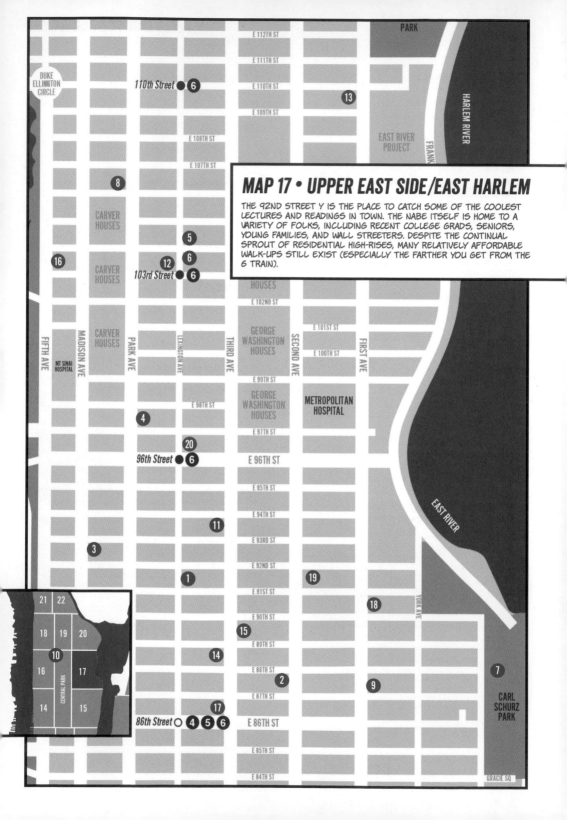

MAP 17 • UPPER EAST SIDE/EAST HARLEM

THE 92ND STREET Y IS THE PLACE TO CATCH SOME OF THE COOLEST LECTURES AND READINGS IN TOWN. THE NABE ITSELF IS HOME TO A VARIETY OF FOLKS, INCLUDING RECENT COLLEGE GRADS, SENIORS, YOUNG FAMILIES, AND WALL STREETERS. DESPITE THE CONTINUAL SPROUT OF RESIDENTIAL HIGH-RISES, MANY RELATIVELY AFFORDABLE WALK-UPS STILL EXIST (ESPECIALLY THE FARTHER YOU GET FROM THE 6 TRAIN).

1 92ND STREET Y
1395 LEXINGTON AVENUE
COMMUNITY HUB FOR FILM, THEATER, AND INTERESTING
LECTURES.

2 CAFE D'ALSACE
1695 2ND AVENUE
CHIC ALSATIAN BISTRO WITH AN ACTUAL BEER SOM-
MELIER.

3 CORNER BOOKSTORE
1313 MADISON AVENUE
TINY, OLD-SCHOOL SHOP. GREAT SELECTION.

4 EARL'S BEER & CHEESE
1259 PARK AVENUE
BEST BEER SELECTION FOR MILES. AND AWESOME
FOOD.

5 EAST HARLEM CAFE
1651 LEXINGTON AVENUE
GREAT COFFEE AND EVEN BETTER COMMUNITY VIBE.

6 EL PASO
1643 LEXINGTON AVENUE
FANTASTIC AND UPSCALE MEXICAN. TRY THE SPICY
GUACAMOLE.

7 GRACIE MANSION
EAST END AVENUE & EAST 88TH STREET
OUR OWN BUCKINGHAM PALACE, RIGHT ABOVE THE
FDR DRIVE.

8 GRAFFITI HALL OF FAME
PARK AVENUE & EAST 106TH STREET
THIS STREET ART WILL BLOW YOU AWAY.

9 GLASER'S BAKE SHOP
1670 1ST AVENUE
OLD WORLD TREASURE WITH THE BEST BLACK-AND-
WHITE COOKIES FOR MORE THAN A CENTURY.

10 GUGGENHEIM MUSEUM
1071 5TH AVENUE
FRANK LLOYD WRIGHT'S ONLY NYC BUILDING, BUT
IT'S ONE OF THE BEST IN THE WORLD.

11 KINSALE TAVERN
1672 3RD AVENUE
A FRIENDLY IRISH STAFF BEHIND THE BAR. GOOD BEERS.

12 LA CASA AZUL BOOKSTORE
143 EAST 103RD STREET
SPANISH AND ENGLISH BOOKS, ART GALLERY AND A
LOVELY BACKYARD.

13 LA TROPEZIENNE
2131 1ST AVENUE
EXCELLENT FRENCH BAKERY. IN EL BARRIO, OF
COURSE.

14 MILANO MARKET
1582 3RD AVENUE
GEM OF AN ITALIAN MARKET.

15 MISTER WRIGHT'S LIQUORS
1593 3RD AVENUE
GOOD STORE WITH HUGE SELECTION AND TASTINGS.

16 MUSEUM CITY OF NEW YORK
1220 5TH AVENUE
FASCINATING EXHIBITIONS ON LIFE IN THE BIG CITY.
EXCELLENT GIFT SHOP FOR METROPOLIS LOVERS.

17 PAPAYA KING
179 EAST 86TH STREET
DISHING OUT DAMN GOOD DOGS SINCE 1932.

18 PIO PIO
1746 1ST AVENUE
THE MATADOR CHICKEN COMBO WILL FEED THE WHOLE
FAMILY.

19 REIF'S TAVERN
302 EAST 92ND STREET
DIVE-O-RAMA SINCE 1942. WITH A BACKYARD FOR
FRESH AIR.

20 VINYL WINE
1491 LEXINGTON AVENUE
EXCELLENT HAND-PICKED SELECTION. AND A RECORD
PLAYER.

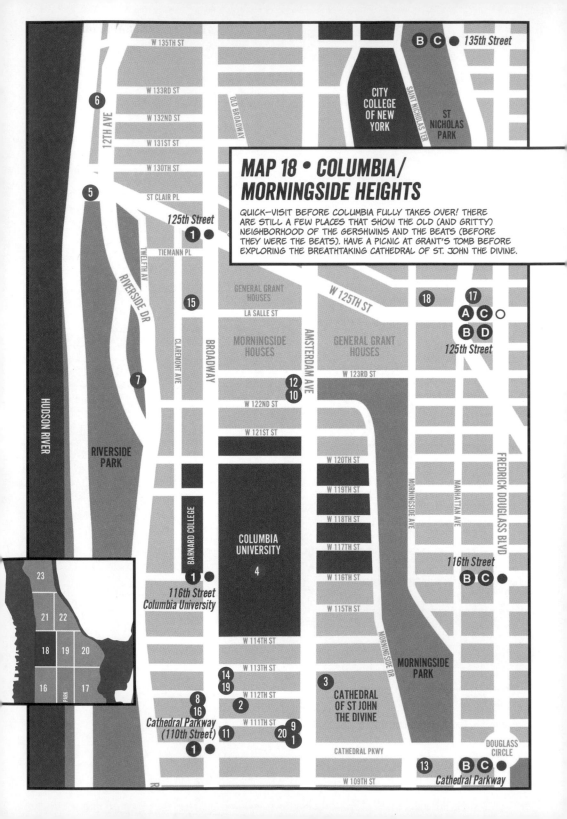

MAP 18 • COLUMBIA/ MORNINGSIDE HEIGHTS

QUICK—VISIT BEFORE COLUMBIA FULLY TAKES OVER! THERE ARE STILL A FEW PLACES THAT SHOW THE OLD (AND GRITTY) NEIGHBORHOOD OF THE GERSHWINS AND THE BEATS (BEFORE THEY WERE THE BEATS). HAVE A PICNIC AT GRANT'S TOMB BEFORE EXPLORING THE BREATHTAKING CATHEDRAL OF ST. JOHN THE DIVINE.

1 1020 BAR
1020 AMSTERDAM AVENUE
COLUMBIA DIVE WITH SUPER CHEAP BEER.

2 BOOK CULTURE
536 WEST 112TH STREET
EXCELLENT BOOKSTORE SERVICING
COLUMBIA/BARNARD STUDENTS.

3 CATHEDRAL OF ST. JOHN THE DIVINE
1047 AMSTERDAM AVENUE
OUR FAVORITE CATHEDRAL. COMPLETELY UNFINISHED
AND USUALLY IN DISARRAY, JUST THE WAY WE LIKE IT.

4 COLUMBIA UNIVERSITY
2960 BROADWAY
A NICE LITTLE SANCTUARY AMID THE ROILING MASSES.

5 DINOSAUR BAR-B-QUE
700 WEST 125TH STREET
OFF-THE-BEATEN-PATH MEAT PALACE WITH GOOD
PRICES.

6 FAIRWAY MARKET
2328 12TH AVENUE
SO BIG. SO GOOD. SO NEW YORK.

7 GRANT'S TOMB
RIVERSIDE DRIVE & WEST 122ND STREET
A TOTALLY UNDERRATED EXPERIENCE, INTERESTING,
GREAT GROUNDS.

8 THE HEIGHTS BAR & GRILL
2867 BROADWAY
HANG OUT ON THE ROOFTOP WITH COLUMBIA
STUDENTS.

9 HUNGARIAN PASTRY SHOP
1030 AMSTERDAM AVENUE
PROFESSORS AND GRAD STUDENTS LOVE TO READ
HERE. AND GUZZLE COFFEE AND EAT SWEETS.

10 KITCHENETTE
1272 AMSTERDAM AVENUE
COZY AND GOOD FOR EVERYTHING.

11 KORONET PIZZA
2848 BROADWAY
JUST ONE SLICE. REALLY. THAT'S ALL YOU'LL NEED.

12 MAX SOHA
1274 AMSTERDAM AVENUE
HOMEY ITALIAN SPOT. CASH-ONLY.

13 MISS MAMIE'S SPOONBREAD TOO
366 WEST 110TH STREET
SOUL FOOD SPECTACULAR.

14 OREN'S DAILY ROAST
2882 BROADWAY
HIP STAFF POURS SUPERIOR JAVA AT LOCAL MINI-CHAIN.

15 PISTICCI
125 LA SALLE STREET
WONDERFUL, FRIENDLY ITALIAN. A TRUE GEM.

16 SAMAD'S GOURMET
2867 BROADWAY
HARD TO FIND MIDDLE EASTERN AND WORLD
DELICACIES.

17 SEA & SEA FISH MARKET
310 ST. NICHOLAS AVENUE
FISH AND MORE FISH. THEY'LL FRY IT UP FOR YOU!

18 SHOWMAN'S
375 WEST 125TH STREET
LIVE JAZZ. IN HARLEM. NO COVER. THAT'S ALL YOU
NEED TO KNOW.

19 TOM'S RESTAURANT
2880 BROADWAY
YES. THIS IS THE SEINFELD DINER WHERE THEY ALL
HUNG OUT. CAN WE GO NOW?

20 V&T PIZZERIA
1024 AMSTERDAM AVENUE
PIES AND PASTA. FAMILY FRIENDLY WITH RED CHECK-
ERED TABLE CLOTHS.

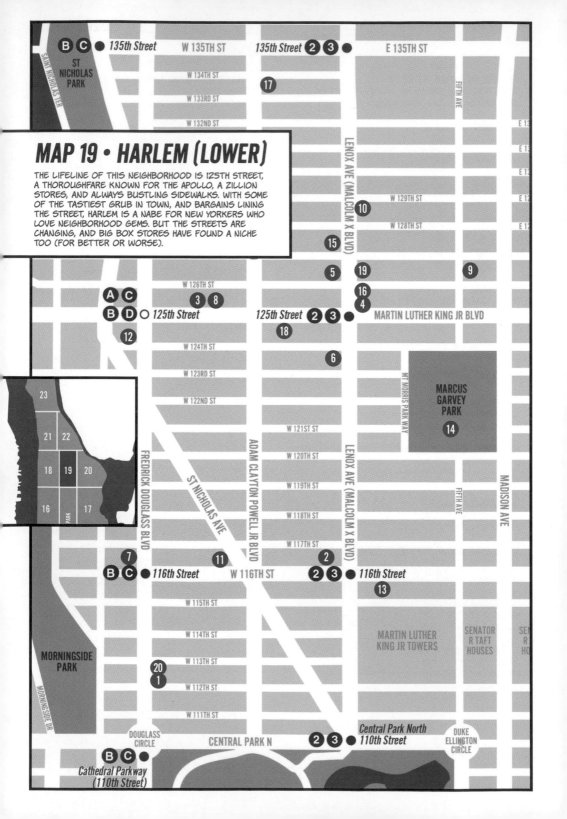

MAP 19 • HARLEM (LOWER)

THE LIFELINE OF THIS NEIGHBORHOOD IS 125TH STREET, A THOROUGHFARE KNOWN FOR THE APOLLO, A ZILLION STORES, AND ALWAYS BUSTLING SIDEWALKS. WITH SOME OF THE TASTIEST GRUB IN TOWN, AND BARGAINS LINING THE STREET, HARLEM IS A NABE FOR NEW YORKERS WHO LOVE NEIGHBORHOOD GEMS. BUT THE STREETS ARE CHANGING, AND BIG BOX STORES HAVE FOUND A NICHE TOO (FOR BETTER OR WORSE).

1 67 ORANGE STREET
2082 FREDERICK DOUGLASS BOULEVARD
CLASSY COCKTAIL BAR WITH SPEAKEASY STYLE.

2 AMY RUTH'S
113 WEST 116TH STREET
SOUL FOOD. NOTHING BEATS FRIED CHICKEN AND
WAFFLES FOR BREAKFAST.

3 APOLLO THEATER
253 WEST 125TH STREET
THE ONE AND ONLY. WHERE BOOING IS NOT ONLY
ALLOWED, IT'S ENCOURAGED!

4 CHEZ LUCIENNE
308 MALCOLM X BOULEVARD
COZY LITTLE FRENCH BISTRO. AUTHENTIC AND
AFFORDABLE.

5 CORNER SOCIAL
321 LENOX AVENUE
A SOLID BACKUP WHEN THE ROOSTER IS PACKED
ACROSS THE STREET.

6 HARLEM SHAKE
100 WEST 124TH STREET
SHAKES AND BURGER JOINT WITH THROWBACK LOOK.

7 HARLEM TAVERN
2153 FREDERICK DOUGLASS BOULEVARD
HYBRID DUTIES: BEER GARDEN, SPORT BAR, AND
PUB FOOD.

8 JIMMY JAZZ
132 WEST 125TH STREET
URBAN STREETWEAR EMPORIUM.

9 LANGSTON HUGHES PLACE
20 EAST 127TH STREET
WHERE THE PROLIFIC POET LIVED AND WORKED
1947-1967.

10 LENOX COFFEE
60 WEST 129TH STREET
CLASSY CAFE WITH LOTS OF LATTES AND LAPTOPS.

11 MAKE MY CAKE
121 ST. NICHOLAS AVENUE
RED. VELVET. CHEESECAKE. BONUS: IN-STORE WIFI.

12 MAGIC JOHNSON HARLEM 9
2309 FREDERICK DOUGLASS BOULEVARD
OWNED BY MAGIC. BEST CHOICE FOR BLOCKBUSTERS
IN HARLEM.

13 MALCOLM SHABAZZ HARLEM MARKET
58 WEST 116TH STREET
AN AFRICAN OPEN-AIR MARKET.

14 MARCUS GARVEY PARK
EAST 120TH STREET & MADISON AVENUE
APPEALINGLY MOUNTAINOUS PARK WITH OUTDOOR
THEATER.

15 MAYSLES CINEMA
343 MALCOLM X BOULEVARD
AMAZING INDIES AND DOCUMENTARIES FROM LOCAL
FILM-MAKERS.

16 RED ROOSTER
310 LENOX AVENUE
THE UPTOWN DINING AND DRINKING CRAZE FROM CHEF
STAR MARCUS SAMUELSSON.

17 SHRINE
2271 ADAM CLAYTON POWELL JR. BOULEVARD
VIBRANT LIVE MUSIC VENUE WITH ECLECTIC LINEUP.

18 STUDIO MUSEUM
144 WEST 125TH STREET
HIGHLIGHTING LOCAL & FAR-FLUNG ARTISTS OF
AFRICAN DESCENT. PLUS GREAT PUBLIC PROGRAMS
AND EVENTS.

19 SYLVIA'S
328 MALCOLM X BOULEVARD
SOUL FOOD INSTITUTION. WORTH A TRIP UPTOWN.
NOT OVERRATED.

20 ZOMA
2084 FREDERICK DOUGLASS BOULEVARD
TASTY ETHIOPIAN IN A TASTEFUL SETTING.

MAP 20 • EL BARRIO/EAST HARLEM

EL BARRIO IS INCREDIBLY RICH AND VIBRANT IN HISTORY AND CULTURE. PUERTO RICAN, AFRICAN-AMERICAN, MEXICAN, DOMINICAN, ITALIAN...IT'S ALL HERE. ABUNDANT COMMUNITY GARDENS PROVIDE LOCALS WITH THE PERFECT SUMMER CHILL OUT SPOTS. EXPLORING THIS NEIGHBORHOOD IS HIGHLY RECOMMENDED.

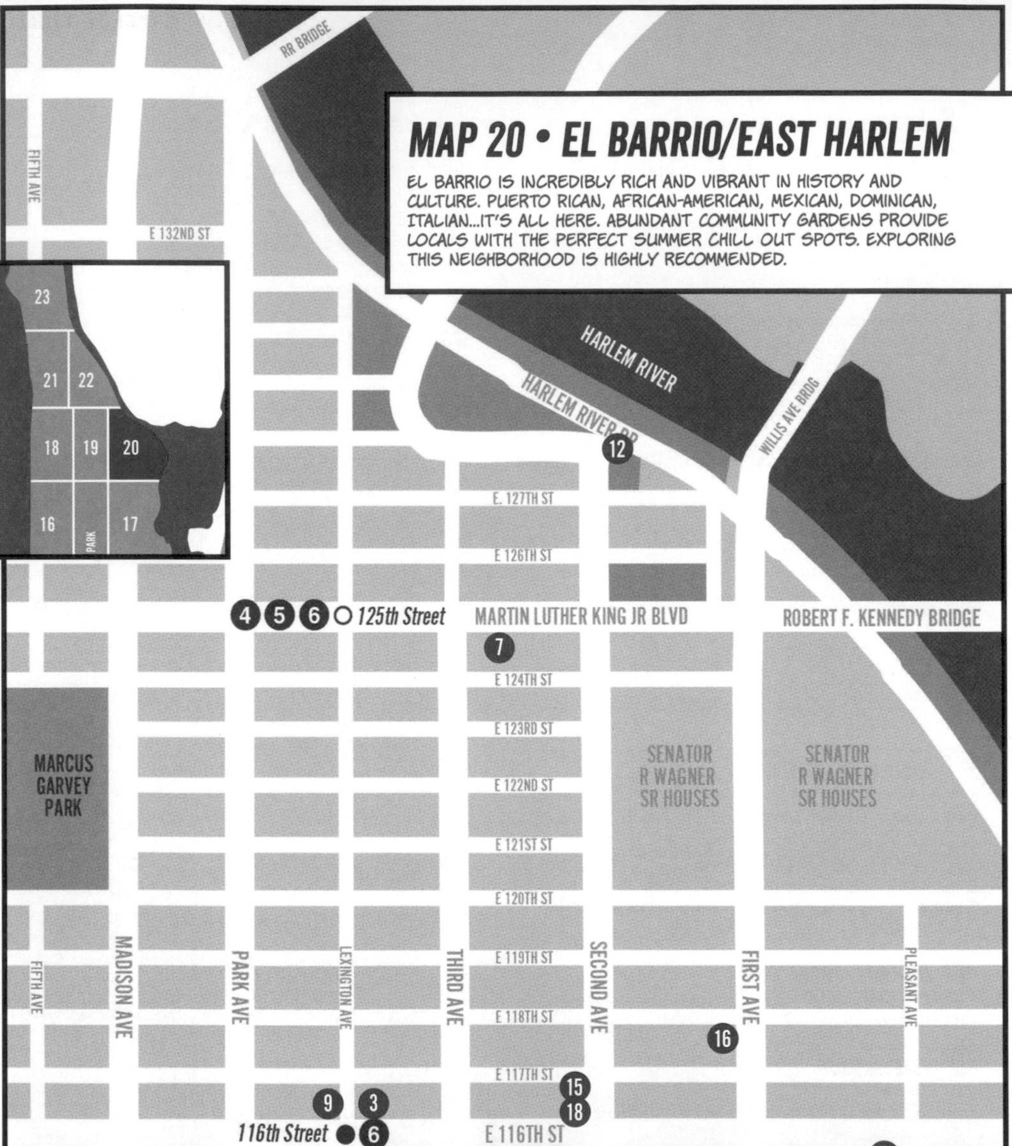

1 AMOR CUBANO
2018 3RD AVENUE
GREAT FOOD AND THE HOUSE BAND ALWAYS HAS THIS PLACE GROOVING.

2 CAMARADAS
2241 1ST AVENUE
ECLECTIC LIVE MUSIC & DJS AND TASTY BAR FOOD. THE GREAT NEIGHBORHOOD VIBE DOESN'T HURT EITHER.

3 CASA LATINO MUSIC SHOP
151 EAST 116TH STREET
EL BARRIO'S OLDEST RECORD STORE.

4 CASABLANCA MEAT MARKET
125 EAST 110TH STREET
THE LINE OUT THE DOOR EVERY SATURDAY SAYS IT ALL.

5 CHURCH OF OUR LADY MT CARMEL
448 EAST 116TH STREET
THE FIRST ITALIAN PARISH IN NYC.

6 CUCHIFRITOS
168 EAST 116TH STREET
PUERTO RICAN AND DOMINICAN FRIED TREATS. HAVE A SEAT AT THE COUNTER AND FILL UP.EITHER.

7 DEMOLITION DEPOT
216 EAST 125TH STREET
AMAZING SELECTION OF ARCHITECTURAL SALVAGE.

8 THE DUCK
2171 2ND AVENUE
UPTOWN COUNTRY DIVE. WEIRD AS IT SOUNDS.

9 EL AGUILA
137 EAST 116TH STREET
PORKTASTIC BUSTLING TACO JOINT. OPEN 24-7!

10 EL NUEVO CARIDAD
2257 2ND AVENUE
DOMINICAN BASEBALL STARS APPROVE OF THIS CHICKEN.

11 KAHLUA'S CAFE
2117 3RD AVENUE
AWESOME MEXI-GRUB. TINY, LOUD, AND FUN.

12 KEITH HARING "CRACK IS WACK" MURAL
2ND AVENUE & EAST 127TH STREET
CLASSIC STREET ART. KEITH WAS RIGHT.

13 LA MARQUETA
1590 PARK AVENUE
HISTORIC PUBLIC MARKET WITH A MIX OF OLD-SCHOOL AND NEW-SCHOOL TENANTS.

14 LOVE CAFE
283 PLEASANT AVENUE
SUPER FRIENDLY INDIE SHOP ALMOST TOO GOOD TO BE TRUE.

15 MI MEXICO LINDO BAKERY
2267 2ND AVENUE
GRAB A TRAY AND LOAD UP ON SWEETS AT THIS LOCAL BAKERY.

16 PATSY'S PIZZA
2287 1ST AVENUE
COAL-OVEN, ICONIC, WORTH-THE-TRIP PIZZA. PLUS, BEST TAKE-OUT SLICES IN NY.

17 RAO'S
455 EAST 114TH STREET
AN ITALIAN INSTITUTION, BUT YOU'LL NEVER GET IN.

18 SANDY RESTAURANT
2261 2ND AVENUE
NEIGHBORHOOD DOMINICAN JOINT. TRY THE LECHON ASADO.

19 TACO MIX
234 EAST 116TH STREET
A TINY TAQUERIA SLINGING THE BEST TACOS IN EL BARRIO. GO FOR THE AL PASTOR.

MAP 21 • MANHATTANVILLE/ HAMILTON HEIGHTS

THIS CLOSELY KNIT COMMUNITY MAINTAINS ITS TRADITIONAL ESSENCE WITH ITS NEO-GOTHIC CITY COLLEGE, GORGEOUS ETHNIC GARB, MEMORIAL GARDENS, AND, OF COURSE, BREATHTAKING BROWNSTONES. JUST TO KEEP THINGS INTERESTING, THE NATIONAL PARK SERVICE MOVED HAMILTON GRANGE TO ST. NICHOLAS PARK A FEW YEARS BACK.

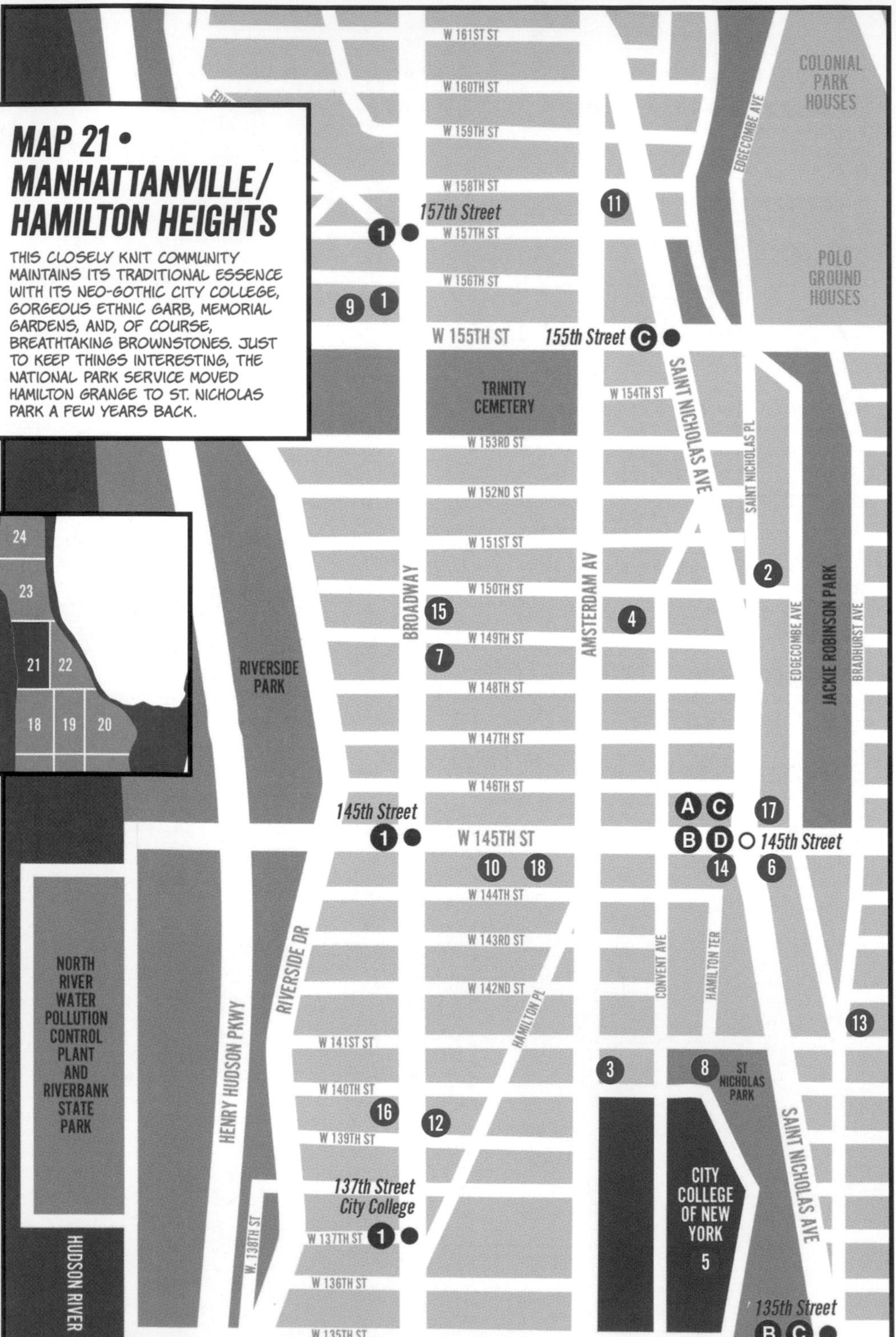

COLONIAL PARK HOUSES

POLO GROUND HOUSES

W 161ST ST
W 160TH ST
W 159TH ST
W 158TH ST
157th Street
W 157TH ST
W 156TH ST
W 155TH ST
155th Street
W 154TH ST
TRINITY CEMETERY
W 153RD ST
W 152ND ST
W 151ST ST
W 150TH ST
W 149TH ST
W 148TH ST
W 147TH ST
W 146TH ST
145th Street
W 145TH ST
145th Street
W 144TH ST
W 143RD ST
W 142ND ST
W 141ST ST
W 140TH ST
W 139TH ST
137th Street City College
W 137TH ST
W 136TH ST
135th Street
W 135TH ST

BROADWAY
AMSTERDAM AV
SAINT NICHOLAS AVE
SAINT NICHOLAS PL
EDGECOMBE AVE
EDGECOMBE AVE
BRADHURST AVE
JACKIE ROBINSON PARK
CONVENT AVE
HAMILTON TER
HAMILTON PL
RIVERSIDE DR
HENRY HUDSON PKWY
W. 138TH ST
RIVERSIDE PARK

NORTH RIVER WATER POLLUTION CONTROL PLANT AND RIVERBANK STATE PARK

HUDSON RIVER

ST NICHOLAS PARK

CITY COLLEGE OF NEW YORK

24
23
21 22
18 19 20

1 AUDUBON TERRACE
BROADWAY & WEST 155TH STREET
PLEASANT, IF LONELY, BEAUX ARTS COMPLEX.

2 BAILEY HOUSE
10 ST. NICHOLAS PLACE
ROMANESQUE REVIVAL MANSION FROM PT BARNUM'S
PARTNER JAMES BAILEY.

3 CAFE ONE
1619 AMSTERDAM AVENUE
FREE WI-FI, QUALITY PASTRIES AND RELIABLE JAVA.

4 CHURCH OF THE CRUCIFIXION
459 WEST 149TH STREET
WHACKED-OUT CONCRETE CHURCH BY COSTAS
MACHLOUZARIDES, CIRCA 1967.

5 CITY COLLEGE
160 CONVENT AVENUE
PEACEFUL GOTHIC CAMPUS.

6 FAMOUS FISH MARKET
684 ST. NICHOLAS
DEEP FRIED AND FROM THE SEA.

7 HARLEM PUBLIC
3612 BROADWAY
GOOD FOOD, GOOD DRINKS, EXCITING ADDITION TO
NEIGHBORHOOD.

8 HAMILTON GRANGE NATIONAL MEMORIAL
414 WEST 141ST STREET
ALEXANDER HAMILTON'S HOUSE, TWICE RELOCATED
AND NOW FACING THE WRONG WAY. DAMN THOSE
JEFFERSONIANS!

9 HISPANIC SOCIETY
613 WEST 155TH STREET
FREE MUSEUM (TUES-SAT) WITH SPANISH
MASTERPIECES.

10 JIMBO'S HAMBURGER PALACE
528 WEST 145TH STREET
CHEAP, FAST, EASY BURGERS.

11 LA OAXAQUENA RESTAURANT
1969 AMSTERDAM AVENUE
ONE OF THE BEST IN A PARADE OF TAQUERIAS.

12 PICANTE
3424 BROADWAY
ARGUABLY MANHATTANVILLE'S BEST MEXICAN, PLUS
AFFORDABLE MARGS.

13 QUEEN SHEBA
317 WEST 141ST STREET
CAFETERIA STYLE MIDDLE EASTERN THAT'S FRIENDLY
ON THE WALLET.

14 SUNSHINE KITCHEN
695 ST. NICHOLAS AVENUE
JAMAICAN EATS LIKE PATTIES AND DELICIOUS CURRIED
GOAT.

15 TONALLI CAFE BAR
3628 BROADWAY
RARE ITALIAN BISTRO CUISINE IN HAMILTON HEIGHTS.

16 TRUFA
3431 BROADWAY
BISTRO FEATURING PASTAS AND NEW AMERICAN
ENTREES.

17 UNITY LIQUORS
708 ST. NICHOLAS AVENUE
RIGHT BY THE SUBWAY, WHERE ALL LIQUOR STORES
SHOULD BE.

18 VIM
508 WEST 145TH STREET
STREET WEAR-JEANS, SNEAKERS, TOPS-FOR ALL.

MAP 22 • HARLEM (UPPER)

UPPER HARLEM IS THE CENTER OF BLACK CULTURE IN NEW YORK. THERE ARE MANY HISTORIC BUILDINGS TO VISIT, INCLUDING NEW YORK'S OLDEST BLACK CONGREGATION, ABYSSINIAN BAPTIST CHURCH, AND THE SCHOMBURG CENTER FOR RESEARCH IN BLACK CULTURE WHICH HAS RESOURCES DOCUMENTING THE HISTORY OF PEOPLE OF AFRICAN DESCENT. ALSO CHECK OUT THE DUNBAR HOUSES.

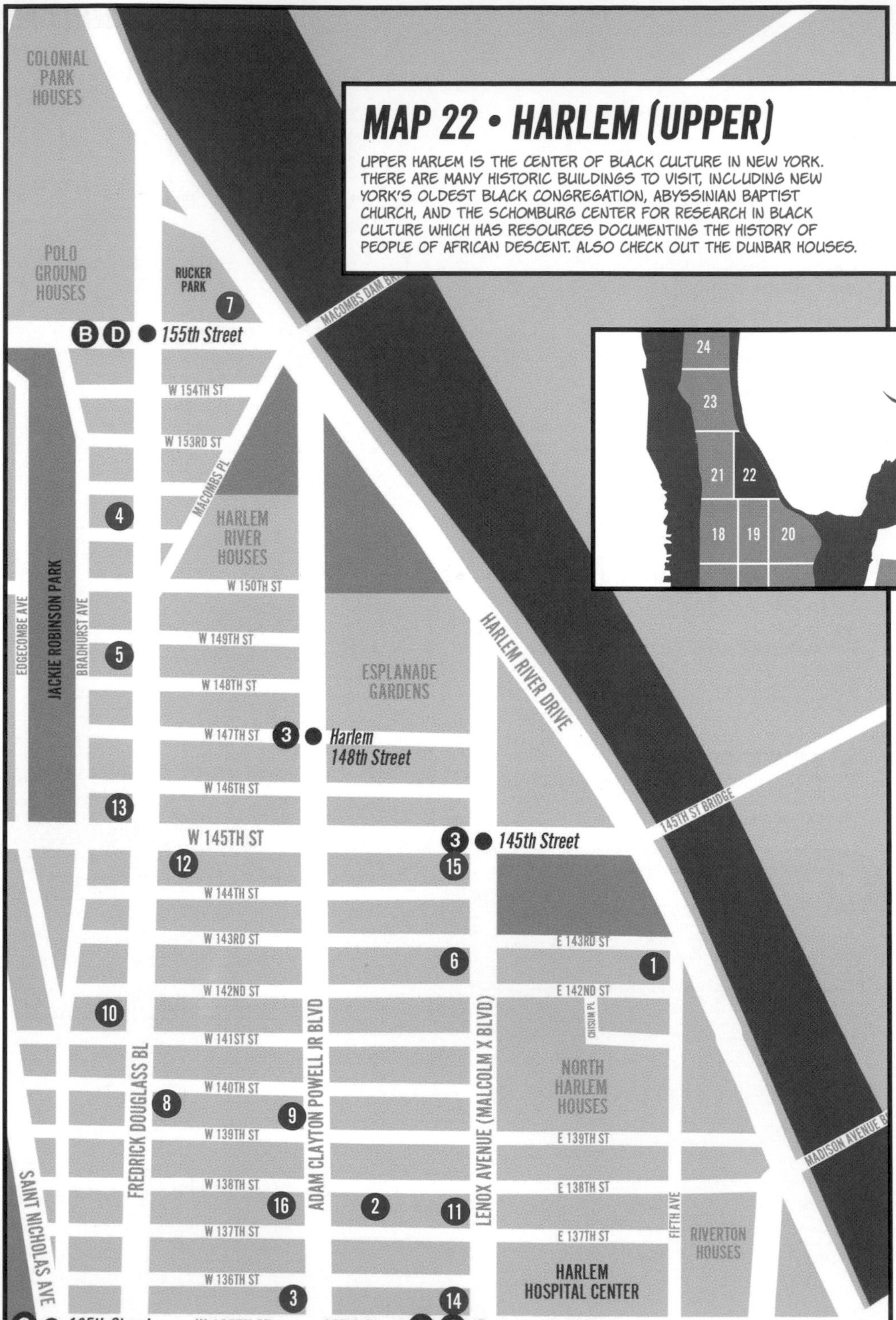

COLONIAL PARK HOUSES

POLO GROUND HOUSES

RUCKER PARK

7

B D ● 155th Street

W 154TH ST

W 153RD ST

MACOMBS DAM BRIDGE

MACOMBS PL

HARLEM RIVER HOUSES

4

W 150TH ST

JACKIE ROBINSON PARK

EDGECOMBE AVE

BRADHURST AVE

W 149TH ST

5

W 148TH ST

ESPLANADE GARDENS

HARLEM RIVER DRIVE

3 ● Harlem 148th Street
W 147TH ST

W 146TH ST

13

W 145TH ST

3 ● 145th Street
15

12

W 144TH ST

145 ST BRIDGE

W 143RD ST

E 143RD ST

1

6

W 142ND ST

E 142ND ST

10

W 141ST ST

CHISUM PL

NORTH HARLEM HOUSES

FREDRICK DOUGLASS BL

ADAM CLAYTON POWELL JR BLVD

LENOX AVENUE (MALCOLM X BLVD)

W 140TH ST

8

9

E 139TH ST

W 139TH ST

MADISON AVENUE BRIDGE

W 138TH ST

16

2

11

E 138TH ST

W 137TH ST

FIFTH AVE

E 137TH ST

RIVERTON HOUSES

SAINT NICHOLAS AVE

W 136TH ST

HARLEM HOSPITAL CENTER

3

14

C ● 135th Street   W 135TH ST   135th Street 2 3 ●   E 135TH ST

24

23

21 22

18 19 20

1 369TH REGIMENT ARMORY
2366 5TH AVENUE
1933 BEAUTY THAT WAS HOME TO THE FAMOUS "HARLEM HELLFIGHTERS" FROM WWI.

2 ABYSSINIAN BAPTIST CHURCH
132 ODELL CLARK PLACE
NYC'S OLDEST BLACK CONGREGATION.

3 B. OYAMA
2312 ADAM CLAYTON POWELL JR. BOULEVARD
FASHION FOR MEN.

4 CHARLES COUNTRY PAN FRIED CHICKEN
2839 FREDERICK DOUGLASS BOULEVARD
THE FRIED CHICKEN THEY SERVE IN HEAVEN.

5 DUNBAR HOUSES
FREDERICK DOUGLASS BOULEVARD & WEST 149TH ST.
HISTORIC, MULTI-FAMILY APARTMENT BUILDINGS FROM THE 1920S.

6 GRINI'S GRILL
100 WEST 143RD STREET
THIS "TAPAS BAR" ACTUALLY SERVES HEAPING PLATES OF MEAT AND RICE

7 HOLCOMBE RUCKER PARK
FREDERICK DOUGLASS BOULEVARD & WEST 155TH ST.
FAMOUS BASKETBALL COURT THAT BIRTHED THE LIKES OF KAREEM ABDUL-JABBAR AND MORE.

8 LONDEL'S SUPPER CLUB
2620 FREDERICK DOUGLASS BOULEVARD
GOOD SOUTHERN FOOD WITH GREAT LIVE MUSIC ON THE WEEKENDS.

9 MAKE MY CAKE
2380 ADAM CLAYTON POWELL JR. BOULEVARD
FRESHLY BAKED CAKES FROM A SOUTHERN FAMILY RECIPE.

10 MAMA TINA'S PIZZA
2649 FREDERICK DOUGLASS BOULEVARD
DECENT PIZZA FOR LATE-NIGHT PANGS.

11 MISS MAUDE'S SPOONBREAD TOO
547 LENOX AVENUE
HARLEM FOOD FOR THE SOUL.

12 O'FISHOLE SEAFOOD
274 WEST 145TH STREET
FRIED FISH PLATTERS & BURGERS. OPEN LATE ON WEEKENDS.

13 PEOPLE'S CHOICE
2733 FREDERICK DOUGLASS BOULEVARD
JERK CHICKEN AND OXTAIL STEWS WORTH A TASTE.

14 SCHOMBURG CENTER FOR RESEARCH IN BLACK CULTURE
515 MALCOLM X BOULEVARD
FOCUSES ON PRESERVING THE HISTORY OF PEOPLE OF AFRICAN DESCENT WORLDWIDE.

15 SNEAKER Q
693 LENOX AVENUE
GET YOUR KICKS AT THIS LENOX STOREFRONT.

16 ST. NICHOLAS HISTORIC DISTRICT
202 WEST 138TH STREET
BEAUTIFUL NEO-GEORGIAN TOWNHOUSES.

MAP 23 · WASHINGTON HEIGHTS

THEY DIDN'T NAME A MUSICAL AFTER THE 'HEIGHTS' FOR NOTHING.
THIS NORTHERN TIP OF MANHATTAN IS THE CENTRAL AMERICA-CUM-
HARDWARE CAPITAL OF NEW YORK. COMPLETE WITH BODEGAS AND
SHOPS WITH BUILDING MATERIALS AND HOME IMPROVEMENT TOOLS,
THE HEIGHTS GETS YOU HIGH OFF FUN AND HARD WORK.

1 181 CABRINI
854 WEST 181ST STREET
SEASONAL AMERICAN BISTRO.

2 THE ARMORY
216 FORT WASHINGTON AVENUE
WORLD CLASS RUNNING FACILITY HOUSES TRACK & FIELD HALL OF FAME.

3 COOGAN'S
4015 BROADWAY
JOIN DOCTORS, PROFESSORS AND OFF-DUTY COPS FOR A COLD ONE.

4 GEORGE WASHINGTON BRIDGE
WEST 178TH STREET & HENRY HUDSON PARKWAY
TRY TO SEE IT WHEN IT'S LIT UP. DRIVE DOWN FROM RIVERDALE ON THE HENRY HUDSON AT NIGHT AND YOU'LL UNDERSTAND.

5 JIMMY ORO RESTAURANT
711 WEST 181ST STREET
CHINESE/SPANISH. HUGE VARIETY.

6 JOU JOU CAFE
3959 BROADWAY
SERVING YOUR SOUP, SANDWICH AND ESPRESSO NEEDS ALL DAY AND NIGHT.

7 LE CHEILE
839 WEST 181ST STREET
NICE-LOOKING IRISH BAR WITH GOOD BEER & FOOD.

8 THE LITTLE RED LIGHTHOUSE
FORT WASHINGTON PARK
ENTER FROM 181ST STREET. IT'S THERE, REALLY!

9 MALECON
4141 BROADWAY
FABULOUS ROAST CHICKEN.

10 MARCHA COCINA & BAR
4055 BROADWAY
TASTY TRIFECTA OF TAPAS, BRUNCH AND COCKTAILS.

11 MARGOT RESTAURANT
3822 BROADWAY
ARGUABLY, THE HEIGHTS' VERY BEST DOMINICAN.

12 MIKE'S BAGELS
4003 BROADWAY
MORE LIKE BOB'S THAN MURRAY'S.

13 MORRIS-JUMEL MANSION
65 JUMEL TERRACE
THE OLDEST BUILDING IN NEW YORK, AT LEAST UNTIL SOMEONE CHANGES IT AGAIN.

14 MOSCOW ON THE HUDSON
801 WEST 181ST STREET
COMRADES, THIS PLACE IS RUSSIAN CULINARY HEAVEN.

15 PARRILLA STEAKHOUSE
3920 BROADWAY
ARGENTINEAN GRILLED MEATS.

16 RED ROOM LOUNGE
1 BENNETT AVENUE
DIONYSUS WOULD BE PROUD.

17 SAGGIO
829 WEST 181ST STREET
EVERY GOOD NEIGHBORHOOD NEEDS A SOLID ITALIAN TRATTORIA.

18 SYLVAN TERRACE
BETWEEN JUMEL TERRACE & ST NICHOLAS AVENUE
THE MOST UN-MANHATTANLIKE PLACE IN ALL THE WORLD.

19 TIPICO DOMINICANO
4172 BROADWAY
FAMILY PLACE TO WATCH THE GAME. GOOOOAL.

20 UNITED PALACE THEATER
4140 BROADWAY
MOVIE THEATER, THEN CHURCH, NOW ROCK VENUE. GORGEOUS INSIDE.

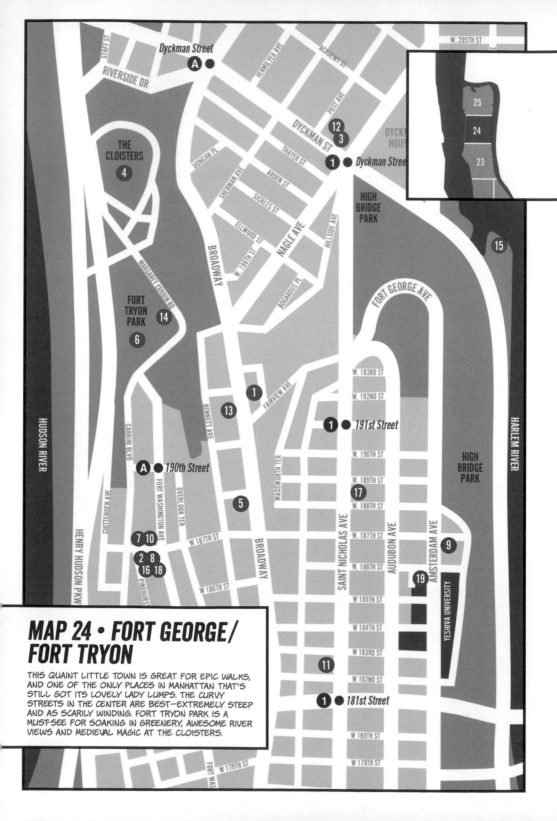

MAP 24 • FORT GEORGE/ FORT TRYON

THIS QUAINT LITTLE TOWN IS GREAT FOR EPIC WALKS, AND ONE OF THE ONLY PLACES IN MANHATTAN THAT'S STILL GOT ITS LOVELY LADY LUMPS. THE CURVY STREETS IN THE CENTER ARE BEST—EXTREMELY STEEP AND AS SCARILY WINDING. FORT TRYON PARK IS A MUST-SEE FOR SOAKING IN GREENERY, AWESOME RIVER VIEWS AND MEDIEVAL MAGIC AT THE CLOISTERS.

1 BUDDHA BEER BAR
4476 BROADWAY
NICE SET OF TAPS AND KOREAN/MEXI FUSION WORTH THE TRIP.

2 CAFE BUUNNI
213 PINEHURST AVENUE
ESPRESSO DRINKS AND ETHIOPIAN FOODS.

3 CACHAPAS Y MAS
107 DYCKMAN STREET
FRIED LATIN TASTINESS IN CORN AND MEAT FORM.

4 THE CLOISTERS
99 MARGARET CORBIN DRIVE
THE MET'S STOREHOUSE OF MEDIEVAL ART. GREAT HERB GARDEN, NICE VIEWS.

5 FOOD PALACE
4407 BROADWAY
YOUR LOCAL RUSSIAN SUPERMARKET.

6 FORT TRYON PARK
WEST 181ST STREET & HUDSON RIVER GREENWAY
A TOTALLY BEAUTIFUL AND SCENIC GREEN SPACE ON THE CITY'S NORTH EDGE.

7 FRANK'S MARKET
807 W 187TH STREET
GOURMET MEATS, CHEESES, AND GROCERIES. A NEIGHBORHOOD INSTITUTION.

8 GIDEON'S BAKERY
810 WEST 187TH STREET
KOSHER SUGAR COMA.

9 GOLAN HEIGHTS
2552 AMSTERDAM AVENUE
TASTY ISRAELI FALAFEL AND SHAWARMA. POPULAR FOR LUNCH.

10 KISMAT INDIAN
603 FORT WASHINGTON AVENUE
THROW YOUR TASTE BUDS A SURPRISE PARTY.

11 LA CASA DEL MOFONGO
1447 ST NICHOLAS AVENUE
THE OBVIOUS: HAVE THE MOFONGO.

12 LA SALA 78
111 DYCKMAN STREET
ENJOY SOME ART WITH YOUR LATTE.

13 LOCKSMITH WINE & BURGER BAR
4463 BROADWAY
FRIENDLY SPOT TO GRAB A GLASS OF WINE OR BEER.

14 NEW LEAF RESTAURANT
1 MARGARET CORBIN DRIVE
UPTOWN HAVEN FOR A FANCIER DINNER OR BRUNCH.

15 PETER JAY SHARP BOATHOUSE
SWINDLER COVE PARK
SEE THE WEST BRONX BY BOAT.

16 RUSTY MACKEREL
209 PINEHURST AVENUE
CREATIVE NEW AMERICAN WITH SMALL PLATES AND A DOWNTOWN VIBE.

17 TACOS EL PAISA
1548 ST. NICHOLAS AVENUE
FANTASTIC HOLE-IN-THE-WALL MEXICAN.

18 VINES ON PINE
814 WEST 187TH STREET
ONE-OF-A-KIND WINE SELECTIONS.

19 YESHIVA UNIVERSITY ZYSMAN HALL
2540 AMSTERDAM AVENUE
INTERESTING BYZANTINE-STYLE BUILDING.

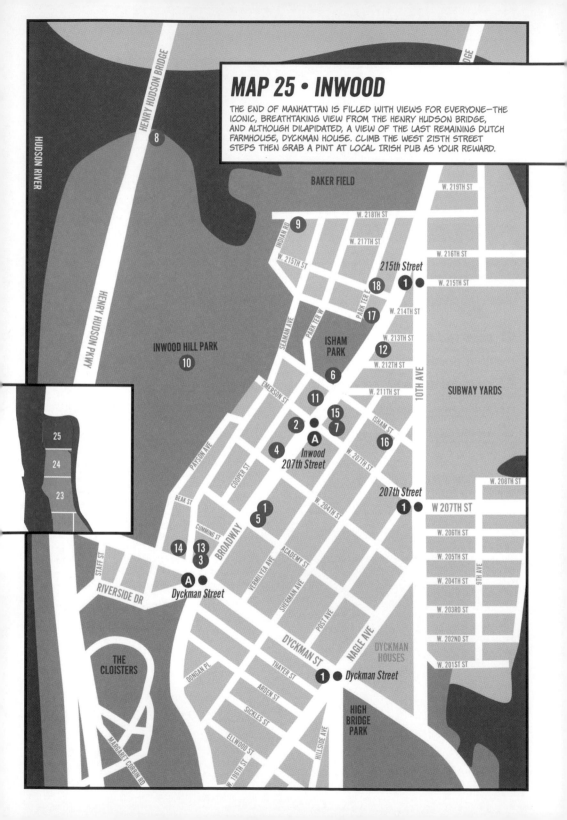

MAP 25 · INWOOD

THE END OF MANHATTAN IS FILLED WITH VIEWS FOR EVERYONE—THE ICONIC, BREATHTAKING VIEW FROM THE HENRY HUDSON BRIDGE, AND ALTHOUGH DILAPIDATED, A VIEW OF THE LAST REMAINING DUTCH FARMHOUSE, DYCKMAN HOUSE. CLIMB THE WEST 215TH STREET STEPS THEN GRAB A PINT AT LOCAL IRISH PUB AS YOUR REWARD.

1 BEANS & VINES
4842 BROADWAY
COZY COFFEE SHOP AND WINE BAR SERVING FOOD.

2 CAPITOL RESTAURANT
4933 BROADWAY
NICE NEIGHBORHOOD DINER.

3 CORCHO
231 DYCKMAN STREET
COZY SPOT TO SIP AND NIBBLE; HAPPY HOUR AND WINE CLASSES A BONUS.

4 DYCKMAN HOUSE
4881 BROADWAY
OLDEST FARMHOUSE IN MANHATTAN, NOW RESTORED AS A MUSEUM.

5 ELSA LA REINA DEL CHICHARRON
4840 BROADWAY
IT'S WORTH THE CORONARY BYPASS.

6 GRANDPA'S BRICK OVEN PIZZA
4973 BROADWAY
PERSONAL BRICK-OVEN PIES AND CATERING.

7 GUADALUPE
597 WEST 207TH STREET
HIGH CLASS MEXICAN.

8 HENRY HUDSON BRIDGE
HENRY HUDSON PARKWAY
AFFORDS A NICE VIEW FROM THE INWOOD HILL PARK SIDE.

9 INDIAN ROAD CAFE
600 WEST 218TH STREET
FRIENDLY NEIGHBORHOOD CAFE.

10 INWOOD HILL PARK
DYCKMAN STREET & PAYSON AVENUE
THE LAST NATURAL FOREST AND SALT MARSH IN MANHATTAN!

11 INWOOD LOCAL
4957 BROADWAY
BEER GARDEN, WINE BAR, AND SPORTS PUB WITH A SIDE OF TASTY GRUB.

12 IRISH EYES
5008 BROADWAY
KNOCK ON THE WINDOW IF THE LIGHT IS ON.

13 MAMA SUSHI
237 DYCKMAN STREET
AS GOOD AS UPTOWN RAW FISH GETS.

14 MAMAJUANA CAFE
247 DYCKMAN STREET
TASTY NUEVO LATINO CUISINE.

15 PIPER'S KILT
4946 BROADWAY
IRISH PUB WITH FRIENDLY LOCALS AND A SOLID BURGER.

16 POST BILLIARDS CAFE
154 POST AVENUE
WHEN YOU NEED TO SHOOT POOL WAY WAY UPTOWN.

17 Q CIGARS
5009 BROADWAY
FRESH OUT OF THE HAND CIGARS.

18 WEST 215TH STREET STEPS
WEST 215TH STREET & PARK TERRACE EAST
ELEVATION OF SIDEWALK REQUIRES STEPS. NOW GET A MOVE ON IT!

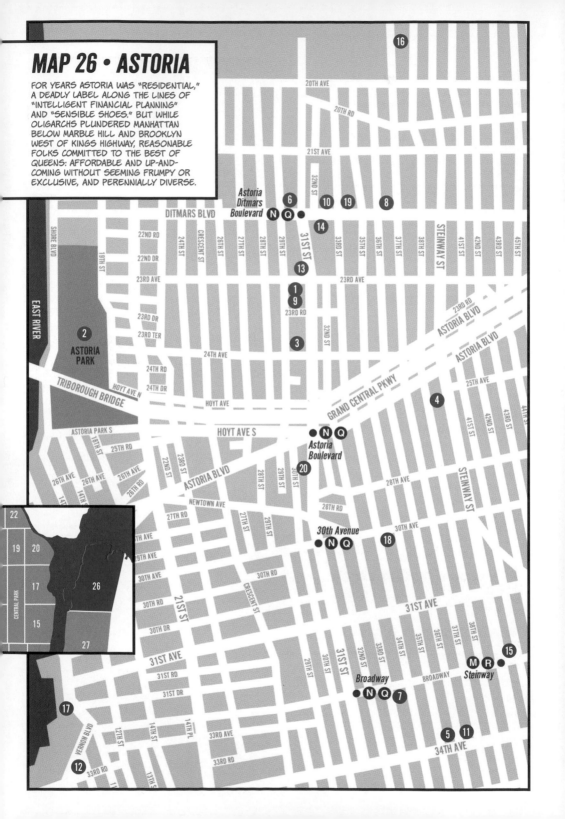

MAP 26 • ASTORIA

FOR YEARS ASTORIA WAS "RESIDENTIAL," A DEADLY LABEL ALONG THE LINES OF "INTELLIGENT FINANCIAL PLANNING" AND "SENSIBLE SHOES." BUT WHILE OLIGARCHS PLUNDERED MANHATTAN BELOW MARBLE HILL AND BROOKLYN WEST OF KINGS HIGHWAY, REASONABLE FOLKS COMMITTED TO THE BEST OF QUEENS: AFFORDABLE AND UP-AND-COMING WITHOUT SEEMING FRUMPY OR EXCLUSIVE, AND PERENNIALLY DIVERSE.

❶ ARTOPOLIS BAKERY
23-18 31ST STREET

DELICIOUS GREEK DESSERTS, ESPECIALLY THE BAKLAVA PIE.

❷ ASTORIA PARK AND POOL
19TH STREET & 23RD DRIVE

60 ACRES OF WATERFRONT PARKLAND AND AN AWE-SOME POOL.

❸ BOHEMIAN HALL & BEER GARDEN
29-19 24TH AVENUE

OVER 100 YEARS OLD; ROOM FOR 500 IN THE GARDEN.

❹ KABAB CAFÉ
25-12 STEINWAY STREET

HAUTE EGYPTIAN COOKED TO ORDER BY FRIENDLY CHEF-OWNER, ALI.

❺ KAUFMAN ASTORIA STUDIOS
34-12 36TH STREET

US'S LARGEST STUDIO OUTSIDE OF LA, AND JUST AS HISTORIC.

❻ LA GULI PASTRY SHOP
29-15 DITMARS BOULEVARD

OLD-SCHOOL ITALIAN PASTRY SHOP. A NEIGHBORHOOD INSTITUTION.

❼ LOCKWOOD SHOP
32-15 33RD STREET

LIFESTYLE SHOP RUN BY ASTORIA BOOSTERS; GOOD EVENTS AND EXTRAS.

❽ MARTHA'S COUNTRY BAKERY
36-21 DITMARS BOULEVARD

BEST POUND CAKE AROUND, AND EVERYTHING ELSE IS GOOD, TOO.

❾ MEDITERRANEAN FOODS
23-18 31ST STREET

GREAT SPOT FOR MEDITERRANEAN-IMPORTED GROCERIES.

❿ MP TAVERNA
31-29 DITMARS BOULEVARD

MICHAEL PSILAKIS' MODERN TAKE ON A TRADITIONAL GREEK TAVERNA.

⑪ MUSEUM OF THE MOVING IMAGE
36-01 35TH AVENUE

FANTASTIC INTERACTIVE FILM/TV MUSEUM, WITH SCREENINGS OF CLASSIC FILMS.

⑫ THE NOGUCHI MUSEUM
9-01 33RD ROAD

NOGUCHI'S CONVERTED FACTORY STUDIO WITH REPRE-SENTATIVE WORKS AND BEAUTIFUL GARDEN.

⑬ ORNELLA TRATTORIA ITALIANA
29-17 23RD AVENUE

INSPIRED EXPERIMENTAL ITALIAN TRATTORIA WITH GREAT PIZZA.

⑭ PARROT COFFEE
31-12 DITMARS BOULEVARD

GOURMET EUROPEAN FOOD, MOSTLY EASTERN EU-ROPE, PLUS FRESH ROASTED COFFEE.

⑮ THE QUEENS KICKSHAW
40-17 BROADWAY

THE HIPSTER TRIFECTA OF ARTISANAL COFFEE, BEER AND GRILLED CHEESE.

⑯ SINGLECUT BEERSMITHS
19-33 37TH STREET

QUEENS' FIRST BREWERY IN DECADES; VISIT TAP ROOM FOR GROWLERS.

⑰ SOCRATES SCULPTURE PARK
32-01 VERNON BOULEVARD

COOL, GRITTY SCULPTURE PARK WITH EVENTS AND FILMS.

⑱ SWEET AFTON
30-09 34TH STREET

SALVAGED WOOD, COMFORT FOOD, AND FANCY DRINKS.

⑲ TAVERNA KYCLADES
33-07 DITMARS BOULEVARD

CONSISTENT, HOMEY GREEK SEAFOOD; WORTH THE WAIT.

⑳ TITAN FOODS
25-56 31ST STREET

THE ZABAR'S OF ASTORIA.

MAP 27 • LONG ISLAND CITY

LONG ISLAND CITY HAS SOME EXCELLENT WATERFRONT FEATURES, BUT IT'S ALSO ONE OF QUEENS' MOST DEVELOPED, MANHATTANISH NEIGHBORHOODS, PLUS WHEN THE 7 TRAIN IS ACTING UP, IT TURNS A 5-SECOND RIDE BETWEEN BOROUGHS INTO A THRASHING NIGHTMARE. THANKFULLY, YOU CAN ALWAYS CHILL OUT WITH MIND-BLOWING SKYLINE VIEWS IN CIVILIZED GANTRY PLAZA STATE PARK.

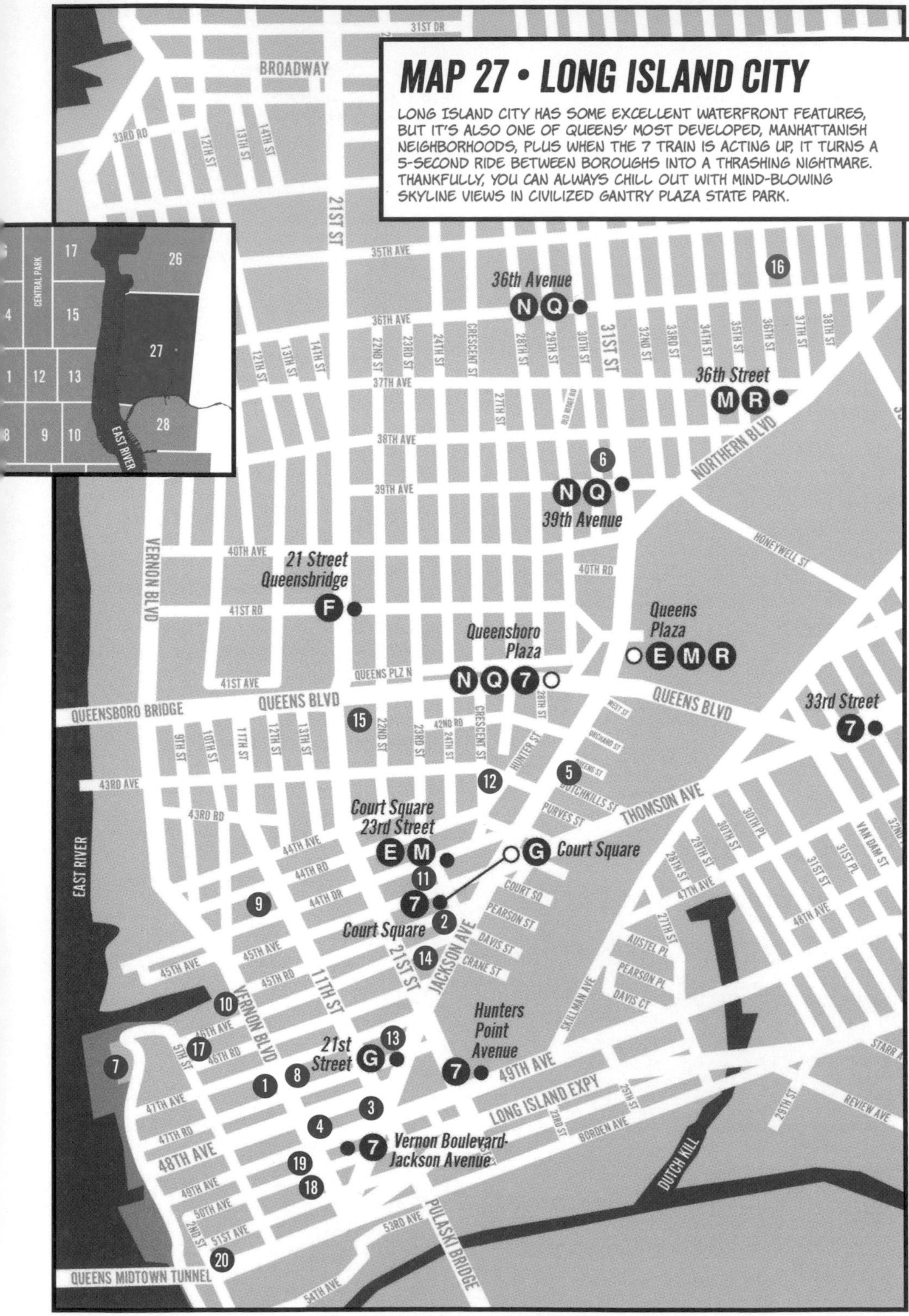

36th Avenue N Q
36th Street M R
39th Avenue N Q
21 Street Queensbridge F
Queensboro Plaza N Q 7
Queens Plaza E M R
33rd Street 7
Court Square 23rd Street E M
Court Square G
Court Square 7
Hunters Point Avenue 7
21st Street G
Vernon Boulevard-Jackson Avenue 7

BROADWAY
31ST DR
33RD RD
35TH AVE
36TH AVE
37TH AVE
38TH AVE
39TH AVE
40TH AVE
40TH RD
41ST RD
41ST AVE
QUEENS PLZ N
QUEENS BLVD
QUEENSBORO BRIDGE
43RD AVE
43RD RD
44TH AVE
44TH RD
44TH DR
45TH AVE
45TH RD
46TH AVE
47TH AVE
47TH RD
48TH AVE
49TH AVE
50TH AVE
51ST AVE
53RD AVE
54TH AVE
QUEENS MIDTOWN TUNNEL
PULASKI BRIDGE
LONG ISLAND EXPY
THOMSON AVE
NORTHERN BLVD
HONEYWELL ST
VERNON BLVD
EAST RIVER
21ST ST

CENTRAL PARK
EAST RIVER

1 CORNER BISTRO
47-18 VERNON BOULEVARD
LEGENDARY VILLAGE BURGER MAINSTAY'S LIC OUTPOST.

2 COURT SQUARE DINER
45-30 23RD STREET
RELIABLE GRUB AVAILABLE 24 HOURS.

3 THE CREEK AND THE CAVE
10-93 JACKSON AVENUE
SUBTERRANEAN LOUNGE WITH MUSIC AND PERFORMANCE NIGHTS.

4 DOMINIE'S HOEK
48-17 VERNON BOULEVARD
NO-FRILLS BAR WITH BACKYARD PATIO AND LIVE MUSIC.

5 DUTCH KILLS
27-24 JACKSON AVENUE
OLD TIME SALOON DECOR AND A CLASSIC COCKTAIL MENU.

6 FISHER LANDAU CENTER
38-27 30TH STREET
FREE ADMISSION, TOP-NOTCH CONTEMPORARY ART COLLECTION.

7 GANTRY PLAZA STATE PARK
EAST RIVER BETWEEN ANABLE BASIN AND 50TH AVENUE
WATERFRONT PARK AND PIERS WITH BREATHTAKING SKYLINE VIEWS.

8 HUNTER'S POINT WINE & SPIRITS
47-07 VERNON BOULEVARD
TRUST THE OWNER TO RECOMMEND GREAT WINES FROM $5 TO $50. ALSO A WELL-EDITED LIQUOR SELECTION.

9 JOHN BROWN'S SMOKEHOUSE
10-43 44TH DRIVE
KANSAS CITY-STYLE BARBECUE JUST OFF THE E TRAIN.

10 LIC BAR
45-58 VERNON BOULEVARD
VINTAGE NEW YORK SALOON WITH SERENE BACKYARD BBQ PATIO AND PHOTO BOOTH.

11 LIC MARKET
21-52 44TH DRIVE
HANDSOME SPACE WITH SEASONAL DISHES AND WINE BAR.

12 M. WELLS STEAKHOUSE
43-15 CRESCENT STREET
MORE BOFFO DISHES FROM STRANGE ANIMAL PARTS AT THIS HIPSTER MEAT PALACE.

13 MANDUCATIS
13-27 JACKSON AVENUE
CLASSIC ITALIAN CUISINE EXPERTLY PREPARED; A BELOVED NEIGHBORHOOD INSTITUTION.

14 MOMA PS1
22-25 JACKSON AVENUE
NYC'S SHOWCASE FOR CONTEMPORARY ART HOSTS DANCE PARTIES IN SUMMER.

15 SILVERCUP STUDIOS
42-22 22ND STREET
FORMER BAKERY IS NOW A BUSY FILM AND TELEVISION STUDIO.

16 STUDIO SQUARE
35-33 36TH STREET
HUGE, NEW-SCHOOL BEER GARDEN WITH PLENTY OF SPACE FOR GROUPS.

17 SWEETLEAF
10-93 JACKSON AVENUE
STUMPTOWN COFFEE AND TASTY HOMEMADE SWEETS.

18 TOURNESOL
50-12 VERNON BOULEVARD
COZY FRENCH BISTRO, A NEIGHBORHOOD GEM.

19 TUK TUK
49-06 VERNON BOULEVARD
HIP SPACE. GOOD THAI FOOD.

20 WATERFRONT CRAB HOUSE
2-03 BORDEN AVENUE
SNACK ON COMPLIMENTARY PEANUTS IN THE BAR BEFORE A SEAFOOD FEAST.

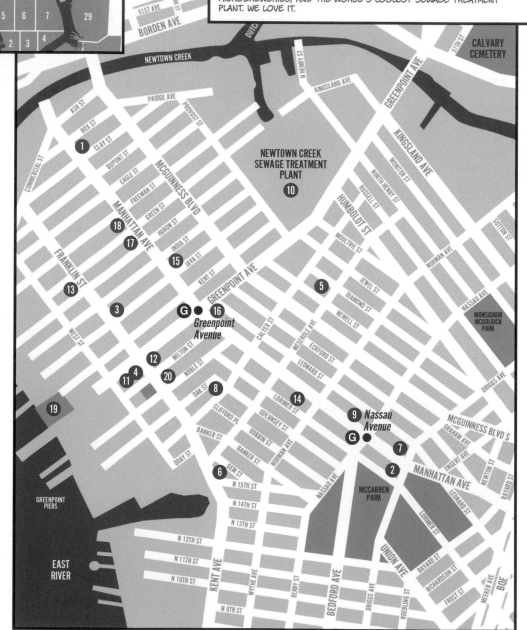

MAP 28 • GREENPOINT

THE PERFECT DICHOTOMY: A LONG-STANDING ETHNIC (POLISH!)
COMMUNITY WITH TONS OF SHOPS AND RESTAURANTS ON BUSTLING
MANHATTAN AVENUE VERSUS A JOHNNY-COME-LATELY HIPSTER
COMMUNITY WITH TONS OF BARS AND RESTAURANTS ON EVER-
EXPANDING FRANKLIN STREET. PLUS, NEW WATERFRONT PARKS,
MICROBREWERIES, AND THE WORLD'S COOLEST SEWAGE TREATMENT
PLANT. WE LOVE IT.

1 ACAPULCO DELI & RESTAURANT
1116 MANHATTAN AVENUE
AUTHENTIC MEXICAN INCLUDES HOMEMADE CHIPS AND TELENOVELLAS AT FULL VOLUME.

2 BAR MATCHLESS
557 MANHATTAN AVENUE
WEEKLY MUSIC SHOWCASES, HEAVY METAL KARAOKE, AND FOOSBALL.

3 BROOKLYN LABEL
180 FRANKLIN STREET
SCRUMPTIOUS SANDWICHES AND COFFEE IN THE STATELY ASTRAL BUILDING.

4 BROUWERIJ LANE
78 GREENPOINT AVENUE
FOR BEER JUNKIES. GLOBAL BOTTLES OR POUR YOUR OWN GROWLER.

5 CAFE GRUMPY
193 MESEROLE AVENUE
THE FINEST COFFEEHOUSE IN BROOKLYN NOW HAS ITS OWN ROASTERY.

6 DIRCK THE NORSEMAN
7 NORTH 15TH STREET
EXCELLENT BREWED-ON-SITE BEER WITH GERMAN FOOD AS A BONUS. GREAT SPACE, TOO.

7 ENID'S
560 MANHATTAN AVENUE
GREENPOINT'S FINEST HIPSTER STAND-BY.

8 GREENPOINT HISTORIC DISTRICT
OAK STREET & GUERNSEY STREET
CHARMING ROWHOUSES THAT WERE BUILT FOR WORKERS OF EARLY MERCHANTS.

9 LOMZYNIANKA
646 MANHATTAN AVENUE
GET YOUR KITSCHY POLISH FIX DIRT CHEAP.

10 NEWTOWN CREEK WASTEWATER TREATMENT PLANT
GREENPOINT AVENUE & PROVOST STREET
A SEWAGE FACILITY WITH A NATURE PARK. WE KID YOU NOT.

11 PAULIE GEE'S
60 GREENPOINT AVENUE
TOP BRICK-OVEN 'ZA RIGHT BY THE RIVER. NICE.

12 PENCIL FACTORY BAR
142 FRANKLIN STREET
GREAT BEER; GREAT VIBE. PERFECTLY UNDERSTATED.

13 PERMANENT RECORDS
181 FRANKLIN STREET
STELLAR SELECTION OF NEW AND USED VINYL, FRIENDLY SERVICE.

14 PETER PAN DOUGHNUTS
727 MANHATTAN AVENUE
POLISH GIRLS IN SMOCKS SERVING TASTY DONUTS.

15 RZESZOWSKA BAKERY
948 MANHATTAN AVENUE
AUTHENTIC POLISH BAKERY; MOBBED AROUND HOLIDAYS YOU WERE UNAWARE OF.

16 SAINT ANTHONY OF PADUA CHURCH
862 MANHATTAN AVENUE
BEAUTIFUL CHURCH STICKING OUT LIKE A HEALTHY THUMB ON CONGESTED AVENUE.

17 THE THING
1001 MANHATTAN AVENUE
UNUSUAL SECOND-HAND STORE OFFERS THOUSANDS OF USED LPS.

18 TOMMY'S TAVERN
1041 MANHATTAN AVENUE
SUPER-DIVE WITH LIVE MUSIC ON WEEKENDS.

19 TRANSMITTER PARK
WEST ST BETWEEN KENT ST AND GREENPOINT AVE
GREENPOINT'S WATERFRONT PARK; FORMER HOME OF WNYC TRANSMITTER TOWERS.

20 WORD
126 FRANKLIN AVENUE
LITERARY FICTION, NON-FICTION, AND KIDS' BOOKS.

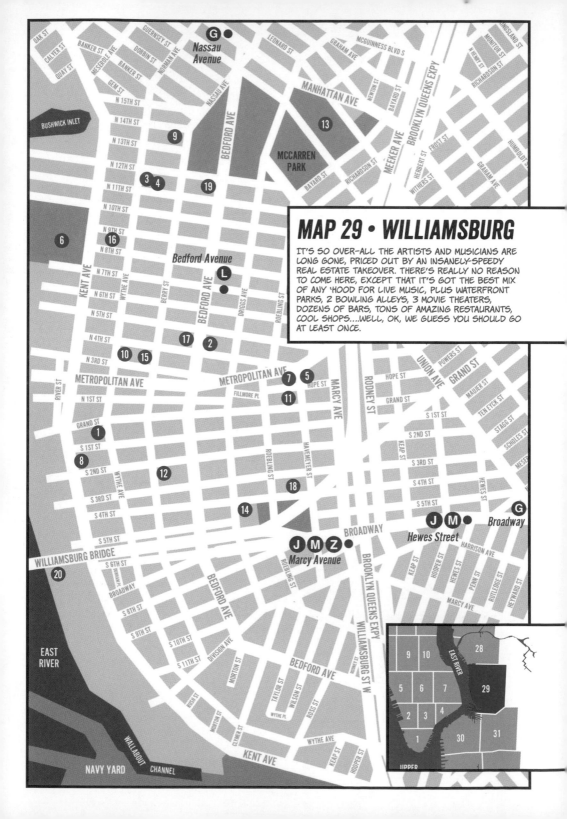

MAP 29 • WILLIAMSBURG

IT'S SO OVER—ALL THE ARTISTS AND MUSICIANS ARE LONG GONE, PRICED OUT BY AN INSANELY-SPEEDY REAL ESTATE TAKEOVER. THERE'S REALLY NO REASON TO COME HERE, EXCEPT THAT IT'S GOT THE BEST MIX OF ANY 'HOOD FOR LIVE MUSIC, PLUS WATERFRONT PARKS, 2 BOWLING ALLEYS, 3 MOVIE THEATERS, DOZENS OF BARS, TONS OF AMAZING RESTAURANTS, COOL SHOPS....WELL, OK, WE GUESS YOU SHOULD GO AT LEAST ONCE.

1 AURORA
70 GRAND STREET
WARM, FRIENDLY RUSTIC ITALIAN. JUST ABOUT PERFECT.

2 BEDFORD CHEESE SHOP
229 BEDFORD AVENUE
BEST CHEESE SELECTION IN THE BOROUGH.

3 BROOKLYN BOWL
61 WYTHE AVENUE
BOWL (16 LANES), EAT (BLUE RIBBON!), AND ROCK OUT (MUSIC VENUE TOO).

4 BROOKLYN BREWERY
79 NORTH 11TH STREET
CONNECT WITH YOUR BEER BY WITNESSING ITS BIRTH; FREE SAMPLES ALSO ENCOURAGE CLOSENESS.

5 CITY RELIQUARY
370 METROPOLITAN AVENUE
ARTIFACTS FROM NEW YORK'S VAST AND RICH HISTORY.

6 EAST RIVER STATE PARK
KENT AVENUE AND NORTH 9TH STREET
SWATH OF WATERFRONT GREENSPACE + SMORGASBURG, WILLIAMSBURG STYLE.

7 FETTE SAU
354 METROPOLITAN AVENUE
ENJOY POUNDS OF MEAT AND CASKS OF BEER IN A FORMER AUTO-BODY REPAIR SHOP.

8 GLASSLANDS GALLERY
289 KENT AVENUE
COMMUNITY EXPERIMENTAL MUSIC AND ART VENUE.

9 THE GUTTER
200 NORTH 14TH STREET
VINTAGE STYLE BOWLING ALLEY WITH GREAT BREWS ON TAP - WHAT COULD BE BETTER?

10 KCDC SKATESHOP
252 WYTHE AVENUE
SHOP AND GALLERY FEATURING LOCALLY DESIGNED GEAR.

11 LARRY LAWRENCE BAR
295 GRAND STREET
LAID-BACK BAR WITH A LOVELY LOFT FOR SMOKERS.

12 LA SUPERIOR
295 BERRY STREET
AUTHENTIC MEXICAN STREET FOOD.

13 MCCARREN PARK POOL
LORIMER STREET & BAYARD STREET
MASSIVE WPA-ERA POOL AND RECREATION CENTER.

14 PIES 'N' THIGHS
166 SOUTH 4TH STREET
COMFORTABLY SOUTHERN STYLE WHERE THE CHICKEN BISCUITS REIGN SUPREME.

15 RADEGAST HALL & BIERGARTEN
113 NORTH 3RD STREET
GERMAN BEER HALL WITH RETRACTABLE ROOF. ONLY IN WILLIAMSBURG.

16 ROUGH TRADE
64 NORTH 9TH STREET
NYC OUTPOST OF FAMOUS LONDON RECORD STORE; MANY LIVE EVENTS.

17 SPOONBILL & SUGARTOWN
218 BEDFORD AVENUE
ART, ARCHITECTURE, DESIGN, PHILOSOPHY, AND LITERATURE BOOKS. A GREAT ONE.

18 TRAIF
229 SOUTH 4TH STREET
SMALL PLATES BRILLIANCE UNDER THE WILLIAMSBURG BRIDGE. GO.

19 TURKEY'S NEST TAVERN
44 BEDFORD STREET
BEST DIVE IN WILLIAMSBURG.

20 WILLIAMSBURG BRIDGE
DRIGGS STREET & SOUTH 5TH STREET
CONNECTING WILLIAMSBURG TO THE LOWER EAST SIDE BY FOOT OR BIKE.

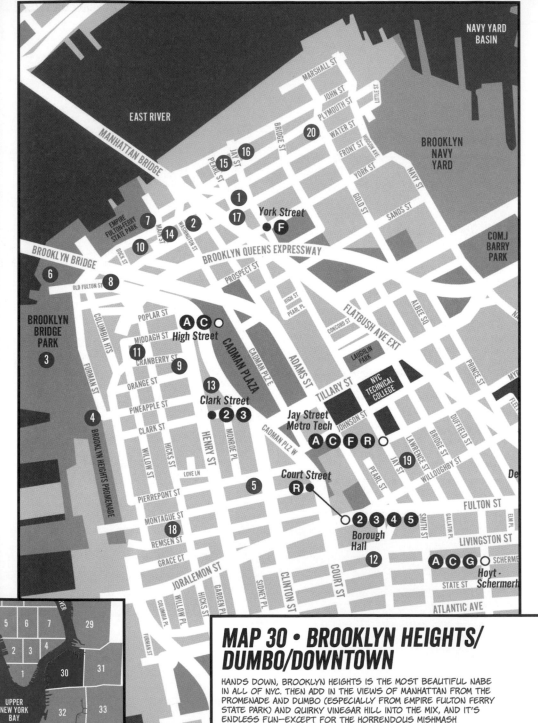

MAP 30 • BROOKLYN HEIGHTS/ DUMBO/DOWNTOWN

HANDS DOWN, BROOKLYN HEIGHTS IS THE MOST BEAUTIFUL NABE IN ALL OF NYC. THEN ADD IN THE VIEWS OF MANHATTAN FROM THE PROMENADE AND DUMBO (ESPECIALLY FROM EMPIRE FULTON FERRY STATE PARK) AND QUIRKY VINEGAR HILL INTO THE MIX, AND IT'S ENDLESS FUN—EXCEPT FOR THE HORRENDOUS MISHMASH THAT IS "DOWNTOWN BROOKLYN."

1 68 JAY STREET BAR
68 JAY STREET
ARTY LOCAL BAR.

2 ALMAR
111 FRONT STREET
CAVERNOUS, FRIENDLY, COMMUNAL-TABLE ITALIAN IN DUMBO. GO TO HANG.

3 BROOKLYN BRIDGE PARK
OLD FULTON STREET & FURMAN STREET
WATERFRONT PARK WITH STELLAR VIEWS AND MANY ACTIVE RECREATIONAL AMENITIES.

4 BROOKLYN HEIGHTS PROMENADE
ABOVE BQE BETWEEN REMSEN AND ORANGE STREETS
THE BEST PLACE TO REALLY SEE MANHATTAN. IT'S THE VIEW THAT'S IN ALL THE MOVIES.

5 BROOKLYN HISTORICAL SOCIETY
128 PIERREPONT STREET
WANT TO REALLY LEARN ABOUT BROOKLYN? GO HERE.

6 BROOKLYN ICE CREAM FACTORY
1 WATER STREET
GET YOUR ICE CREAM FIX ON THE BROOKLYN WATERFRONT.

7 GALAPAGOS ART SPACE
16 MAIN STREET
HIP, ARTY ENTERTAINMENT EMPORIUM. CHECK OUT THE CABARET SHOWS.

8 GRIMALDI'S
1 FRONT STREET
EXCELLENT, RESPECTED, ARGUABLY AMONG THE BEST NYC PIZZA JOINTS.

9 HENRY STREET ALE HOUSE
62 HENRY STREET
COZY, DARK SPACE WITH GOOD SELECTIONS ON TAP.

10 JACQUES TORRES CHOCOLATE
66 WATER STREET
THE PLATONIC IDEAL OF CHOCOLATE.

11 JACK THE HORSE TAVERN
66 HICKS STREET
OUTSTANDING UPSCALE PUB/NEW AMERICAN CUISINE, GREAT FEEL.

12 NEW YORK TRANSIT MUSEUM
130 LIVINGSTON STREET
RIDE VINTAGE SUBWAY CARS THROUGH FORMERLY ABANDONED TUNNELS? YES, PLEASE!

13 PARK PLAZA RESTAURANT
220 CADMAN PLAZA WEST
NFT-APPROVED NEIGHBORHOOD DINER.

14 POWERHOUSE ARENA
37 MAIN STREET
ONE OF OUR FAVORITE GALLERY/BOOKSTORES.

15 RECYCLE-A-BICYCLE
35 PEARL STREET
BIKES TO THE CEILING.

16 ST. ANN'S WAREHOUSE
29 JAY STREET
BE CAREFUL NOT TO CUT YOURSELF ON THE EDGINESS.

17 SUPERFINE
126 FRONT STREET
MEDITERRANEAN-INSPIRED MENU, BI-LEVEL BAR, LOCAL ART AND MUSIC. NFT PICK.

18 TERESA'S RESTAURANT
80 MONTAGUE STREET
POLISH-AMERICAN COMFORT FOOD. COME HUNGRY.

19 TKTS BOOTH
1 METROTECH CENTER
SHHH...DON'T TELL ANYONE THERE'S ONE IN BROOKLYN!

20 VINEGAR HILL
WATER STREET & HUDSON AVENUE
NYC'S COOLEST MICRO-NEIGHBORHOOD. PROMISE.

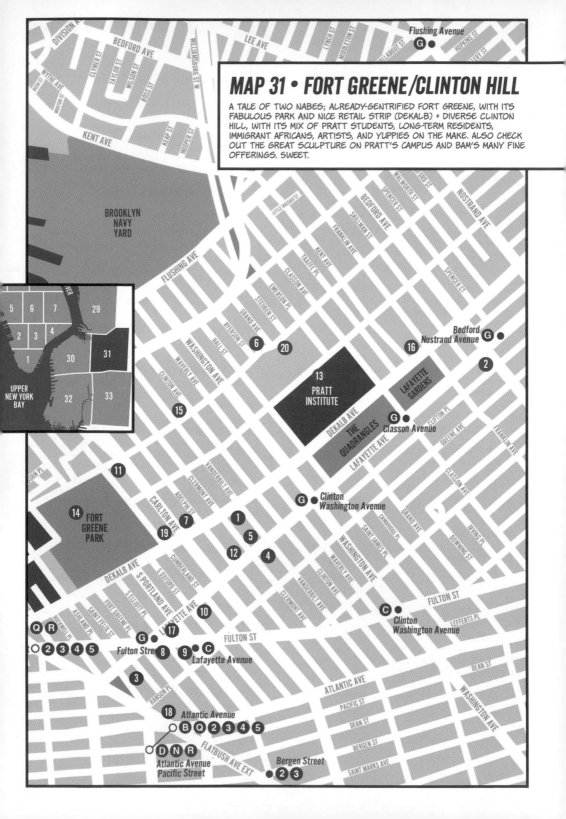

MAP 31 • FORT GREENE/CLINTON HILL

A TALE OF TWO NABES; ALREADY-GENTRIFIED FORT GREENE, WITH ITS FABULOUS PARK AND NICE RETAIL STRIP (DEKALB) + DIVERSE CLINTON HILL, WITH ITS MIX OF PRATT STUDENTS, LONG-TERM RESIDENTS, IMMIGRANT AFRICANS, ARTISTS, AND YUPPIES ON THE MAKE. ALSO CHECK OUT THE GREAT SCULPTURE ON PRATT'S CAMPUS AND BAM'S MANY FINE OFFERINGS. SWEET.

1 THE ALIBI
242 DEKALB AVENUE
REAL DEAL NEIGHBORHOOD BAR.

2 BLACK SWAN
1048 BEDFORD AVENUE
GREAT PUB, LONG MENU, LATE-NIGHT BITES...
ABOUT PERFECT.

3 BROOKLYN ACADEMY OF MUSIC (BAM)
30 LAFAYETTE AVENUE
AMERICA'S OLDEST CONTINUOUSLY OPERATING PERFORMING ARTS CENTER. NEVER DULL.

4 BROOKLYN FLEA
CLERMONT AVENUE & LAFAYETTE AVENUE
ALREADY-FAMOUS FLEA MARKET WITH ROTATING VENDORS & KILLER FOOD.

5 BROOKLYN MASONIC TEMPLE
317 CLERMONT AVENUE
MASONS + INDIE ROCK = SMILES ALL AROUND.

6 CASTRO'S
511 MYRTLE AVENUE
BURRITOS DELIVERED CON CERVESAS, IF YOU LIKE.

7 DICK & JANE'S BAR
266 ADELPHI STREET
A VERY, VERY COOL SPEAKEASY HIDDEN BEHIND FOUR GARAGE DOORS. SSSSHHHH...

8 FRANK'S COCKTAIL LOUNGE
660 FULTON STREET
WHEN YOU NEED TO GET FUNKY.

9 GREENLIGHT BOOKSTORE
686 FULTON STREET
FT. GREENE'S NEWEST AND IMMEDIATELY BEST BOOKSTORE.

10 LAFAYETTE AVENUE PRESBYTERIAN CHURCH
85 SOUTH OXFORD STREET
NATIONALLY KNOWN CHURCH WITH PERFORMING ARTS; FORMER UNDERGROUND RAILROAD STOP.

11 LULU & PO
154 CARLTON AVENUE
SMALL-PLATES GOODNESS ARRIVES IN FORT GREENE. SWEET(BREADS)!

12 OLEA
171 LAFAYETTE AVENUE
FRIENDLY, BUZZING NEIGHBORHOOD TAPAS/MEDITERRANEAN. GET THE BRONZINO.

13 PRATT INSTITUTE STEAM TURBINE POWER PLANT
200 WILLOUGHBY AVENUE
THIS AUTHENTIC STEAM GENERATOR GETS FIRED UP A FEW TIMES A YEAR TO IMPRESS THE PARENTS. COOL.

14 PRISON SHIP MARTYRS' MONUMENT
FORT GREENE PARK
CRYPT HOLDS REMAINS OF THOUSANDS OF REVOLUTIONARY WAR-ERA PRISONERS.

15 PUTNAM'S PUB & COOKER
419 MYRTLE AVENUE
BUZZING BAR, OYSTERS, BURGERS, MUSSELS, TWO LEVELS, OUTDOOR SEATING...WE LOVE IT.

16 RUSTIK TAVERN
471 DEKALB AVENUE
NEIGHBORHOOD TAP DRAWS COZY CLIENTELE.

17 THE SMOKE JOINT
87 SOUTH ELLIOTT PLACE
SPEND THE $16 AND GET THE SHORT RIB. THANK US LATER.

18 TARGET
139 FLATBUSH AVENUE
THE EVERYTHING STORE. SERIOUSLY.

19 THIRST WINE MERCHANTS
187 DEKALB AVENUE
BRILLIANT WINE AND ALCOHOL SELECTION, PLUS BAR.

20 UTRECHT ART SUPPLIES
536 MYRTLE AVENUE
CAVERNOUS ART STORE SERVICING PRATT STUDENTS & LOCAL ARTISTS.

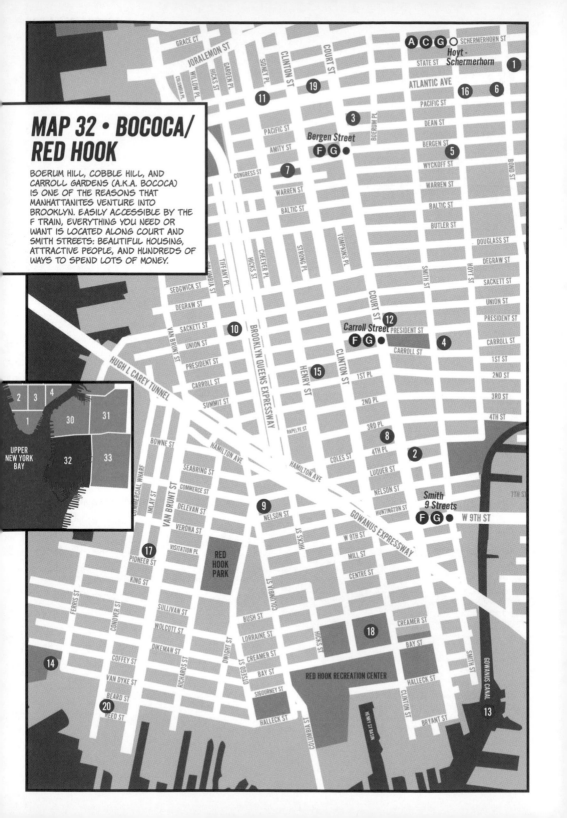

MAP 32 • BOCOCA/ RED HOOK

BOERUM HILL, COBBLE HILL, AND CARROLL GARDENS (A.K.A. BOCOCA) IS ONE OF THE REASONS THAT MANHATTANITES VENTURE INTO BROOKLYN. EASILY ACCESSIBLE BY THE F TRAIN, EVERYTHING YOU NEED OR WANT IS LOCATED ALONG COURT AND SMITH STREETS: BEAUTIFUL HOUSING, ATTRACTIVE PEOPLE, AND HUNDREDS OF WAYS TO SPEND LOTS OF MONEY.

1 BEDOUIN TENT
405 ATLANTIC AVENUE
TWO WORDS: LAMB SANDWICH. NO, FOUR: BEST LAMB SANDWICH EVER.

2 BLACK GOLD
461 COURT STREET
COFFEE, RECORDS, ANTIQUES, BAKED GOODS. ALL THEY'RE MISSING IS CHEESE.

3 BOOKCOURT
163 COURT STREET
CLASSIC COBBLE HILL BOOKSTORE W/ GREAT READINGS, SELECTION, ETC.

4 BROOKLYN SOCIAL
335 SMITH STREET
OLD BOY'S LOUNGE REVAMPED. COCKTAILS STILL THE SAME. NFT PICK.

5 THE BROOKLYN INN
148 COURT STREET
WHEN YOU'RE FEELING NOSTALGIC.

6 BUILDING ON BOND
112 BOND STREET
PUB GRUB, COFFEE, DRINKS—SPEND THE WHOLE DAY THERE!

7 COBBLE HILL PARK
CLINTON STREET & VERANDAH PLACE
ONE OF THE CUTEST PARKS IN ALL OF NEW YORK.

8 CAPUTO'S FINE FOODS
460 COURT STREET
ITALIAN GOURMET SPECIALTIES. THE REAL DEAL.

9 DEFONTE'S SANDWICH SHOP
379 COLUMBIA STREET
CRAZY-ASS ITALIAN HERO SHOP.

10 FERDINANDO'S FOCACCERIA
151 UNION STREET
SICILIAN SPECIALTIES YOU WON'T FIND ANYWHERE ELSE! GET THE PANELLE SPECIAL.

11 FLOYD
131 ATLANTIC AVENUE
INDOOR BOCCE BALL COURT!

12 G. ESPOSITO & SONS
357 COURT STREET
SOPRESSATA AND SAUSAGES DIRECT FROM THE GODHEAD.

13 GOWANUS CANAL
SMITH STREET & 9TH STREET
BROOKLYN'S ANSWER TO THE SEINE.

14 LOUIS VALENTINO JR. PARK & PIER
COFFEY STREET & FERRIS STREET
ESCAPE GENTRIFICATION-INDUSTRIAL COMPLEX WITH PERFECT VIEW STATUE OF LIBERTY.

15 LUCALI
575 HENRY STREET
ONE MAN MAKES EVERY PERFECT PIZZA BY HAND. BE PREPARED TO WAIT.

16 MILE END
97 HOYT STREET
JEWISH DELI, MONTREAL-STYLE. TWO WORDS: SMOKED MEAT.

17 RED HOOK BAIT & TACKLE
320 VAN BRUNT STREET
KITSCHY, COMFY PUB WITH CHEAP DRINKS AND GOOD BEERS ON TAP.

18 RED HOOK BALLFIELDS
CLINTON STREET & BAY STREET
WATCH FUTBOL AND EAT CENTRAL AMERICAN STREET FOOD EVERY SATURDAY FROM SPRING THROUGH FALL.

19 SAHADI'S
187 ATLANTIC AVENUE
TOTALLY BRILLIANT MIDDLE EASTERN SUPERMARKET—OLIVES, CHEESE, BREAD, ETC.

20 SUNNY'S
253 CONOVER STREET
NO LONGER PAY-WHAT-YOU-WISH, BUT STILL CHEAP AND GOOD.

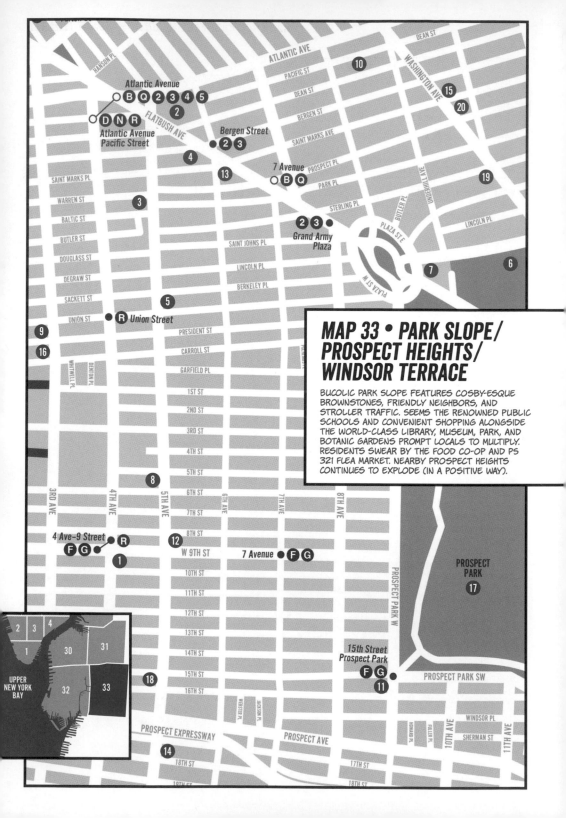

MAP 33 • PARK SLOPE/ PROSPECT HEIGHTS/ WINDSOR TERRACE

BUCOLIC PARK SLOPE FEATURES COSBY-ESQUE
BROWNSTONES, FRIENDLY NEIGHBORS, AND
STROLLER TRAFFIC. SEEMS THE RENOWNED PUBLIC
SCHOOLS AND CONVENIENT SHOPPING ALONGSIDE
THE WORLD-CLASS LIBRARY, MUSEUM, PARK, AND
BOTANIC GARDENS PROMPT LOCALS TO MULTIPLY.
RESIDENTS SWEAR BY THE FOOD CO-OP AND PS
321 FLEA MARKET. NEARBY PROSPECT HEIGHTS
CONTINUES TO EXPLODE (IN A POSITIVE WAY).

1 BARBES
376 9TH STREET
SMART-LOOKING SPACE WITH ECLECTIC
ENTERTAINMENT. RECOMMENDED.

2 BARCLAYS CENTER
420 ATLANTIC AVENUE
WORLD-CLASS ARENA IN THE HEART OF BROOKLYN.

3 BEACON'S CLOSET
92 5TH AVENUE
RAD RESALE WITH LOTS OF GEMS.

4 BERGEN STREET COMICS
470 BERGEN STREET
EXCELLENT SMALL SHOP W/ EVENTS, SIGNINGS, ETC.

5 BIERKRAFT
191 5TH AVENUE
CHEESE, CHOCOLATE, AND NEARLY 1000 VARIETIES
OF BEER.

6 BROOKLYN MUSEUM
200 EASTERN PARKWAY
BREATHTAKINGLY BEAUTIFUL BUILDING, EXCELLENT
COLLECTION.

7 BROOKLYN PUBLIC LIBRARY
10 GRAND ARMY PLAZA
FABULOUS ART DECO TEMPLE TO KNOWLEDGE.

8 BROOKLYN SUPERHERO SUPPLY CO.
372 5TH AVENUE
CAPES, TREASURE MAPS, AND BOTTLED SPECIAL POW-
ERS. ALSO, MCSWEENEY'S PUBLICATIONS.

9 CANAL BAR
270 3RD AVENUE
DIVE NEAR THE GOWANUS, BUT NOT INTO IT.

10 THE CO-CATHEDRAL OF ST. JOSEPH
856 PACIFIC STREET
CHECK OUT THE STUNNING JUST-RENOVATED INTERIOR
OF THIS 1912 CATHEDRAL. WOW.

11 DOUBLE WINDSOR
210 PROSPECT PARK WEST
GOOD FOOD. GREAT BEER.

**12 FIFTH AVENUE RECORD
& TAPE CENTER**
439 5TH AVENUE
UNASSUMING LOCALE FOR SURPRISING FINDS.

13 FLATBUSH FARM
76 ST. MARK'S AVENUE
GREAT BAR, GREAT FOOD, GREAT EVERYTHING,
REALLY.

14 FREDDY'S BAR AND BACKROOM
627 5TH AVENUE
IT LIVES AGAIN! AND WITH GREAT AVANT-JAZZ
BOOKINGS, TOO.

15 GEN RESTAURANT
659 WASHINGTON AVENUE
DELICIOUS, FRESH JAPANESE CUISINE AND
LAID-BACK SERVICE.

16 LITTLENECK
288 3RD AVENUE
HIP OYSTERS AND SEAFOOD STEPS FROM THE PAS-
TORAL GOWANUS.

17 PROSPECT PARK
PROSPECT PARK WEST/GRAND ARMY PLAZA
OLMSTED & VAUX'S TRUE MASTERPIECE.

18 SIDECAR
560 5TH AVENUE
YUMMY COMFORT DINING WITH EQUALLY COMFORTING
COCKTAILS.

19 TOM'S
782 WASHINGTON AVENUE
OLD-SCHOOL MOM-AND-POP DINER SINCE 1936.
A CHOLESTEROL LOVE AFFAIR.

20 THE WAY STATION
683 WASHINGTON AVENUE
STEAMPUNK BAR W/ DR. WHO TARDIS, AND SCREEN-
INGS. LOVIN' BABE.

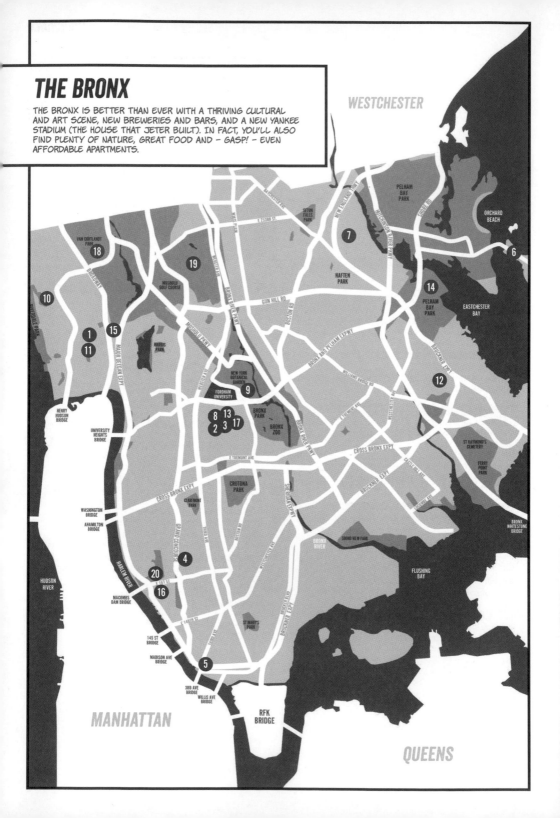

THE BRONX

THE BRONX IS BETTER THAN EVER WITH A THRIVING CULTURAL
AND ART SCENE, NEW BREWERIES AND BARS, AND A NEW YANKEE
STADIUM (THE HOUSE THAT JETER BUILT). IN FACT, YOU'LL ALSO
FIND PLENTY OF NATURE, GREAT FOOD AND – GASP! – EVEN
AFFORDABLE APARTMENTS.

1 AN BEAL BOCHT CAFE
445 WEST 238TH STREET

CAFE/BAR/COFFEE SHOP HANGOUT FOR THE HIP, YOUNG, AND IRISH.

2 ARTHUR AVENUE
STILL AN AUTHENTIC LITTLE ITALY WORTH VISITING, EVEN THOUGH MANY BUSINESSES NOW BELONG TO ALBANIANS.

3 ARTHUR AVENUE RETAIL MARKET
2344 ARTHUR AVENUE

NEW DEAL-ERA SHOPPING TREASURE; DON'T LIMIT YOURSELF TO COLD CUTS.

4 BRONX MUSEUM OF THE ARTS
1040 GRAND CONCOURSE

CHECK OUT CONTEMPORARY WORK FROM ARTISTS OF AFRICAN, ASIAN, AND LATIN AMERICAN DESCENT.

5 BRUCKNER BAR & GRILL
1 BRUCKNER BOULEVARD

FRIENDLY BAR/ART GALLERY A STONE'S THROW FROM MANHATTAN.

6 CITY ISLAND
IMAGINE A NEW ENGLAND FISHING VILLAGE CROSSED WITH A NEW JERSEY SUBURB.

7 CO-OP CITY
INTERSTATE 95 & THE HUTCHINSON RIVER PARKWAY

WITH 15,372 UNITS, THIS TOWERING COMPLEX IS RIGHTLY CALLED A CITY WITHIN THE CITY.

8 DOMINICK'S
2335 ARTHUR AVENUE

OLD-SCHOOL ITALIAN-AMERICAN SERVED FAMILY STYLE. OH YEAH, ALSO NO MENUS OR PRICES. TOTALLY GREAT.

9 NEW YORK BOTANICAL GARDEN
2900 SOUTHERN BOULEVARD

A 250-ACRE SERENE ESCAPE FROM THE CITY. FAMOUS FOR THEIR ANNUAL HOLIDAY TRAIN SHOW.

10 WAVE HILL
WEST 249TH STREET AND INDEPENDENCE AVENUE

PUBLIC GARDEN OASIS WITH VIEWS OVERLOOKING THE HUDSON RIVER.

11 LIEBMAN'S KOSHER DELICATESSEN
552 WEST 235TH STREET

JUST TASTY OLD-FASHIONED JEWISH SPECIALTIES.

12 LOUIE & ERNIE'S PIZZA
1300 CROSBY AVENUE

DOWN-HOME PARLOR WITH THIN CRUST BEAUTIES THAT ARE THE BEST IN THE BOROUGH.

13 MADONIA'S BROTHERS BAKERY
2348 ARTHUR AVENUE

ITALIAN SWEETS HEAVEN. TAKE THE CANNOLI.

14 PELHAM BAY PARK
THE CITY'S LARGEST AT 2,764 ACRES WITH THE THOMAS PELL WILDLIFE SANCTUARY, TWO NATURE CENTERS, AND THE IMMENSELY POPULAR ORCHARD BEACH.

15 S&S CHEESECAKE
222 WEST 238TH STREET

THE BEST CHEESECAKE IN NEW YORK.

16 STAN'S SPORTS BAR
836 RIVER AVENUE

PRE- AND POST-GAME YANKEE FAN DIVE THAT PACKS 'EM LIKE SARDINES.

17 TRATTORIA ZERO OTTE NOVE
2357 ARTHUR AVENUE

AMAZING HIGH-END PIZZA WORTH LEAVING MANHATTAN FOR.

18 VAN CORTLANDT PARK
OFFERING PLAYGROUNDS, BALL FIELDS, TENNIS AND BASKETBALL COURTS, HIKING, HORSEBACK RIDING, AND ONE OF GOLF'S CLASSIC COURSES, "VANNY."

19 WOODLAWN CEMETERY
WEBSTER AVENUE & EAST 233RD STREET

GET YOUR GOTH ON AT THIS HOME TO FIORELLO LA GUARDIA, DUKE ELLINGTON AND HERMAN MELVILLE JUST TO NAME A FEW.

20 YANKEE STADIUM
1 EAST 161ST STREET

JUST NEXT TO WHERE THE HOUSE THAT RUTH BUILT WAS IS NOW THE HOUSE THAT JETER BUILT.

BROOKLYN

UNTIL "THE GREAT MISTAKE OF 1898," BROOKLYN WAS ITS OWN
THRIVING CITY. TODAY, THE BOROUGH OF KINGS COULD STILL MAKE A
DAMN FINE CITY ALL ON ITS OWN. ALTHOUGH MANHATTAN WILL MOST
LIKELY OVERSHADOW BROOKLYN FOR ALL OF ETERNITY, IT'S STILL
PACKED WITH MANY OF THE COOLEST SPORTS IN TOWN. HERE ARE A
FEW IN THE OUTLYING AREAS WORTH A TRIP.

1 BRIGHTON BEACH
WELCOME TO THE THRIVING COMMUNITY OF MOSCOW, BROOKLYN. BRING A RUSSIAN DICTIONARY.

2 BROOKLYN CYCLONES AT MCU PARK
1904 SURF AVENUE

MINOR LEAGUE BASEBALL FUNHOUSE STEPS FROM THE CONEY ISLAND BOARDWALK.

3 CONEY ISLAND
THE CYCLONE ROLLERCOASTER, BUSTLING BOARDWALK AND TEEMING MASSES ON THE BEACH. SUMMER PERFECTION.

4 DI FARA PIZZA
1424 AVENUE J
TOP NYC PIZZA; WELL WORTH THE WAIT. SAY HI TO DOM.

5 THE FARM ON ADDERLY
1108 CORTELYOU ROAD

AN UNLIKELY GEM IN A REVIVING 'NABE. KILLER DESSERTS AND A HEATED GARDEN.

6 GREEN-WOOD CEMETERY
500 25TH STREET

LOTS OF WINDING PATHS AND GREENERY GOOD FOR CONTEMPLATION.

7 L&B SPUMONI GARDENS
2725 86TH STREET

ASTOUNDING SICILIAN SLICE FACTORY. LONG LIVE L&B!

8 MELODY LANES
461 37TH STREET

NFFAPPROVED BOWLING AND BAR. THE REAL DEAL.

9 NATHAN'S FAMOUS HOT DOGS
1310 SURF AVENUE

FAMOUS FOR DELICIOUSNESS AND QUICK DESPITE THE LINE.

10 NORTHEAST KINGDOM
18 WYCKOFF AVENUE

COZY, HIP SKI LODGE-STYLE EATERY IN GRITTY NABE.

11 PEPPA'S JERK CHICKEN
738 FLATBUSH AVENUE

SCRUMPTIOUS AND SPICY HOLE-IN-THE-WALL.

12 RANDAZZO'S CLAM BAR
2017 EMMONS AVENUE

HISTORIC CAFETERIA-STYLE CLAM BAR. JUST TRY TO SCORE CHEAPER OR TASTIER STEAMED LOBSTER.

13 RUBY'S
1213 RIEGELMAN BOARDWALK

COLORFUL REGULARS, KICKIN' JUKE, BEACH VIEW... WE LOVE SUMMERTIME.

14 ROBERTA'S
261 MOORE STREET

SOLID WOOD OVEN PIZZA IN AN INDUSTRIAL SETTING. THE CLINTONS ATE HERE.

15 SYCAMORE
1118 CORTELYOU ROAD
FLOWER SHOP BY DAY, BARROOM BY NIGHT.

16 TACOS MATAMOROS
4508 5TH AVENUE
YOU CAN'T GET MORE MEXICAN THAN THIS!

17 TANOREEN
7704 3RD AVENUE
MIDDLE EASTERN WITH BIG, BOLD FLAVORS.

18 TATIANA RESTAURANT
3152 BRIGHTON 6TH STREET
MOSCOW MEETS VEGAS.

19 TOTONNO'S PIZZA
1524 NEPTUNE AVENUE
THIN AS PAPER, GO EARLY-THEY RUN OUT. AWESOME.

20 VERRAZANO-NARROWS BRIDGE
92ND STREET & GATLING PLACE

THE LONGEST SPAN IN NORTH AMERICA REALLY PUTS THINGS INTO PERSPECTIVE. AWESOME VIEWS BELOW.

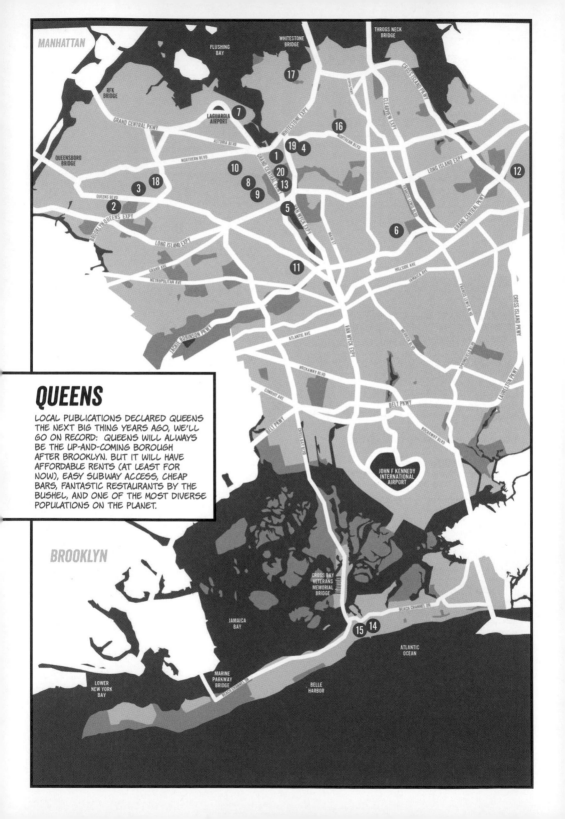

QUEENS

LOCAL PUBLICATIONS DECLARED QUEENS THE NEXT BIG THING YEARS AGO. WE'LL GO ON RECORD: QUEENS WILL ALWAYS BE THE UP-AND-COMING BOROUGH AFTER BROOKLYN. BUT IT WILL HAVE AFFORDABLE RENTS (AT LEAST FOR NOW), EASY SUBWAY ACCESS, CHEAP BARS, FANTASTIC RESTAURANTS BY THE BUSHEL, AND ONE OF THE MOST DIVERSE POPULATIONS ON THE PLANET.

1 CITIFIELD
126-01 ROOSEVELT AVENUE
VERY COMFORTABLE AND FAN-FRIENDLY PLACE TO GO SEE THE METS LOSE.

2 DE MOLE
4502 48TH AVENUE
FRESH, TASTY MEXICAN IN A BISTRO SETTING.

3 DONOVAN'S PUB
57-24 ROOSEVELT AVENUE
A COZY NEIGHBORHOOD TAVERN WITH GREAT BURGERS AND AN IRISH STAFF.

4 FLUSHING MALL FOOD COURT
133-31 39TH AVENUE
HODGEPODGE OF ASIAN CUISINE.

5 FLUSHING MEADOWS-CORONA PARK
HUGE OPEN SPACE THAT WAS HOME TO THE 1964 WORLD'S FAIR.

6 KING YUM
181-08 UNION TURNPIKE
TIKI JOINT SERVING OLD-SCHOOL CHINESE-AMERICAN FARE SINCE 1953. THINK PU PU PLATTER!

7 LAGUARDIA AIRPORT
CONSISTENTLY RATED WORST AIRPORT IN COUNTRY; "THIRD WORLD" TO BIDEN.

8 LEO'S LATTICINI
46-02 104TH STREET
ALSO KNOWN AS MAMA'S. REALLY TASTY SANDWICHES THAT ARE WELL WORTH A TRIP.

9 LEMON ICE KING
52-02 108TH AVENUE
NOTHING BETTER ON A HOT SUMMER DAY THAN THIS SLUSHY GOODNESS.

10 LOUIS ARMSTRONG HOUSE
34-56 107TH ST
TAKE A TOUR OF SATCHMO'S HOME. DON'T MISS THE BLUE KITCHEN AND GOLD-PLATED BATHROOM.

11 NICK'S PIZZA
108-26 ASCAN AVENUE
CONSISTENTLY RATED AMONGST NYC'S TOP PIZZERIAS.

12 QUEENS FARM
73-50 LITTLE NECK PARKWAY
VISIT A DUTCH FARMHOUSE BUILT IN 1772, TAKE SOME FRESH PRODUCE HOME.

13 QUEENS MUSEUM
FLUSHING MEADOWS CORONA PARK
FEATURES WORLD-CLASS EXHIBITIONS AND THE AWE-INSPIRING NYC PANORAMA.

14 ROCKAWAY BEACH
SHORE FRONT PARKWAY & BEACH 90TH STREET
NICE STRETCH OF SAND FOR SURFING AND SWIMMING WITH THE FISHES. AND HIPSTERS.

15 ROCKAWAY TACO
9519 ROCKAWAY BEACH BOULEVARD
TASTY FISH TACOS. ONLY OPEN IN THE SUMMER.

16 SIK GAEK CHUN HA
16129 CROCHERON AVENUE
INSANE KOREAN WITH MASSIVE SEAFOOD PLATTERS OPEN 'TILL 6 AM.

17 SPA CASTLE
131-10 11TH AVENUE
AHHHH, RELAX WITH MULTIPLE POOLS, SAUNAS, AND A KOREAN FOOD COURT. THANK YOU QUEENS.

18 SRIPRAPHAI
64-13 39TH AVENUE
HAIL, HOLY SRIPRAPHAI! WE CROWN THEE THE GREATEST THAI RESTAURANT IN ALL THE CITY!

19 SZECHUAN GOURMET
135-15 37TH AVENUE
THE ORIGINAL FLUSHING LOCATION OF MIDTOWN'S BEST SZECHUAN RESTAURANT.

20 USTA BILLIE JEAN KING NATIONAL TENNIS CENTER
FLUSHING MEADOWS CORONA PARK
SEE THE US OPEN, OR PLAY TENNIS YOURSELF.

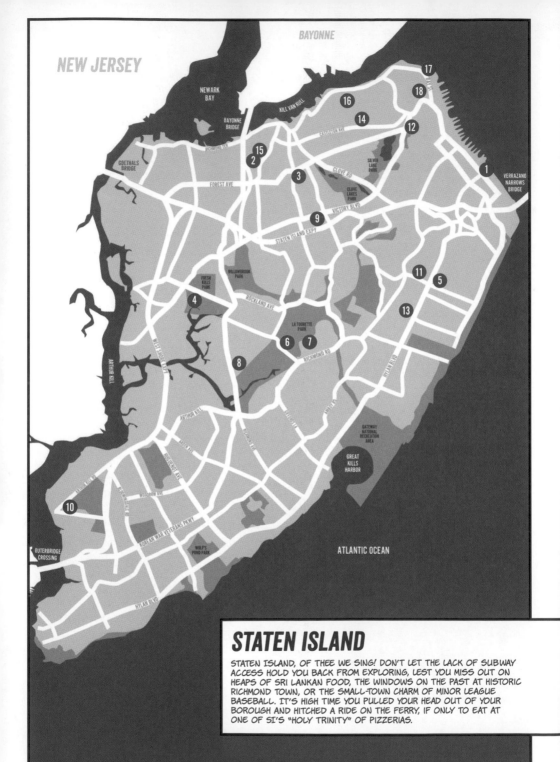

STATEN ISLAND

STATEN ISLAND, OF THEE WE SING! DON'T LET THE LACK OF SUBWAY
ACCESS HOLD YOU BACK FROM EXPLORING, LEST YOU MISS OUT ON
HEAPS OF SRI LANKAN FOOD, THE WINDOWS ON THE PAST AT HISTORIC
RICHMOND TOWN, OR THE SMALL-TOWN CHARM OF MINOR LEAGUE
BASEBALL. IT'S HIGH TIME YOU PULLED YOUR HEAD OUT OF YOUR
BOROUGH AND HITCHED A RIDE ON THE FERRY, IF ONLY TO EAT AT
ONE OF SI'S "HOLY TRINITY" OF PIZZERIAS.

1 ALICE AUSTEN HOUSE
2 HYLAN BOULEVARD
GREAT VIEWS FROM THIS HOME AND ARCHIVES OF AN
EARLY 20TH-CENTURY PHOTOGRAPHER.

2 DENINO'S
524 PORT RICHMOND AVENUE
IN THE PANTHEON OF TOP STATEN ISLAND PIZZA.

3 EGGERS ICE CREAM PARLOR
7437 AMBOY ROAD
ICE CREAM COUNTER AND TREMENDOUS SELECTION
OF SWEETS.

4 FRESHKILLS LANDFILL PARK
OFF ROUTE 440.
LANDFILLS BAD. PARKS GOOD.

5 GOODFELLAS PIZZA
1718 HYLAN AVENUE
SO GOOD MAYOR BILL DE BLASIO ATE IT WITH A FORK.

6 HISTORIC RICHMOND TOWN
441 CLARKE AVENUE
STEP BACK INTO THE PAST AT THIS RESTORED VILLAGE
AND LEARN TO CHURN BUTTER!

7 JACQUES MARCHAIS MUSEUM OF TIBETAN ART
338 LIGHTHOUSE AVENUE
WORLD-CLASS COLLECTION BY A WOMAN WHO WENT
BY PSEUDONYM JACQUES. FOR REAL.

8 JADE ISLAND
2845 RICHMOND AVENUE
TIKI PALACE OF OLD. DRINKS WITH UMBRELLAS ETC.

9 JOE & PAT'S
1758 VICTORY BOULEVARD
THIN, CRISPY CRUST PIZZA SINCE 1960.

10 KILLMEYER'S OLD BAVARIAN INN
4254 ARTHUR KILL ROAD
CHECK OUT THE KREISCHERVILLE-ERA MAHOGANY BAR
AT THIS HISTORIC BEER GARDEN.

11 LEE'S TAVERN
60 HANCOCK STREET
GREAT BAR PIZZA RIGHT OFF THE STATEN ISLAND
RAILROAD.

12 NEW ASHA
322 VICTORY BOULEVARD
GREAT SRI LANKAN FOOD ON THE CHEAP. SPICY!

13 NUNZIO'S
2155 HYLAN AVENUE
IN SOME WAYS, ANY STATEN ISLAND PIE IS BETTER
THAN MOST.

14 NURNBERGER BIERHAUS
817 CASTLETON AVENUE
GERMAN FOOD AND GERMAN BEERS ON TAP.

15 RALPH'S
501 PORT RICHMOND AVENUE
SLINGING SLUSH SINCE 1928.

16 SNUG HARBOR CULTURAL CENTER
1000 RICHMOND TERRACE
FORMER SAILORS' HOME TRANSFORMED INTO A WATER-
FRONT ARTS COMPLEX.

17 STATEN ISLAND YANKEES
75 RICHMOND TERRACE
A LOT CHEAPER AND CHILLER THAN THE BRONX VER-
SION, WITH SKYLINE VIEWS.

18 ST. GEORGE THEATER
35 HYATT STREET
1929 VENUE WITH A NICE MIX OF COMMUNITY EVENTS
AND BIG-NAME CONCERTS.

BATTERY PARK CITY

GENERAL INFORMATION

BATTERY PARK CITY AUTHORITY: 212-417-2000 OR
WWW.BATTERYPARKCITY.ORG
BATTERY PARK CITY PARKS CONSERVANCY:
212-267-9700 OR WWW.BPCPARKS.ORG

OVERVIEW

Welcome to Battery Park City–a master-planned community reminiscent of Pleasantville. Originally the brainchild of Nelson Rockefeller, this urban experiment transformed a WTC construction landfill into a 92-acre planned enclave on the southwestern tip of Manhattan. As space in Manhattan continues to disappear into the stratosphere (literally, the only way to build is up), the idea of BPC requires a doubletake. It's about making public spaces (about 30% of those 92 acres) work within private entities. Imagine taking Central Park, cutting it up, and saying, "Here, your neighborhood can have a chunk of it, and that street down there, and that street over there, too." Admit it: walking among private, commercial spaces day in and day out is enough to make anyone claustrophobic (thank you, Financial District). In BPC you walk through spacious parks with weird statues and brick pavers all on your way to work, the grocery store, the gym, or the movie theater. BPC will have you asking: "What's outside Battery Park City?"

Those looking for all -night eateries and party spots should pass it up, but if you've got kids this is the place for you. Many NY families–roughly 25,000 people–occupy the 40% of BPC that's dedicated residential space, including a future-forward "green" building, the Solaire. Robert F. Wagner Jr. and Rector are good choices for a picnic; The Esplanade or South Cove to walk along the Hudson; Nelson A. Rockefeller to play Frisbee; North Cove to park your yacht; and Teardrop Park for the kids. People of all ages have welcomed the ever-popular Shake Shack (the cheapest meal in the neighborhood), live music at the World Financial Center, and Manhattan's first green LEED-certified branch library.

Seeing: Amazing sculptures by Bourgeois, Otterness, Puryear, Dine, and Cragg.

Inspired architecture: Stuyvesant High School, Siah Armajani's Tribeca Bridge, Kevin Roche's Museum of Jewish Heritage, Cesar Pelli's Winter Garden, and the World Financial Center.

If you like things nice, neat, and compartmentalized, this 'hood is for you.

EMPIRE STATE BUILDING

GENERAL INFORMATION

NFT MAP: *9*
ADDRESS: *350 FIFTH AVE (& 34TH ST)*
PHONE: *212-736-3100*
WEBSITE: *WWW.ESBNYC.COM*
TWITTER: *@EMPIRESTATEBLDG*
OBSERVATORY HOURS: *OPEN DAILY 365 DAYS A YEAR 8 AM–2 AM. LAST ELEVATORS GO UP AT 1:15 AM*
OBSERVATORY ADMISSION: *$27 FOR ADULTS, $21 FOR KIDS, $24 FOR SENIORS, $50 IF YOU WANT TO BE A SHOW OFF AND CUT IN FRONT OF EVERYONE TO THE FRONT OF THE LINE (WE'RE NOT LYING WITH THIS ONE, FOLKS...OUR SOCIETY IS INDEED MORALLY BANKRUPT).*

OVERVIEW

There may not be a gorilla climbing it, but if you don't already know the "World's Most Famous Office Building," the jig is up, Mac. Put down the NFT and back away slooowly. You're not a true Manhattanite; you're not even a well -researched tourist. So, folks, how did the giant end up perching on our block? In 1930, at the hands of raw men compounding raw material day after day, four-and-a-half stories were erected per week. Those ravaged from the Depression and eager to put their minds to work built the 1,500-foot structure in just 14 months, way ahead of schedule. We used to make stuff in this country. Quickly.

A year later, it served as an ambassador to visiting dignitaries like Queen Elizabeth and, years later, your Aunt Elizabeth. These days it is one of New York City's (and the world's) most famous landmarks. Movies have been shot there. Big shots work there. Wherever you are in Manhattan (and sometimes Brooklyn or Queens), it's there to orient you. And you can take plenty of snapshots from the reason-you-go-there observation deck on the 86th floor. No trick questions asked. Some New Yorkers think it's hip to have never been to the Empire State Building. These people are nuts. Whether you choose to go during the day or at night, it's a totally different but amazing experience either way.

THE LIGHTS

As far away as downtown and all the way uptown, the lights of the Empire State Building soar above the clouds, signifying an international holiday and/or an interminable disease. On the 86th floor, a man with binoculars and a direct line to the lighting engineers waits. His raison d'etre? Close-flying flocks of birds. One phone call, and the lights go out, lest the poor suckers smash their beaks and plunge to their death from the mesmerizing lights. True story.

CENTRAL PARK

GENERAL INFORMATION

CENTRAL PARK CONSERVANCY: 212-310-6600
WEBSITE: WWW.CENTRALPARKNYC.ORG
TWITTER: @CENTRALPARKNYC

OVERVIEW

Taking a stroll through Central Park is something that tourists and residents can always agree on. This world-class sanctuary is a huge, peaceful lush oasis in the concrete jungle, and who hasn't skipped therapy once or twice in favor of clearing your mind the old-fashioned way, by taking a long walk in the park? On any given day, you'll see people disco roller skating, playing jazz, juggling, walking their dogs, running, making out, meditating, playing softball, whining through soccer practice, getting married, picnicking, and playing chess.

Designed by Frederick Law Olmsted and Calvert Vaux in the 1850s, Central Park has a diverse mix of attractions. The Central Park Conservancy leads walking tours, and you can always hail a horse-drawn carriage or bike taxi for a ride through the park if you want to look like a true tourist.

PRACTICALITIES

Central Park is easily accessible by subway, since the A, C, B, D, N, R, Q, 1, 2 and 3 trains all circle the park. Parking along CPW is harder, so try side streets. Unless you're heading to the park for a big concert, a softball game, or Shakespeare in the Park, walking or hanging out (especially alone!) in the park at night is not recommended.

NATURE

Central Park is the place to see and be seen, for birds, actually; 230 species can be spotted and The Ramble is a good place to stake out. There are an amazing number of both plant and animal species that inhabit the park, including the creatures housed at the zoo. Some people forage for edible plants throughout the park, perhaps out of curiosity, though officials tend to discourage this practice. A good source of information on all of the park's flora and fauna is NYC school teacher Leslie Day's book, *Field Guide to the Natural World of New York City*.

ARCHITECTURE & SCULPTURE

Central Park was designed to thrill visitors at every turn. The Bethesda Fountain, designed by Emma Stebbins, is one of the main attractions

of the park. Don't miss the view of Turtle Pond from Belvedere Castle. The Arsenal is a wonderful ivy-clad building that houses the Parks Department headquarters. The original Greensward plan for Central Park is located in the Arsenal's third-floor conference room—if there isn't a meeting going on, you might be able to sneak a peek. Two of the most notable sculptures in the park are Alice in Wonderland and the Obelisk. Oh, and one other tiny point of interest...the Metropolitan Museum of Art also happens to be in the park.

OPEN SPACES

New Yorkers covet space. Since they rarely get it in their apartments, they rely on large open areas such as the Great Lawn and Sheep Meadow. The Ramble is stocked with trees and is great for hiking around—just use common sense after dark. When it snows, you can find great sledding on Cedar Hill, which is otherwise perfect for picnicking and sunbathing.

PERFORMANCE

In warmer weather, Central Park is a microcosm of the great cultural attractions New York has to offer. The Delacorte Theater is the home of Shakespeare in the Park, a New York tradition begun by famous director Joseph Papp. SummerStage is the city's best outdoor concert venue for all types of music, including killer rock shows. Free opera and classical concerts happen all summer long on the Great Lawn. Or just enjoy a sing-along with some dude with an acoustic guitar for as long you can stand at the Imagine memorial to John Lennon at Strawberry Fields.

SPORTS

Rollerblading and roller skating are still popular, as is jogging, especially around the reservoir (1.57 mi). The Great Lawn boasts well-maintained softball fields. Central Park has 30 tennis courts (if you make a reservation, you can walk right on to the clay court with tennis shoes only—212-280-0205), fishing at Harlem Meer, gondola rides and boat rentals at the Loeb Boathouse, model boat rentals at the Conservatory Water, chess and checkers at the Chess & Checkers House, two ice skating rinks, croquet and lawn bowling just north of Sheep Meadow, and basketball courts at the North Meadow Rec Center. You will also see volleyball, basketball, skateboarding, bicycling, and many pick-up soccer, Frisbee, football, and kill-the-carrier games to join. During heavy snows, bust out your snowboard, cross-country skis, or homemade sled. Finally, Central Park is where the NYC Marathon ends each year.

COLUMBIA UNIVERSITY

GENERAL INFORMATION

NFT MAP: 18

MORNINGSIDE HEIGHTS: 2960 BROADWAY & 116TH ST

MEDICAL CENTER: 601 W 168TH ST

PHONE: 212-854-1754

WEBSITE: WWW.COLUMBIA.EDU

TWITTER: @COLUMBIA

STUDENTS ENROLLED: 29,250 (2013)

ENDOWMENT: $8.2 BILLION (2013)

OVERVIEW

Yearning for those carefree days spent debating nihilism in the quad and wearing pajamas in public? Look no further than a quick trip to the Ivy League haven of Columbia University. Unlike the other collegiate institutions that pepper Manhattan's real estate, Columbia actually has a campus. The main campus, located in Morningside Heights, spans six blocks between Broadway and Amsterdam Avenues. Most of the undergraduate classes are held here, along with several of the graduate schools. Other graduate schools, including the Law School and School of International and Public Affairs, are close by on Amsterdam Avenue. The main libraries, Miller Theater, and St. Paul's Chapel are also located on the Morningside Heights campus. You can even get your intramural fix on a few fields for Frisbee-throwing and pick-up soccer games.

Founded in 1754 as King's College, Columbia University is one of the country's most prestigious academic institutions. The university is well known for its core curriculum, a program of requirements that gives students an introduction to the most influential works in literature, philosophy, science, and other disciplines. It also prepares them for the rigors of those pesky dinner parties.

After residing in two different downtown locations, Columbia moved to its present campus (designed by McKim, Mead, and White) in 1897. Low Library remains the focal point of the campus as does the Alma Mater statue in front–a landmark that continues to inspire student superstitions (find the hidden owl and you might be the next valedictorian) thanks to a thwarted plot to blow it up by the radical Weather Underground in the '60s. Students line the stairs in front of the library on sunny days, eating lunch and chatting with classmates. Columbia even has its own spooky network of underground tunnels (third largest in the world) that date back to the old Morningside mental asylum and were utilized by students and police during the 1968 strike.

Town/gown relations in Morningside Heights are quite controversial. While Columbia students show local businesses the money, the university continues to relentlessly buy up property and expand into the community, to the chagrin of many New Yorkers city-wide. The most famous of these struggles came in response to Columbia's plans to build a gymnasium in Morningside Park. Contentious proposals, approved in 2009, for a 17-acre expansion into Manhattanville (the area north of 125th Street) by 2030 still cause tension and fear of evictions, and the debate between the university and old-time residents continues.

Columbia's medical school is the second oldest in the nation, and the world's first academic medical center. The school is affiliated with the Columbia-Presbyterian Medical Center in Washington Heights and encompasses the graduate schools of medicine, dentistry, nursing, and public health. Columbia is the only Ivy League university with a journalism school, which was founded at the bequest of Joseph Pulitzer in 1912. (The prize is still administered there.) The school is also affiliated with Barnard College, Jewish Theological

Seminary, Teachers College, and Union Theological Seminary.

Numerous movies have been filmed on or around the campus including *Ghostbusters*, *Hannah and Her Sisters*, and various iterations of *Spiderman*.

Notable alums and faculty include artists James Cagney, Art Garfunkel, Georgia O'Keeffe, Rodgers and Hammerstein, Paul Robeson, and Twyla Tharp; critic Lionel Trilling; baseball player Lou Gehrig; and writers Isaac Asimov, Joseph Heller, Carson McCullers, Eudora Welty, Zora Neale Hurston, and Herman Wouk. Business alumni include Warren Buffet, Alfred Knopf, Joseph Pulitzer, and Milton Friedman, while government officials Madeline Albright, Dwight Eisenhower, Alexander Hamilton, Robert Moses, Franklin Delano Roosevelt, and Teddy Roosevelt all graced the university's classrooms. In the field of law, Benjamin Cardozo, Ruth Bader Ginsburg, Charles Evans Hughes, and John Jay called Columbia home, and Stephen Jay Gould, Margaret Mead, and Benjamin Spock make the list of notable science alumni.

TUITION

Undergraduate tuition is approximately $50,000 per year plus room, board, books, illegal substances, therapy for your inferiority/superiority complex, etc. We suggest: Shacking up with your Aunt Agatha on the Upper West Side for the duration.

SPORTS

The Columbia Marching Band plays "Roar, Lion, Roar" after every touchdown, but their instruments remain tragically roarless most of the time. The Lions almost set the record for straight losses by a major college football team when they dropped 44 consecutive games between 1983 and 1988. Not much has changed—their 0-10 record in 2013 was par for the course. The Lions play their mostly Ivy League opponents at Lawrence A. Wien Stadium (Baker Field), located way up at the top of Manhattan.

Columbia excels in other sports including crew, fencing, golf, tennis, and sailing (silver spoon not included). The university is represented by 29 men's and women's teams in the NCAA Division I. It also has the oldest wrestling team in the country.

CULTURE ON CAMPUS

The ire evoked by its controversial immigration speech, when students stormed the stage, pales when compared to Columbia's 2007 invitation to Iranian president Mahmoud Ahmadinejad to participate in a debate. Good or bad, it created much hype and put the campus in the spotlight for a day or two. Columbia does, however, feature plenty of other less volatile dance, film, music, theater, lectures, readings, and talks. Venues include: the Macy Gallery at the Teacher's College, which exhibits works by a variety of artists, including faculty and children's artwork; the fabulous Miller Theatre at 2960 Broadway, which primarily features musical performances and lectures; the student-run Postcrypt Art Gallery in the basement of St. Paul's Chapel; the Theatre of the Riverside Church for theatrical performances from their top-rated graduate program; and the Wallach Art Gallery on the 8th floor of Schermerhorn Hall, featuring art and architecture exhibits. Check the website for a calendar of events.

EAST RIVER PARK

OVERVIEW

East River Park is a thin slice of land sandwiched between the FDR Drive and the East River, and running from Montgomery Street up to 12th Street. Built in the late 1930s as part of the FDR Drive, the park's sporting facilities are some of the best Manhattan has to offer. The East River Esplanade welcomes runners, rollerbladers, dog-walkers, and those who just want to enjoy up-close views of the Williamsburg Bridge and across to Brooklyn. Long-term plans call for waterfront parkland from The Battery to Harlem, and in fact East River Park is part of an overall plan to someday create one continuous green stretch from Maine to Florida, known as the East Coast Greenway.

ATTRACTIONS

The park comes alive in the summer and on weekends, when hundreds of families barbecue in the areas between the athletic fields, blaring music and eating to their hearts' content. Others take leisurely strolls or jogs along the East River Esplanade, which offers dramatic views of the river and Brooklyn. Many have turned the park's unused areas into unofficial dog runs, places for pick-up games of ultimate Frisbee or soccer, and sunbathing areas. And aside from bathing beauties, you'll even find fishermen waiting patiently for striped bass (not that we have to tell you, but nothing caught in the East River should be eaten—while the water quality has improved dramatically, it's still full of pollutants).

SPORTS

The sports facilities at East River Park have undergone heavy reconstruction. The park now includes facilities for football, softball, basketball, soccer, tennis, and even cricket. Thankfully, many of the fields have been resurfaced with a resilient synthetic turf—a smart move given the amount of use the park gets by all the different sports leagues.

FACILITIES

There are three bathroom facilities located in the park–one at the tennis courts, one at the soccer/track field, and one up in the northern part of the park by the playground. The reconstruction has provided East River Park with new benches, game tables, seal sprinklers for the kids, and new water fountains. Aside from the occasional guy with a cart full of cold drinks, there are no food or drink options close by. Your best bet is to arrive at the park with any supplies you might need–if that's too difficult, try a bodega on Avenue D.

ESOTERICA

Built in 1941, the Corlears Hook Pavilion was the original home of Joseph Papp's Shakespeare in the Park. However, it closed in 1973, and has never quite returned to its glory days. Plans for the fancy $3.5 million amphitheater/restaurant that was to replace the sad-looking, abandoned, graffiti-covered Corlears Hook Pavilion band shell have been canned. A less ambitious reconstruction took place in 2001, however, and with new seating, a renovated band shell, and a good scrubbing, the facility is currently open for use.

HOW TO GET THERE

Two FDR Drive exits will get you very close to East River Park–the Houston Street exit and the Grand Street exit. Technically, cars are not allowed in the park. There is some parking available at the extreme south end of the park by Jackson Street off the access road, but it's hard to get to and poorly marked. Plan to find street parking just west of the FDR and cross over on a footbridge.

If you are taking the subway, you'd better have your hiking boots on–the fact that the closest subways (them J, M, Z, F at Delancey/Essex St and the L at First Ave) are so far away (at least four avenue blocks) is one of the reasons East River Park has stayed mainly a neighborhood park. Fortunately, if you're into buses, the M22, M21, M14 and M8 and get you pretty close. Regardless of the bus or subway lines, you will have to cross one of the five pedestrian bridges that traverse the FDR Drive, unless you approach via the East River Esplanade.

THE HIGH LINE

GENERAL INFORMATION

NFT MAPS: *5 & 8*
WEBSITE: *WWW.THEHIGHLINE.ORG*
TWITTER: *@HIGHLINENYC*

OVERVIEW

Built on top of a disused portion of elevated freight train tracks, The High Line is at once both an escape from the chaos of the city's streets and a celebration of Manhattan's West Side, especially its architecture. The first section between Gansevoort Street and West 20th Street opened in 2009 and was an instant success, proving that open space could be hip and stylish, and causing the city tax assessor's heart to race at the thought of all the surrounding property that suddenly deserved a second look. Section 2, which opened in June 2011, doubled the length of the park up to 30th Street. Section 3, opened in 2014, follows the elevated track to its end at 34th Street.

The rail line was built in the 1930s as part of the West Side Improvement project that eliminated dangerous at-grade railroad crossings and alleviated terrible traffic along Manhattan's West Side. The same project expanded Riverside Park on the Upper West Side. As trucking became more efficient, train traffic on the rail line slowed. By 1980 the entire line shut down and quickly fell into disrepair. Many wanted to demolish the line, which was prohibitively expensive, but a grassroots group, Friends of the High Line, slowly built support that became a groundswell, thanks in part to a mayoral administration

that didn't mind investing in high-end development. The final cost of sections 1 and 2 was $152.3 million, including $112 million from the city, $20 million from the federal government and nearly $50 million in privately raised funds.

The High Line is open from 7 am to 10 pm daily (7 pm during winter and 11 pm during summer). The entire thing is wheelchair accessible although there are limited access points along the way. Dogs and bicycles are strictly prohibited, though there are bike racks at street level at various access points. Closest subway access is the A, C, and E along Eighth Avenue or the 1 along Seventh Avenue. The M11, M14, M23 and M34 buses also travel toward the park.

The park has several environmentally friendly touches. The flora planted along the High Line is representative of the region's native ecology. Half of the plants are native to North America and 30% are native to the Northeast, making the park a natural home to birds and butterflies. The park also absorbs and uses rainwater that would otherwise be finding its way into gutters. Although the philosophy is low impact, the High Line has had a decidedly high impact on the surrounding neighborhood. In addition to providing an aesthetically pleasing path from the Meatpacking District north into the heart of Chelsea's art galleries, the High Line has attracted people and businesses to a part of the city that was perhaps better known for its untz-untz dance clubs and Scores. The High Line has been a catalyst for both architectural and cultural development in the area, including The Whitney's new second home in the Meatpacking District.

Take a quick survey of the architecture by simply looking up; *The Standard*, which straddles the High Line just south of 14th Street, sports a posh restaurant as well as a beer garden, both directly underneath the High Line. Two other stunning architectural gems visible from the High Line (looking west) are Frank Gehry's first commercial office building in New York, Barry Diller's *IAC Building*, and Jean Nouvel's *100 Eleventh Avenue* condo building right across the street. The IAC is one of the most wonderfully luminescent buildings in all of New York, and Nouvel's façade of hundreds of differently sized panes of glass became an instant classic. Of course, the work on the High Line itself, by architects Diller Scofidio + Renfro and landscape architects James Corner Field Operations, is simply amazing. The 10th Avenue Square area, with amphitheater-style seating and a living-room-window view of the northbound traffic of Tenth Avenue, is a favorite as well as a perfect place for a picnic (hit up the nearby Chelsea Market food vendors).

While weekend days during summer on the High Line is already a madhouse, we recommend an early-morning or evening stroll during spring and fall. The cityscape views at night are stunning; early morning is quiet and generally cool, until the sun moves above the skyscrapers to the east of the park. Really, there is no bad time to visit the High Line. The views will be great no matter what time of day it is.

Great food options abound nearby, including hip *Cookshop* (Map 8), French haven *La Lunchonette* (Map 8), neighborhood standby *Red Cat* (Map 8), Jean-Georges Vongerichten's *Spice Market* (Map 5), and warm Italian *Bottino* (Map 8). Want cheaper fare? Hit greasy spoon *Hector's*(-Map 5) or wait for one of the gourmet trucks to pull up around the corner from the Gansevoort stairs, or go DIY by buying food at *Chelsea Market* (Map 8). On the High Line itself, look out for stands selling artisanal popsicles, ice cream, tacos and coffee.

At night, you can hang around to rock out at The *Highline Ballroom* (Map 8), or drink at pubs *The Half King* (Map 8), *Brass Monkey* (Map 5), or The Standard's *Biergarten* (Map 5), or, better yet, walk the streets of the West 20s in search of gallery openings (read: free wine and cheese). No matter how you slice it, a visit to the High Line will only make you happier. We promise.

HUDSON RIVER PARK

GENERAL INFORMATION

HUDSON RIVER PARK TRUST
PHONE: 212-627-2020
WEBSITES: WWW.HUDSONRIVERPARK.ORG OR WWW.FRIENDSOFHUD-SONRIVERPARK.ORG
TWITTER: @HUDSONRIVERPARK

OVERVIEW

It's up for debate whether Hudson River Park is a beacon for downtown joggers or a Bermuda triangle that pilots should fly away from. In a matter of months, this western stretch of green torpedoed into infamy when two planes and a helicopter crash-landed off the banks of the park. Most famously, the U.S. Airways "Miracle on the Hudson" skidded to a safe water landing in early 2009. Seven months later, a helicopter and a small plane collided in nearly the same spot and killed nine people.

Of course, we'd rather talk about the park's safer aerial acrobatics, like the trapezes and half-pipes that define this 550-acre, $330 million park development along the south and southwest coastline of Manhattan, stretching from Battery Place to West 59th Street.

As part of the New York State Significant Coastal Fish and Wildlife Habitat, 400 acres of the total 550 thrive as estuarine sanctuary. This means the 70 fish species (there are fish in the Hudson?) and 30 bird species on the waterfront won't go belly up or beak down with all the marine preservation. Thanks to this effort, you'll be able to enjoy the winter flounder, white perch, owls, hawks, and songbirds for generations

to come. (That's fantastic! Bob, tell them what else they've won...) What downtown, nature-loving, organic -eating savers of the planet have won is in what they've lost. As a mandate, office buildings, hotels, casino gambling boats, and manufacturing plants are prohibited from the HRP, as are residences (sorry, no waterfront property next to your yacht) and jet skis (better to leave them in the Caymans). Check out the Intrepid aircraft carrier/sea-air-space museum, especially during Fleet Week each year (usually the week of Memorial Day, in May). You'll get to see teeming Navy personnel and much more modern vessels, some of which absolutely dwarf the Intrepid itself. A sight not to be missed.

ART

HRP takes its culture cue from the surrounding downtown art scene of TriBeCa, SoHo, and Chelsea. Perhaps you saw one of Merce Cunningham Dance Company's final performances before they shut down. Or maybe you were waiting in line to see Ashes and Snow, Gregory Colbert's rendition of the interactions between animals and humans took form in the temporary Nomadic Museum on Pier 54. Or maybe you checked out Malcolm Cochran's Private Passage on Clinton Cove (55th–57th St). Similar to your late-night antics, you peered into a gigantic wine bottle. There, from portholes carved on the sides, you could see the interior of the stateroom of the Queen Mary. Or, hearkening back to an early time, the Shadow of the Lusitania. Justen Ladda recreated the shadow of the famous ship on the south side of Pier 54 (also home to reconstructed historic

ships, not just their shadows), its original docking place, with glass and planters. Jutting out where Pier 49 used to sit is one of the park's more somber exhibits, the New York City AIDS memorial. Dedicated on World AIDS Day in 2008 after 14 years of fundraising and planning, the 42-foot-long memorial is both a striking accomplishment and a sober nod to those whose lives have been lost to the disease. A more permanent piece in HRP: Salinity Gradient in TriBeCa. Paver stones spanning 2,000 feet take the shape of Hudson marine creatures. Striped bass included. Not impressed? HRP Trust hired different designers for each segment of the five-mile park, with only the esplanade and waterfront railing as universal pieces. Check out the landscape design of each segment.

ATTRACTIONS

Season-specific events are held year-round at HRP. During the summer, experience fight-night basics on Pier 84 for Rumble on the River with live blood splattering with each KO. Sundays in the summer host MoonDances on Pier 84 with free dance lessons before live New York bands play. Wednesday and Fridays in the summer boast River Flicks on Pier 54 and Pier 84 with throwback films like The Goonies. Pier of Fear is mainly a Halloween party for the kiddies, but if you're still down with dressing up as the Scream guy, hey, no one will stop you. An estuarium (dedicated to the science of the river) and a TriBeCa dog run, among other projects, are next on the list of improvements for HRP.

SPORTS

Think of sports in terms of piers. You already know about ritzy Chelsea Piers, but soon enough "Pier 40" or "Pier 63" will also become vernacular to sports freaks. And there are far less expensive piers beyond CP. Most crucial to athletic -minded souls, a five-mile running/biking/blading path that threads through the piers. It's a miniature divided highway–smooth, simple, and super crowded during peak times (early evening and weekends). You'll find sunbathing lawns throughout (the most sport some will ever do). Pier 40: three and a half ball fields. Area south of Houston: three tennis courts. Mini-golf. Batting cages. Skateboard park. Beach volleyball. Trapeze lessons. Pier 40, CP, Pier 63, Pier 96: free kayaking. Those are the highlights; for more that's up your particular sports alley, check out the website.

HOW TO GET THERE

Hmmm. How to most efficiently make your way through all the concrete to the shoreline? The 1 and A, C, E between Chambers and 59th Streets will get you the closest. Go west 'til you hit water. You're there.

GENERAL INFORMATION

NFT MAP: 14

WEBSITE: WWW.LINCOLNCENTER.ORG OR

TWITTER: @LINCOLNCENTER

GENERAL INFORMATION: 212-875-5000

GUIDED TOURS: 212-875-5350

CENTERCHARGE: 212-721-6500

VENUES

ALICE TULLY HALL: 212-671-4050

AVERY FISHER HALL: 212-875-5030

DAVID H. KOCH THEATER: 212-870-5570

WALTER READE THEATER: 212-875-5610

ORGANIZATIONS

THE CHAMBER MUSIC SOCIETY: 212-875-5775

FILM SOCIETY OF LINCOLN CENTER: 212-875-5367

JAZZ AT LINCOLN CENTER: 212-258-9800

THE JULLIARD SCHOOL: 212-799-5000

LINCOLN CENTER THEATER: 212-362-7600

THE METROPOLITAN OPERA HOUSE: 212-362-6000

NEW YORK CITY BALLET: 212-496-0600

NEW YORK PHILHARMONIC: 212-875-5656

NEW YORK PUBLIC LIBRARY FOR THE PERFORMING ARTS: 917-275-6975

OVERVIEW

Lincoln Center is the largest performing arts center in the world, which means it's a beloved icon, but it's also guilty of some cultural Disneyfication. It sets the gold standard, but it also needs to make money, which it does by presenting the same venerable artists performing the same standard works, geared toward an aging, wealthy, elitist audience. However, that shouldn't stop you from seeing the Met Opera, hearing the New York Philharmonic, and taking a photo by the fountain at least once in your life. Go ahead, wear jeans to the ballet, in the name of the people!

In 2012 LC completed a massive $1.2 billion renovation, which included a much-needed facelift (inside and out) for Alice Tully Hall and the addition of a lawn-covered café, among other worthy attractions. Don't miss out on discount tickets at the new Atrium, one small step toward lowering LC's snob factor. (But not for long, as LC now hosts Mercedes-Benz Fashion Week.) Jazz at Lincoln Center, opened in 2004, benefits from having Wynton Marsalis as its artistic director; the trumpet god has done wonders for promoting jazz education. That said, JALC embodies the same disparity as the rest of LC: it's an esteemed heavyweight in the jazz world, but it caters to the 1%, despite jazz having been conceived as accessible music for regular folks like you and me.

WHO LIVES WHERE

A mecca of tulle, tin, and strings, Lincoln Center houses companies upon troupes upon societies. Matching the performing group to the building means you won't end up watching Swan Lake when you should be listening to Mozart. The most confusing part about Lincoln Center is that "Lincoln Center Theater" is actually two theaters–the Vivian Beaumont and the Mitzi E. Newhouse theaters. Jazz at Lincoln Center moved into the Frederick P. Rose Hall in the Time Warner Center.

AMERICAN BALLET THEATER–*METROPOLITAN OPERA HOUSE*

CHAMBER MUSIC SOCIETY–*ALICE TULLY HALL*

FILM SOCIETY OF LINCOLN CENTER–*WALTER READE THEATER*

JAZZ AT LINCOLN CENTER–*FREDERICK P. ROSE HALL*

JULLIARD ORCHESTRA & SYMPHONY–*ALICE TULLY HALL*

METROPOLITAN OPERA COMPANY–*METROPOLITAN OPERA HOUSE*

LINCOLN CENTER THEATER–*VIVIAN BEAUMONT THEATER AND MITZI E. NEWHOUSE THEATER*

MOSTLY MOZART FESTIVAL –*AVERY FISHER HALL*

NEW YORK CITY BALLET–*DAVID H. KOCH THEATER*

NEW YORK PHILHARMONIC –*AVERY FISHER HALL*

SCHOOL OF AMERICAN BALLET–*SAMUEL B. AND DAVID ROSE BUILDING*

COLUMBUS CIRCLE

The crazy-making subterranean **Whole Foods** in the Time Warner Center is probably the reason most trek over to Columbus Circle, but don't miss the intriguing **Museum of Arts and Design**, which opened up on the south side of the circle in 2008 following an expansive and controversial renovation of 2 Columbus Circle. Check out its sublime permanent collection, excellent temporary exhibits, and cool design shop. As for the **Time Warner Center**, the shops therein cohere into something resembling a mall, a Manhattan rarity, though one with a great view of Central Park. Elsewhere there is the **Mandarin Oriental Hotel**, featuring 18,000-count sheets on which your out-of-town guests will not sleep unless they own a small kingdom. Ditto for eating at Thomas Keller's **Per Se** ($300-plus per person, not including wine), though his **Bouchon Bakery** is more within reach. See also the uptown outpost of TriBeCa's cool **Landmarc** restaurant. The **Trump International Hotel and Tower** rises up across the street, next to the riff on the Unisphere; Nougatine, of Jean-Georges fame, is its premier lunch spot...ahh...the other reason you go to Columbus Circle.

HOW TO GET THERE

Lincoln Center is right off Broadway and only a few blocks north of Columbus Circle, which makes getting there easy. The closest subway is the 66th Street 1 stop, which has an exit right on the edge of the center. It's also an easy walk from the trains that roll into Columbus Circle. If you prefer above-ground transportation, the M5, M7, M10, M11, M20, M66, and M104 bus lines all stop within one block of Lincoln Center. There is also a parking lot underneath the complex.

NEW YORK UNIVERSITY

GENERAL INFORMATION

NFT MAP: *6*
PHONE: *212-998-1212*
WEBSITE: *WWW.NYU.EDU*
TWITTER: *@NYUNIVERSITY*
ENROLLMENT: *44,599 (2013)*
ENDOWMENT: *$3.1 BILLION (2013)*

OVERVIEW

Founded in 1831, one of the nation's largest private universities sprawls throughout Manhattan, though its most recognizable buildings border Washington Square. Enrollment hovers around 45,000 (about half undergrads), many of whom will flood the city with their artistic product upon graduation, as if there wasn't enough competition for young folks here.

The expansion of NYU during recent years has been controversial. Some Village folks blame NYU's sprawl for higher rents and diminished neighborhood character. On the other hand, the students are a great boon to area businesses, the school is one of the city's largest private employers, and—to the ostensible point of many of the university's detractors—many historical buildings, such as the row houses on Washington Square, are owned and kept in good condition by the university.

NYU comprises 14 colleges, schools, and divisions, including the well-regarded Stern School of Business, the School of Law, and the Tisch School of Arts. It also has a school of Continuing and Professional Studies, with offerings in publishing, real estate, and just about every other city-centric industry you could imagine. Oh, and somehow they have the only Chick-fil-A this side of Paramus.

TUITION

If you squint, tuition for undergraduates runs around $50,000, plus $15,000 for room and board. Presented without comment.

SPORTS

NYU isn't big on athletics, but its fencing teams are highly competitive, with a long list of Olympians. The school competes in Division III and its mascot is the Bobcat, although all of their teams are nicknamed the Violets. "Violets" comes from the cute purple flowers that grew in Washington Square Park. Preferring a more robust identity, in the early 1980s the school turned to the Bobcat, inspired by—no kidding—its new computerized Bobst Library Catalog system dubbed "BobCat." Somewhere Albert Gallatin was all like, "SMH," but it stuck and here we are today...

CULTURE ON CAMPUS

The Grey Art Gallery usually has something cool (www.nyu.edu/greyart), and the Skirball Center for the Performing Arts hosts live performances (nyuskirball.org). Still, NYU doesn't have nearly as many events as a typical liberal arts school. But then again, why would they? NYU is in Greenwich Village, surrounded by some of the world's best music clubs, and on the same island as 700+ art galleries, thousands of restaurants, and tons of revival and new cinema. This is both the blessing and the curse of NYU—no true "campus," but situated in the middle of the greatest cultural square mileage in the world.

TRANSPORTATION

NYU runs its own campus transportation service for students, faculty, staff, and alumni with school ID cards. They run 7 am to 12 midnight weekdays and 10 am to 12 midnight weekends. During fall and spring session, free overnight Safe Ride Van Service is available to and from NYU facilities. NYU also has its own free bike share program.

GENERAL PHONE NUMBERS

GOULD WELCOME CENTER: 212-998-4550

OFFICE OF FINANCIAL AID: 212-998-4444

UNIVERSITY DEVELOPMENT AND ALUMNI RELATIONS: 212-998-6900

BOBST LIBRARY INFORMATION: 212-998-2500

MAIN BOOKSTORE: 212-998-4667

THE NEW SCHOOL

GENERAL INFORMATION

NFT MAPS: *5 & 6*
WELCOME CENTER: *72 FIFTH AVE (AT 13TH ST)*
PHONE: *212-229-5600*
WEBSITE: *WWW.NEWSCHOOL.EDU*
TWITTER: *@THENEWSCHOOL*
ENROLLMENT: *10,250 (2013)*
ENDOWMENT: *$295 MILLION (2014)*

OVERVIEW

The New School is a legendary progressive university located in and around Greenwich Village. Founded in 1919 to defy the constraints of a traditional college education, it gained international renown for groundbreaking courses taught by the likes of W.E.B. DuBois, Margaret Mead, Martha Graham, Frank Lloyd Wright, Aaron Copland, John Cage, and W.H. Auden. Today, The New School remains a hothouse for courageous creative thinkers driven (in the words of former New School student Jack Kerouac) to "never say a commonplace thing."

The university annually enrolls more than 10,000 undergraduate and graduate students within its interconnected colleges: Parsons, Eugene Lang College, Mannes College, The New School for Drama, The New School for Jazz and Contemporary Music, The New School for Social Research, and The New School for Public Engagement.

Collaborative problem solving is a core value at The New School, but it isn't about linking arms and singing Kumbaya. It's about mashing up ideas from different disciplines and rigorously challenging conventional wisdom to generate new ideas, new art, new knowledge, and new approaches. In small, seminar classes and intensive studio programs, students have not just the opportunity, but the obligation to take creative risks and speak their mind.

TUITION

Tuition for undergraduates varies by college but is generally around $40,000 per year plus $15,000 or so for student housing. Welcome to NYC real estate, and what may be the nicest living space you'll ever have in the city.

CULTURE ON CAMPUS

Robust and deep public programs—lectures, exhibitions, conferences, and concerts—are The New School's equivalent of a football team (in that campus life revolves around them). Dominating the corner of 14th Street and Fifth Avenue, the funky new University Center is a veritable ant farm of student activity. Of course, there's always the city.

TRANSPORTATION

All the subways that Union Square has to offer: N, Q, R, 4, 5, 6 and the L. See also the F and M trains along Sixth Avenue and the 1, 2 and 3 trains on Seventh Avenue.

GENERAL PHONE NUMBERS

ADMISSION AND FINANCIAL AID INFORMATION: *212-229-5150 OR 800-292-3040*
ALUMNI RELATIONS: *212-229-5662*
CAMPUS SECURITY: *212-229-7001*

ACADEMIC PHONE NUMBERS

PARSONS THE NEW SCHOOL FOR DESIGN: *212-229-8900*
EUGENE LANG COLLEGE THE NEW SCHOOL FOR LIBERAL ARTS: *212-229-5110*
THE NEW SCHOOL FOR SOCIAL RESEARCH: *212-229-5700*
THE NEW SCHOOL FOR PUBLIC ENGAGEMENT: *212-229-5615*
MANNES COLLEGE THE NEW SCHOOL FOR MUSIC: *212-580-0210*
THE NEW SCHOOL FOR DRAMA: *212-229-5859*
THE NEW SCHOOL FOR JAZZ AND CONTEMPORARY MUSIC: *212-229-5896*

RIVERSIDE PARK

GENERAL INFORMATION

WEBSITE: RIVERSIDEPARKNYC.ORG
PHONE: 212-870-3070

OVERVIEW

Riverside Park, stretching from 59th Street to 155th Street along the Hudson River on Manhattan's West Side, is the place where Upper West Siders go to find a little bit of rest and respite in the one of the most crowded neighborhoods in the country. The park also serves as a vital link between Upper Manhattan and Midtown for bicyclists and joggers along the water's edge, and there are ample recreational opportunities all along the way. Oh, and the views to the west across the Hudson from the vistas above are just magnificent.

The park developed in stages. The initial plans, from 72nd to 125th Streets, were conceived in the 1870s by Frederick Law Olmsted, co-designer of Central and Prospect Parks. Those designs were implemented piecemeal into the early part of the 20th century; the garden pathways and vistas along Riverside Drive are part of the original Olmsted plans. In the 1930s the Parks Department under the leadership of so-called master builder Robert Moses undertook a massive expansion of the park when the Henry Hudson Parkway was built along the waterfront and recreational facilities were added, along with the 79th Street Marina and Rotunda. In 1980, the park was designated an official scenic landmark by the City Landmarks Commission; it is one of only a handful of scenic landmarks in the city. The new millennium saw further expansion south of 72nd Street to 59th Street.

SIGHTS & SOUNDS

The thin path between the Henry Hudson Parkway and the water's edge between 100th and 125th Streets is home to dozens of cherry trees, gifts of the Japanese government from 1909, and from the same batch as were planted in D.C's Tidal Basin. In spring the pink flowers are stunning. Speaking of trees, the American Elms along Riverside Drive are a relatively rare living example of a species that has been nearly decimated by disease over the years. Many films and television shows are shot in Riverside Park, but head to the garden at 91st Street to see where Tom Hanks finally met Meg Ryan in *You've Got Mail*. The Soldiers' and Sailors' Monument at 89th Street is the site of the city's annual Memorial Day commemoration. At 122nd Street is the punchline to the old Groucho Marx joke: technically, no one is buried in Grant's Tomb, as the 18th President and his wife lay in rest in two sarcophagi above ground. And if you thought you had a good deal on rent, check out the lucky few who get to dock their houseboats at the 79th Street Boat Basin. But will Zabar's deliver?

RECREATION

In the early part of the 20th century park systems across the country began focusing less on passive recreation in favor of active recreation. Part of the Westside Improvement Project that covered the train tracks and built the Henry Hudson Parkway also added recreation facilities on the land below bluffs. Today Riverside Park has ballfields, basketball, tennis, volleyball and handball courts, and even kayak launches. It's safe to say that Olmsted probably never expected dog runs dotting his park.

PRACTICALITIES

Take the 1, 2, 3 train to any stop between Columbus Circle and 157th and it's just a short walk west to Riverside Park. The M72 bus gets you closest to Riverside Park South and the M5 bus runs up and down Riverside Drive, right at the edge of the park.

GENERAL INFORMATION

RANDALL'S ISLAND PARK ALLIANCE: *212-830-7722*
WEBSITE: *WWW.RANDALLSISLAND.ORG*
TWITTER: *@RANDALLSISLAND*

OVERVIEW

If landfills, minimal food options, and a treacherous mix of the Harlem and East Rivers called "Hell Gate" don't entice you over the RFK Bridge, you probably have good instincts. But put Randall's & Wards Islands' sullied past aside, and its 480 acres of open space just across the bridge will surprise you, not only its abundant recreational facilities but also the large concerts, art fairs and various festivals that set up shop each summer.

The islands, which were actually once two separate features since connected by landfill, were once home to hospitals and various social outreach facilities. In the 1930s the site began to transition to its current use as a public park and recreational hub. Over the years the island's Downing Stadium hosted concerts starring the likes of Duke Ellington and Jimi Hendrix. Jesse Owens competed there in Olympic trials, and Soccer great Pele played there with the Cosmos in the 1970s.

As with many of the city's ambitious 1930s-era projects, by the 1980s Randall's Island fell into disrepair, but since 1999 it has undergone a huge overhaul, and now it again boasts some of the city's top recreational amenities. The Randall's Island Park Alliance public-private conservancy now operates the greenspace and keeps progress humming. The foundation kicked off the park's renovation by replacing Downing Stadium with the state-of-the-art Icahn Track & Field Stadium, opened in 2005. Since then, they've restored dozens of ballfields, marshes, and wetlands, and built new waterfront bike and pedestrian paths. Some ideas have not come to pass: in 2007, local activists put the kibosh on a grand plan to build a fancy suburban-style water park.

No matter what, we hope future plans bring in more food facilities. Currently, the only culinary options are a smattering of food trucks near the Icahn Stadium and the golf center's snack bar. One suggestion: make a Whole Foods/Fairway/Zabar pit stop before enjoying a chill weekend afternoon in the park.

HOW TO GET THERE

By Car: Take the RFK Bridge, exit left to Randall's Island. While you do have to pay the MTA's hefty toll to get on the island, rest assured that it's free to leave!

By Subway/Bus: From Manhattan: take the 4, 5, 6 train to 125th Street, then transfer on the corner of 125th Street and Lexington Avenue for the M35 bus to Randall's Island. There's a bus about every 15-20 minutes during the day.

By Foot: A pedestrian footbridge at 103rd Street was built by Robert Moses in the '50s to provide Harlem residents access to the recreational facilities of the parks after then-City Council President Newbold Morris criticized the lack of facilities in Harlem. The bridge is open to pedestrians and cyclists 24/7.

FACILITIES

RANDALL'S ISLAND GOLF CENTER

The golf center on Randall's Island features a year-round driving range with heated stalls along with grass tees and an area to practice your short game (complete with sand bunkers). See also their 36 holes of mini-golf, nine batting cages, snack bar, and beer garden. Shuttle service is available weekends year-round and weekdays in season ($12 round trip). www.randallsislandgolfcenter.com/

ICAHN TRACK & FIELD STADIUM

Named for financier Carl Icahn (who contributed $10 million for naming rights), the 5,000-seat stadium is the only state-of-the-art outdoor track and field venue in New York City with a 400-meter running track and a regulation-size soccer field.

FIRE DEPARTMENT TRAINING CENTER

The NYC Fire Academy is located on 27 acres of landfill on the east side of Randall's Island. In an effort to keep the city's bravest in shape, the academy utilizes 68 acres of parkland for physical fitness programs. The ultra-cool training facility includes 11 Universal Studios-like buildings for simulations training, a 200,000 gallon water supply tank, gasoline and diesel fuel pumps, and a 300-car parking lot. In addition, the New York Transit Authority installed tracks and subway cars for learning and developing techniques to battle subway fires and other emergencies. They're clearly missing an opportunity here...

Sportime Tennis Center 20 year-round courts, including courts heated for winter use, a training facility and cafe. www.sportimeny.com/Manhattan

ROBERT MOSES BUILDING

Perhaps a few urban planning students have made a pilgrimage here, the one-time home of Moses' power-consolidating Triborough Bridge and Tunnel Authority.

NYPD

They launch cool-looking police boats from here.

ROCKEFELLER CENTER

GENERAL INFORMATION

NFT MAP: *12*
PHONE: *212-332-6868*
WEBSITE: *WWW.ROCKEFELLERCENTER.COM*
TWITTER: *@ROCKCENTERNYC*
RINK PHONE: *212-332-7655*
RINK WEBSITE: *WWW.THERINKATROCKCENTER.COM*
NBC TOUR PHONE: *212-664-3700*
TOP OF THE ROCK:
WWW.TOPOFTHEROCKNYC.COM

OVERVIEW

Perhaps you've been blinded five streets away by 25,000 Swarovski crystals. Or maybe you've glimpsed a gargantuan King Kong of a tree shooting seventy feet in the air and wondered how on earth such vegetation could grow in concrete. Regardless how you fall for antics, arrive in bewilderment at Rockefeller Center, and stay for the ice skating rink, services at St. Patrick's, and the Rockettes at Radio City Music Hall. When there's not a huge pine tree to distract you, you'll note that Rockefeller Center occupies three square blocks with a slew of retail, dining, and office facilities. Midtown corporate just ain't the same without its magic.

The massive Rockefeller Center complex was begun at the height of the Great Depression and reflects the Art Deco architecture of the era. It opened in 1933 and it's notable that most of the iconic Rockefeller Center attractions and features actually date back to those early years: the tree tradition began in 1931, the Rainbow Room opened for business in 1934, the wintertime rink first welcomed skaters in 1936, and Radio City Music Hall and its Rockettes date back to the early days. NBC has been headquartered at 30 Rockefeller Plaza (i.e., "30 Rock") since the very beginning; when you go, you'll recognize the Today Show exterior immediately, and *Saturday Night Live*, *The Tonight Show Starring Jimmy Fallon*, and *Late Night with Seth Meyers* all take place in the NBC studios on the lower floors of the GE Building. NBC offers tours of its facilities; call or visit online for more information.

The Top of the Rock Observation Deck has jaw-dropping, 360-degree views of the skyline from atop the 70-story GE Building. In some ways it's a better view than that from the Empire State Building, if only because it features a great view of the Empire State Building. Top of the Rock is open daily 8 am–12 am (last elevator 11 pm). Tickets are timed entry and cost $27. Guided tours of Rockefeller Center are offered daily throughout the day and combined Top of the Rock/tour tickets are available.

WHERE TO EAT

How hungry are you? Rock Center isn't a prime dining destination, but you won't starve if you find yourself in the area. For cheaper fare, try places down in the Concourse. You'll pay for the view if you eat overlooking the skating rink. For coffee, there is an outpost of **Blue Bottle** on the Concourse level. The **Magnolia Bakery** on 49th and Sixth is one of two architectural holdouts that refused to sell to the Rockefellers. Many restaurants in Rockefeller Center are open on Saturdays, but aside from the "nice" restaurants, only a few open their doors on Sundays.

WHERE TO SHOP

Much of the Rockefeller Center roster could be at a mall nearly anywhere, but there are some fun standouts in the crowd. **FDNY Fire Zone** (50 Rockefeller Plaza) features both interactive fire safety exhibits and official FDNY merch. **La Maison Du Chocolat** (30 Rockefeller Plaza) sells high-end French chocolate and boffo hot chocolate. **Posman Books** (30 Rockefeller Plaza) is a family-owned independent bookstore. **Teuscher Chocolates** (620 Fifth Ave) are Swiss chocolates in the truest sense: they're flown in from Switzerland.

THE RINK

To practice your double loop: The rink opens Columbus Day weekend and closes in April to make way for the Rink Bar. Skating hours are 8:30 am–12 am daily. Rates are $27 for each 90-minute session plus $12 skate rental. Season passes are available. If it all seems a little pricey, keep in mind that only 150 skaters are allowed on the rink at one time, making for a more intimate experience. And that setting, duh.

ROOSEVELT ISLAND

OVERVIEW

Once upon a time, Roosevelt Island was much like the rest of New York—populated by criminals, the sick, and the mentally ill. The difference was that they were the residents of the island's various mental institutions, hospitals, and jails, but these days this slender tract of land between Manhattan and Queens has become prime real estate for families and UN officials.

The 147-acre island, formerly known as "Welfare Island" because of its population of outcasts and the poor, was renamed for Franklin D. Roosevelt in 1973, when the island began changing its image. The first residential housing complex opened in 1975. Some of the old "monuments" remain, including the Smallpox Hospital and the Blackwell House (one of the oldest farmhouses in the city), while the Octagon Building, formerly a 19th-century mental hospital known for its deplorable conditions, has been turned into luxury condos (so yes, you're still in New York). **Four Freedoms Park**, which dusts off a decades-old design by the architect Louis I. Kahn, is a focal point for the southern tip of the island; the putting green-length grass and severe white granite isn't exactly welcoming, but you certainly can't beat that view of East Midtown.

The island's northern tip is a popular destination for fishermen with iron gullets. It's also the home of a lighthouse designed by James Renwick, Jr., of St. Patrick's Cathedral fame. The two rehab/convalescent hospitals on the island don't offer emergency services, so if you're in need of medical attention right away, you're out of luck. The island's main drag, Main Street (where did they come up with the name?), resembles a cement-block college campus circa 1968. Just south, closer to the tram, is a more recent stretch of development that fetches top dollar. Two of these buildings are residences for Memorial Sloan-Kettering Cancer Center and Rockefeller and Cornell University employees.

Perhaps the best way to experience the island is to spend a little while on the local shuttle bus that runs the length of the island. You'll see a wonderful mix of folks, some crazy characters, and have a chance to grill the friendly bus drivers about all things Roosevelt Island. Trust us.

HOW TO GET THERE

Roosevelt Island can be reached by the train, but it's much more fun to take the tram. Plus, your-out-of town friends will love that this is the tram Tobey Maguire saved as Spiderman in the first movie. You can board it with a Metrocard (including an unlimited!) at 60th Street and Second Avenue in Manhattan—look for the big hulking mass drifting through the sky. It takes 4 minutes to cross and runs every 15 minutes (every 7 minutes during rush hour) 6 am–2 am, Sunday through Thursday, and 'til 3:30 am on Fridays and Saturdays. To get there by car, take the Queensboro-Ed Koch Bridge and follow signs for the 21st Street-North exit. Go north on 21st Street and make a left on 36th Avenue. Go west on 36th Avenue and cross over the red Roosevelt Island Bridge. There is limited reliable street parking on Roosevelt Island; hit the Motorgate Plaza garage at the end of the bridge at Main Street instead.

SOUTH STREET SEAPORT

GENERAL INFORMATION

NFT MAPS: 1 & 3
PHONE: 212-732-8257
WEBSITE: WWW.SOUTHSTREETSEAPORT.COM
TWITTER: @THESEAPORT

OVERVIEW

For years New York's modus operandi has been something along the lines of build, tear down, build bigger, tear down again, and build even bigger until it's the biggest, bestest, most badass thing in the Western Hemisphere. Or something like that. Which is what makes the South Street Seaport such an odd and endearing spot in Lower Manhattan. The old-tymey tyme historic ships and intact nineteenth-century buildings take you back to New York's mercantile/shipping past. If you squint, you just might make out Walt Whitman ducking a roving band of Dead Rabbits. Or something like that. Or maybe those are just a few preteens goofing while their folks settle up at the TKTS booth. Same-same.

Indeed, time was you could be forgiven if you assumed South Street Seaport was just a mall and a cobblestoned pedestrian walkway of chain stores. After Superstorm Sandy, however, the area has undergone quite a physical and spiritual change. To-day the Seaport has been rebranded as a spot for container ship pop-ups, artisanal vendors from Brooklyn and a space for live events. Even the bad old mall is scheduled for a major renovation.

Part of the impetus for change has come from the Howard Hughes Corporation, which has plans to shake up what had become a sleepy and, honestly, somewhat stale part of Lower Manhattan. The museum and its picturesque tall ships had been struggling financially for years, the bland shops along Schermerhorn Row amount-ed to a lesser Faneuil Hall Marketplace, and the less said about that strange Pier 17 mall the better. It remains to be seen whether the plans for a giant tower and multi-screen mixed-use fantasia survive first contact, but the ball is definitely rolling. And if they can do something won-derful with the former Fulton Fish Market, which has been waiting for a permanent repurposing since it closed in 2005, then it will all be for the best. Our vote is for the wonderful New Amsterdam Market (www. newamsterdammarket.org) to permanent-ly move in.

For the time being, the area deserves all the support it can get. For years, our favorite stop is friendly and crowded **Nelson Blue**, with its crisp, clean New Zealand cuisine. It can get crowded early evenings with Wall Streeters, but off-times and weekends it's a perfect respite from walking the pavement. **SUteiShi**, right across the street, does excellent sushi rolls, while **Barbalu's** owners proved stronger than the storm. A gourmet cuppa joe can be sipped at **Jack's Stir Brew** or have a glass of wine at Bin 220 before indulging in succulent steaks at **Mark Joseph**. And then there are those great old-old school places that remain awesome–don't miss brunch at 19th-century spot **Bridge café** and drinks at former fishmonger hangout **Paris café**. And **Pasanella** is a great wine store.

The South Street Historic District is at a crossroads, and time will tell whether the development that happens creates some-thing smart and vital or just replicates the same sort of tourist crapola a la Pier 17 mall. Here's hoping for the former–the in-frastructure is just too cool, and the stakes are too high to let this fantastic resource wither.

TIMES SQUARE

GENERAL INFORMATION

NFT MAP: 12

WEBSITE: WWW.TIMESSQUARENYC.ORG

TWITTER: @TIMESSQUARENYC

TRANSIT: TAKE THE 1, 2, 3, 7, N, Q, R, AND S TRAINS TO GET TO THE CENTER OF EVERYTHING AT THE 42ND STREET/TIMES SQUARE STOP, UNDER BROADWAY AND SEVENTH AVENUE. THE A, C, AND E TRAINS STOP AT 42ND STREET ALONG EIGHTH AVENUE.

OVERVIEW

Let's get real: the hand-wringing about whether the "old" "gritty" Times Square was somehow better than the "new" "sanitized" "Disneyfied" Times Square is so three decades ago. Times Square is what it is, and the truth is that if you spend any amount of time in Midtown, or if you've ever go to a theatrical presentation, or if you–god forbid!– happen to happen upon one of the most iconic cityscapes on the planet, then you just might find yourself here. And when that occurs, you can either be a dead-ender about it and spar with Elmo about how Show World was so much better than M&Ms World or you can accept the fact that, duh, healthy cities evolve. That said, no one's debating the idea that those Hard Gump Planet Fieri ShrimpZone theme restaurants are and always will be patently absurd. Granted. And of course you dislike Times Square–of course you do, we get it. But now that you are here, let's talk about how to make the most of it.

For starters, now that Broadway between 42nd Street and 47th Street is permanently closed to traffic, Times Square is a lot less of a headache to walk through. Now there is ample space to gawk at the underwear ads above. The street preachers have lost their narrow sidewalk gauntlet. Some days you can even walk from one end to the other without once ever having to consider whether you like comedy. The "pilot" project that began in 2009 was made permanent, or permanent enough, by the end of Bloomberg's tenure in 2013.

On the north end of the Times Square district in Duffy Square is the giant red TKTS booth, a sort of ziggurat of cheap Broadway tickets. Climb to the top–don't worry, unlike nearly everything else in the immediate vicinity, it's free–take the customary selfie and admire the view. Come on, admit it: it's pretty neat up there. And now you know what the view is like from the Olive Garden.

SIGHTS

Times Square was known as Longacre Square until 1904, when *The New York Times* moved to the building now known as **One Times Square**, which is also known as the place where the ball drops each New Year's Eve. The paper has since moved twice–first to 229 West 43rd Street and then in 2007 to a new

Renzo Piano-designed 52-story skyscraper on the southeast corner of 42nd Street and Eighth Avenue, just across from the Port Authority Bus Terminal. The Times Building also houses a hip *MUJI* store for all your Japanese design needs. As for the Port Authority, it's not a bad option if you're feeling nostalgic for the gritty days though even it, too, falls into the Latter-Day *Lion King* camp: the dumpy old bowling alley has been rebranded as Frames, with bottle service (!) and the *Port Authority Greenmarket* (!!) is a year-round operation. Or, just embrace the suck, and go for broke at the *View Lounge*, which, not for nothing, features a 360-degree rotating bar at the top of the Marriott. Gripe all you want about the overpriced drinks, but you can't beat the view.

RESTAURANTS & NIGHTLIFE

Far be it from us to speculate about what compels people to travel all the way to New York, with its tens of thousands of restaurants, some of which being actually very good, only to spend several meals' worth of calories (and a not inconsequential wad of cash) at one of the chains in Times Square. Which is to say, those places exist, but that's not all there is. Cases in point: *Virgil's Real BBQ* (152 W 44th St) serves up quite good grub, although they rush you out like you're in Chinatown; the 24-hour French haven *Maison* (1700 Broadway, off the map) features an excellent beer selection as well; *Marseille* (630 Ninth Ave, off the map) is another French standby that is a good pre-theater option; and there's a branch of Danny Meyer's *Shake Shack* over on Eighth Avenue and 44th St. After dinner, the *Iridium Jazz Club* (1650 Broadway, off the map) showcases top-notch jazz acts; guitar god Les Paul jammed here every Monday before dying of pneumonia in 2009 at age 94. For a drink, the bar at the *Paramount Hotel* (235 W 46th St) is cool (merci, Monsieur Starck), though (of course) not cheap. Our recommendation: head a few blocks north to the *Russian Vodka Room* (265 W 52nd St, off the map) for a singular experience. You won't remember it, but you'll have fun doing it. And finally, for people who say the old Times Square is gone forever, stop in for a shot, a beer, and some boxing nostalgia at *Jimmy's Corner* (140 W 44th St).

GENERAL INFORMATION

NFT MAPS: 6, 9, & 10

OVERVIEW

Want to find the real pulse of Manhattan? Head straight to Union Square where thousands of people surge through here everyday to hang out on the steps, shop at the excellent farmers market, protest whatever's wrong with our country this week, and watch the city roll on by. Part of the charm is that there's no real attraction here. There's a park with some benches, a few statues, a dog run, the aforementioned market, and that's about it. After 9/11 New Yorkers congregated under the George Washington monument to console each other and remember the perished. Since that fateful day, Union Square has become the de facto living room of Downtown. Between New School and NYU kids rushing to class, crazy street entertainers, lost tourists, and people just trying to get to work, this place is always jumping. Historical note: The first ever Labor Day celebration took place here, so next time you're sitting in the park enjoying your lunch from the Whole Foods salad bar, give thanks that the legal days of working 14-hour shifts are behind us. Or so they say.

SHOPPING

Over the years, the area around Union Square gradually filled with the kind of chains that you can find across the country, but if you look very carefully, you'll find a couple of good shopping options in these parts. High on the list is **The Strand** (828 Broadway), the iconic bookstore that keeps on truckin' (thank goodness) with discounted books and literary readings, and don't forget **Alabaster Bookshop** (122 4th Ave) just around the corner. There's also **Forbidden Planet** (840 Broadway), a comic book nerd's heaven. For the sports nuts **Paragon Sporting Goods** (867 Broadway) is the place to get any kind of racquet, ball, or bat you can think of. If you must choose a big name, **the Barnes & Noble** (33 E 17th) at the north end of the park has an amazing magazine selection and of course an incredible selection of NFTs. But the main draw is the **Union Square Greenmarket**– one of the original NYC greenmarkets dating back to 1976, this is one the best spots in the city to stock up on produce, cheese, baked goods, meat, and flowers. Fantastic.

RESTAURANTS

For a true splurge make reservations at **Union Square café** (21 E 16th St). Established in 1985, this is restaurateur extraordinaire Danny Meyer's first restaurant, not only has it stayed strong and fresh over the years but

many New York chefs have spent time in the kitchen there. For a quick bite that won't break the bank, **Republic** (37 Union Sq W) serves up noisy noodles. To eat really cheap you can't beat **Maoz** (38 Union Sq E) for fast food vegetarian. Or do what it seems most everyone in the universe seems to be doing and make a trip to the **Whole Foods'** (4 Union Sq E) hot and cold food bars. In the warmer months you can sit in the park, but on colder days walk up to the second floor cafeteria and enjoy an amazing panoramic view. For dessert, try the hot chocolate at **Max Brenner Chocolate by the Bald Man** (841 Broadway).

NIGHTLIFE

Ready for a stiff drink? **Old Town Bar** (45 E 18th St) is the prime choice. It has character, cheapish cocktails, and the crowd isn't totally ridiculous (yeah, it's that tough of a neighborhood to find a decent bar). Just west of Union Square is **Park Bar** (15 E 15th St), a perfect place to meet up for an after work blind date—it's small enough to force conversation with your new friend. Or try **Lillie's** (13 E 17th St) just up the block if you have a Irish-Victorian bar décor fetish. You'll know what we're talking about the second you walk in. If you like your bowling alleys with fancy cocktails and a velvet rope, then **Bowlmor** (110 University Pl) will do you just fine. And for live music, the **Irving Plaza** (17 Irving Pl) is a staple on the New York rock scene.

JUST PLAIN WEIRD

See that giant smoking magic wand clocky thingy on the facade on south side of the square? It's actually got a name–*The Metronome*. Installed in 1999, artists Andrew Ginzel and Kristen Jones created something that's supposed to inspire reflection on the pace of time in the city...or something like that. Unfortunately, every time we glance up at it, we feel even more on edge than we already are. The strip of numbers is a sort of clock: the left-hand side counts the hours in the day while the right-hand side subtracts the hours left–the two numbers crash in the middle. On the right side is a moon with the current phase. Somewhere in the middle at the top is a hand, a riff on George Washington's directly across the street.

JUST OFF THE MAP

The post-work rush at **Trader Joe's** (142 E 14th St) is a special kind of torture that we will gladly submit to in order to save a few bucks on Wasabi-Ginger Almonds and Organic Fair Trade Italian Coffee. Ditto for the "Two Buck Chuck" (add a dollar or two in Manhattan) at the adjoining **TJ's Wine Shop** (138 E 14th St). And those dryer chairs seem to be in good working order over at **Beauty Bar** (231 E 14th St), which features smart cocktails in a repurposed hair salon.

UNITED NATIONS

GENERAL INFORMATION

NFT MAP: *13*
ADDRESS: *FIRST AVE B/W 42ND & 48TH STS*
PHONE: *212-963-TOUR(8687)*
WEBSITE: *WWW.UN.ORG*
VISITOR INFORMATION: *VISIT.UN.ORG*
GUIDED TOUR HOURS: *MONDAY-FRIDAY 9:15 AM-4:15 PM.*
GUIDED TOUR ADMISSION: *$18 FOR ADULTS, $11 FOR SENIORS, $11 FOR STUDENTS, AND $9 FOR CHILDREN AGES 5–12. CHILDREN UNDER 5 NOT ADMITTED.*

OVERVIEW

The United Nations Headquarters building, that giant domino teetering on the bank of the East River, opened its doors in 1951. It's here that the 193 member countries of the United Nations meet to fulfill the UN's mandate of maintaining international peace, developing friendly relations among nations, promoting development and human rights, and getting all the free parking they want. The UN is divided into bodies: the General Assembly, the Security Council, the Economic and Social Council, the Trusteeship Council, the Secretariat, and the International Court of Justice (located in the Hague). Specialized agencies like the World Health Organization (located in Geneva) and the UN Children's Fund (UNICEF) (located in New York) are part of the UN family.

The United Nations was founded at the end of World War II by world powers intending to create a body that would prevent war by fostering an ideal of collective security. New York was chosen to be home base when John D. Rockefeller Jr. donated $8.5 million to purchase the 18 acres the complex occupies. The UN is responsible for a lot of good—its staff and agencies have been awarded nine Nobel Peace Prizes over the years. However, the difficult truth is that the United Nations hasn't completely lived up to the ideals of its 1945 charter. Scandals involving abuses by UN troops in Haiti and other countries have certainly not boosted the UN's reputation recently.

That said, this place is definitely worth a tour. After all, the people in this building do change the world, for better or worse. The UN Headquarters complex is an international zone complete with its own security force, fire department, and post office (which issues UN stamps). It consists of four buildings: the Secretariat building (the 39-story tower), the General Assembly building, the Conference building, and the Dag Hammarskjöld Library. Once you clear what feels like airport security, you'll find yourself in the Visitor Centre where there are shops, a coffee shop, and a scattering of topical small exhibits that come and go. The guided tour is your ticket out into important rooms like the Security Council Chambers and the impressive and inspiring General Assembly Hall. Sometimes tour groups are allowed to briefly sit in on meetings, but don't expect to spy the Secretary General roaming the halls. Take a stroll through the Peace Bell Garden (off limits to the public, but it can be seen from the inside during the guided tour). The bell, a gift from Japan in 1954, was cast from coins collected by children from 60 different countries. A bronze statue by Henry Moore, *Reclining Figure: Hand*, is located north of the Secretariat Building. The UN grounds are especially impressive when the 500 prize-winning rose bushes and 140 flowering cherry trees are in bloom.

WORLD TRADE CENTER

GENERAL INFORMATION

NFT MAP: *1*
WEBSITE: *WWW.WTC.COM OR*
TWITTER: *@WTCPROGRESS*

NATIONAL SEPTEMBER 11 MEMORIAL & MUSEUM

WEBSITE: *WWW.911MEMORIAL.ORG*
TWITTER: *@SEPT11MEMORIAL*

OVERVIEW

After years of delay, the neighborhood's ongoing rehabilitation now continues apace. One World Trade Center topped off in 2013. The National September 11th Memorial opened in 2011 and its accompanying museum opened in 2014. Further afield, Chambers, Fulton, Hudson, and other downtown streets have been structurally improved, downtown parks have been revitalized, and various initiatives have welcomed thousands of new residents to Lower Manhattan.

It remains to be seen how many of WTC's five planned towers will be built, and to what height they will rise. The various claims are complex, and it's unclear how much office space is actually needed downtown—tenants are already heavily subsidized and it's difficult to believe that Port Authority tolls won't eventually have to be applied toward either the development or upkeep of the site, no matter how much the PA denies this to be the case. Also unknown is how the site will function as both a place of mourning and a humming civic space. In short, this is not your typical public project.

Transit has been restored to pre–September 11th order, with all subway lines resuming service to the area, along with PATH service to a new PATH station designed by architect Santiago Calatrava.

Even though the end result was pared back somewhat from the original design, the whole thing still cost a cool $3.8 billion.

One World Trade Center, the epic 104-story, 1,776-foot skyscraper whose exact height is no accident, is the tallest building in the Western Hemisphere. Its footprint matches the footprints of the Twin Towers at 200 by 200 feet. The building itself is the same height as the original WTC 1 and 2 and the spire rises to 1,776 feet (remember the early "Freedom Tower" label?), something that caused Chicago boosters much consternation when the spire was deemed an architectural feature part of the building and not just an antenna, and thus higher than the Sears/Willis Tower. The building has 2.6 million square feet of office space, restaurants, an observation deck, and broadcasting facilities for the Metropolitan Television Alliance. Suffice it to say, it was built with security and safety at the fore—some even argue to the exclusion of aesthetics.

The National September 11 Memorial & Museum opened in 2011 and 2014 respectively. The memorial, Michael Arad's *Reflecting Absence* marks the footprints of the Twin Towers with massive waterfalls flowing down into the ground. The museum, designed by Norwegian firm Snohetta, focuses on not only on the events September 11, 2001 but also the original World Trade Center, the first terrorist attack in 1993, the rescue and recovery effort after 9/11, tributes large and small to those who perished and an extensive oral history project. One wall of Foundation Hall is the exposed "slurry wall," part of the original WTC retaining wall that held back the Hudson River. Indeed, the museum is an engineering feat, cited 70 feet underground, and with a price tag to match—the museum and memorial combined are said to cost in excess of $1 billion.

GENERAL INFORMATION

ADDRESS: JFK EXPY JAMAICA, NY 11430

PHONE: 718-244-4444

LOST & FOUND: 718-244-4225 OR JFKLOSTANDFOUND@PANYNJ.GOV

WEBSITE: WWW.KENNEDYAIRPORT.COM

AIRTRAIN: WWW.AIRTRAINJFK.COM

AIRTRAIN PHONE: 877-535-2478

GROUND TRANSPORTATION: 800-AIR-RIDE (247-7433)

LONG ISLAND RAIL ROAD: WWW.MTA.INFO/LIRR

PORT AUTHORITY POLICE: 718-244-4335

TWITTER: @NY_NJAIRPORTS

OVERVIEW

Ah, JFK. It's long been a nemesis to Manhattanites due to the fact that it's the farthest of the three airports from the city. Nonetheless, more than 49 million people go through JFK every year. A $9.5 billion expansion and modernization program is transforming the airport, with JetBlue taking about $900 million of that for its gigantic, 26-gate, new HQ to address the ten million of you who, in spite of JFK's distance, wake up an hour earlier to save a buck. JetBlue's Terminal 5 rises just behind the landmark TWA building, which you should check out if you have time to kill after getting up an hour earlier. Its bubblicious curves make this 1960s gem a glam spaceship aptly prepared to handle any swanky NY soiree. Top that, Newark.

CAR SERVICES, SHARED RIDES & TAXIS

ALL COUNTY EXPRESS: 800-914-4223

CONNECTICUT LIMOUSINE: 203-974-4700 OR 800-472-5466

WESTCHESTER EXPRESS: 914-332-0090 OR 866-914-6800

SUPER SHUTTLE LONG ISLAND: 800-742-9824

SUPER SHUTTLE MANHATTAN: 212-BLUE-VAN OR 800-258-3826

DIAL 7 CAR & LIMO SERVICE: 212-777-7777 OR 800-777-8888

SUPER SAVER BY CARMEL: 866-666-6666

EXECUCAR: 800-253-1443

Taxis from the airport to anywhere in Manhattan cost a flat $52 + tolls and tip, while fares to the airport are metered + tolls and tip. The SuperShuttle (800-258-3826) will drop you anywhere in Manhattan, including all hotels, for $20–$30, but be warned it could end up taking a while, depending on where your fellow passengers are going. Nevertheless, it's a good option if you want door-to-door service and have a lot of time to kill, but not a lot of cash.

HOW TO GET THERE–DRIVING

You can take the lovely and scenic Belt Parkway straight to JFK, as long as it's not rush hour. The Belt Parkway route is about 30 miles long, even though JFK is only 15 or so miles from Manhattan. You can access the Belt by taking the Hugh L. Cary Tunnel to the Gowanus (the best route) or by taking the Brooklyn, Manhattan, or Williamsburg Bridges to the Brooklyn-Queens Expressway to the Gowanus. If you're sick of stop-and-go highway traffic and prefer using local roads, take Atlantic Avenue in Brooklyn and drive east until you hit Conduit Avenue. Follow this straight to JFK–it's direct and fairly simple. You can get to Atlantic Avenue from any of the three downtown bridges (look at one of our maps first!). From midtown, you can take the Queens-Midtown Tunnel

to the Long Island Expressway to the Van Wyck Expressway South (there's never much traffic on the LIE, of course...). From uptown, you can take the Robert F. Kennedy Bridge to the Grand Central Parkway to the Van Wyck Expressway S. Tune into 1630AM for general airport information en route to your next flight. It might save you a headache.

HOW TO GET THERE– MASS TRANSIT

This is your chance to finish *War and Peace*. A one-seat connection to the airport–any of them–is still a far-off dream, but the AirTrain works fairly well. AirTrain runs 24 hours a day between JFK and two off-site stations, one connecting with the A train at Howard Beach and the other connecting with the E, J, and Z trains at the Sutphin/Archer Ave-Jamaica Station stop. The ride takes around 15–25 minutes, depending on which airport terminal you need.

A one-way ride on the AirTrain is $5, so a ride on the subway and then hopping the AirTrain will cost $7.50 combined. If you're anywhere near Penn Station and your time is valuable, the LIRR to Jamaica will cost you $10.50 during peak times ($7 off-peak and $4 on weekends using a MTA CityTicket). The AirTrain portion of the trip will still cost you an additional $5 and round out your travel time to less than an hour. If you want to give your MetroCard a workout, and ridiculously long bus journeys don't make you completely insane–or if you're just a connoisseur of mass transit–you can also take the E or F train to the Turnpike/Kew Gardens stop and transfer to the Q10 bus. Another option is the 3 train to New Lots Avenue, where you can transfer to the B15 bus to JFK. The easiest and most direct option is to take a NYC Airporter bus (718-777-5111) from either Grand Central Station, Penn Station, or the Port Authority for $16. Since the buses travel on service roads, Friday afternoon is not an advisable time to try them out.

PARKING

Daily rates for the Central Terminal Area lots cost $4 for the first half-hour, $8 for up to one hour, $4 for every half-hour after that, up to $33 per 24-hour period. Long-term parking costs $18 for the first 24-hours, then $6 in each 8-hour increment thereafter. The Port Authority website features real -time updates on parking availability, showing what percent of each lot is occupied. Online reservations are available for $5, and EZ-Pass holders can use the tag to pay for parking.

RENTAL CARS (ON-AIRPORT)

The rental car offices are all located along the Van Wyck Expressway near the entrance to the airport. Just follow the signs.

AVIS: 718-244-5406 OR 800-230-4898
BUDGET: 718-656-1890 OR 800-527-0700
DOLLAR: 800-800-4000
ENTERPRISE: 718-553-7013 OR 800-736-8222
HERTZ: 718-656-7600 OR 800-654-3131
NATIONAL: 718-632-8300 OR 888-826-6890

LAGUARDIA AIRPORT

GENERAL INFORMATION

ADDRESS: *LAGUARDIA AIRPORT, FLUSHING, NY 11371*
PHONE: *718-533-3400*
LOST & FOUND: *718-533-3988 OR LGALOSTANDFOUND@PANYNJ.GOV*
WEBSITE: *WWW.LAGUARDIAAIRPORT.COM*
GROUND TRANSPORTATION: *800-AIR-RIDE (247-7433)*
POLICE: *718-533-3900*
TWITTER: *@NY_NJAIRPORTS*

OVERVIEW

The reason to fly from LaGuardia (affectionately known as LGA on your baggage tags) is that it is geographically the closest airport to Manhattan and thus a cheap(er) cab ride when your delayed flight touches down at 1 in the morning. The reason not to fly to and from here is that there is no rail link and the check-in areas are just too darn small to accommodate the many passengers and their many bags that crowd the terminals at just about every hour of the day. Food has gotten better, but it is still not a great option, so eat before you leave home.

HOW TO GET THERE– DRIVING

LaGuardia is mere inches away from Grand Central Parkway, which can be reached from both the Brooklyn-Queens Expressway (BQE) or from the Robert F. Kennedy Bridge. From Lower Manhattan, take the Brooklyn, Manhattan, or Williamsburg Bridges to the BQE to Grand Central Parkway E. From Midtown Manhattan, take FDR Drive to the Robert F. Kennedy Bridge to Grand Central. For a toll-free alternative, take the 59th Street Bridge to 21st Street in Queens. Once you're heading north on 21st Street, you can make a right on Astoria Boulevard and follow it all the way to 94th Street, where you can make a left and drive straight into LaGuardia. This alternate route is good if the FDR and/or the BQE is jammed, although that probably means that the 59th Street Bridge won't be much better.

HOW TO GET THERE– MASS TRANSIT

Alas, no subway line goes directly to LaGuardia. The closest the subway comes is the 7-E-F-M-R Jackson Heights/Roosevelt Avenue/74th Street stop in Queens where you can transfer to the Q70 limited-stop bus which gets you to LaGuardia in 8-10 minutes. Another option is the M60 bus, which runs across 125th Street and the RFK Bridge to the airport, connecting with the N and Q at Astoria Blvd. You could also pay the extra few bucks and ride the NYC Airporter bus ($13 one-way, 718-777-5111) from Grand Central, departing every 30 minutes and taking approximately 45 minutes. Also catch it at Penn Station and the Port Authority Bus Terminal. The SuperShuttle (800-258-3826) will drop you anywhere in Manhattan, including all hotels, for $20–$30.

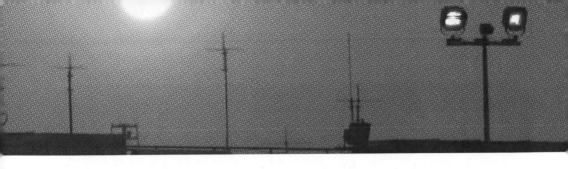

HOW TO GET THERE— REALLY

Taxis to Manhattan run between $25-$37 depending on your final destination, and there is no flat rate from LaGuardia. If you want a taxi, search for the "hidden" cab line tucked around Terminal D as the line is almost always shorter than the others. Alternatively, plan ahead and call a car service to guarantee that you won't spend the morning of your flight fighting for a taxi. Nothing beats door to door service. All County Express: 800-914-4223; Connecticut Limousine: 203-974-4700 or 800-472-5466; Westchester Express: 914-332-0090 or 866-914-6800; Dial 7 Car & Limo Service: 212-777-7777 or 800-777-8888; Super Saver by Carmel: 866-666-6666; ExecuCar: 800-253-1443.

PARKING

Daily parking rates at LaGuardia cost $4 for the first half-hour, $8 for up to one hour, $4 for every hour thereafter, up to $33 per 24-hour period. Long-term parking is $33 per day for the first two 24-hour periods, and $6 for each subsequent 8 hour period. (though only in Lot 3). The Port Authority website features real -time updates on parking availability, showing what percent of each lot is occupied. Online reservations are available for $5, and EZ-Pass holders can use the tag to pay for parking.

Several off-site parking lots serve LaGuardia, including LaGuardia Plaza Hotel (104-04 Ditmars Blvd, 718-457-6300 x295), Clarion Airport Parking (Ditmars Blvd & 94th St, 718-335-2423) and The Parking Spot (23rd Ave & 90th St, 718-507-8162). Each runs its own shuttle from the lots, and they usually charge $14–$25 per day. If all the parking garages onsite are full, follow the "P" signs to the airport exit and park in one of the off-airport locations.

RENTAL CARS

AVIS: LGA; 718-507-3600 OR 800-230-4898
BUDGET: 83-34 23RD AVE; 718 639-6400
DOLLAR: 95-05 25TH AVE; 800-800-4000
ENTERPRISE: 104-04 DITMARS BLVD; 718-457-2900 OR 800-736-8222
HERTZ: LGA; 718-478-5300 OR 800-654-3131
NATIONAL: DITMARS BLVD & 95TH ST; 718-429-5893 OR 888-826-6890

NEWARK LIBERTY AIRPORT

GENERAL INFORMATION

ADDRESS: *10 TOLER PL, NEWARK, NJ 07114*
PHONE: *973-961-6000*
LOST & FOUND: *EWRLOSTANDFOUND@PANYNJ.GOV*
WEBSITE: *WWW.NEWARKAIRPORT.COM*
AIRTRAIN: *WWW.AIRTRAINNEWARK.COM*
GROUND TRANSPORTATION: *800-AIR-RIDE (247-7533)*
TWITTER: *@NY_NJAIRPORTS*

OVERVIEW

Newark Airport is easily the nicest of the three major metropolitan airports. The monorail that connects the terminals and the parking lots, the AirTrain link from Penn Station, and the diverse food court (in Terminal C), make it the city's preferred point of departure and arrival. There are also plenty of international departures, making it a great second option to the miserable experience of doing JFK.

If your flight gets delayed or you find yourself with time on your hands, check out the d-parture Spa to unwind (Terminal C), or, if you're feeling carnivorous after your screaming match with airline personnel, Gallagher's Steakhouse (Terminal C).

HOW TO GET THERE—DRIVING

The route to Newark Airport is easy—just take the Holland Tunnel or the Lincoln Tunnel to the New Jersey Turnpike South. You can use either Exit 14 or Exit 13A. If you want a cheaper and slightly more scenic (from an industrial standpoint) drive, follow signs for the Pulaski Skyway once you exit the Holland Tunnel. It's free, it's one of the coolest bridges in America, and it leads you to the airport just fine. If possible, check a traffic report before leaving Manhattan—sometimes there are viciously long tie-ups, especially at the Holland Tunnel. It's always worth it to see which outbound tunnel has the shortest wait. Tune into 530 AM for information as you arrive or leave the airport.

HOW TO GET THERE—MASS TRANSIT

If you're allergic to traffic, try taking the AirTrain service to and from the Newark Liberty International Airport station on the main Northeast Corridor line into and out of Penn Station. Both Amtrak long-haul trains and NJ Transit commuter trains serve the stop, which is between Newark and Elizabeth. NJ Transit to Penn Station costs $12.50 one way (price includes the $5.50 AirTrain ticket) and takes about 30 minutes. You can also transfer to PATH trains at Newark Penn Station (confusing, we know) to Lower Manhattan. If you use NJ Transit from Penn Station, choose a train that runs on the Northeast Corridor or North Jersey Coast Line with a scheduled stop for Newark Airport, designated with the "EWR" code. If you use Amtrak, choose a train that runs on the Northeast Corridor Line with a scheduled stop for

Newark Airport. The cheapest option is to take the PATH train ($2.50) to Newark Penn Station then switch to NJ Transit bus #62 ($1.50), which hits all the terminals. Why you're skimping on bus fare when you're paying hundreds of dollars to fly is beyond us, however. You can also catch direct buses departing from Port Authority Bus Terminal (with the advantage of a bus-only lane running right out of the station and into the Lincoln Tunnel), Grand Central Terminal, and Penn Station (the New York version–confusing, we know) on the Newark Airport Express Bus for $16 ($28 round trip).

HOW TO GET THERE–CAR SERVICES

Car services are always the simplest option, although they're a bit more expensive for Newark Airport than they are for LaGuardia–expect $50 or more and know you're getting a fair deal for anything under that. Carmel Super Saver (800-924-9954 or 212-666-6666), Dial 7 Car & Limo Service (800-222-9888 or 212-777-7777), and All County Express (800-914-4223 or 516-285-1300) serve all five boroughs. Super Shuttle Manhattan (800-258-3826 or 212-258-3826) and Airlink New York (877-599-8200 or 212-812-9000) serve Manhattan. There are taxis from Newark that charge $40-50 to Hudson County and $50-70 to Manhattan. Yellow cabs from Manhattan are metered fares with a surcharge of $17.50; all tolls to and from the airport are the responsibility of the passenger.

PARKING

Short-term parking directly across from the terminals is $4 for the first half-hour, $8 up to one hour, and $4 for each half-hour increment up to $33 per 24-hour period. Daily lots have the same rates, except up to $24 per day for the P1 and P3 lots, and $27 per day for the P4 garage. The P6 long-term parking lot is served by a 24-hour shuttle bus leaving the lot every 10 minutes and costs $18 for the first 24 hours and $6 for each 8-hour period or part thereafter. High rollers opt for valet parking at lot P4, which costs $40 per day and $20 for each additional 12 hours. There are some off-airport lots that sometimes run under $10 per day. Most of them are on the local southbound drag of Route 1 & 9. The Port Authority website features real -time updates on parking availability, showing what percent of each lot is occupied. Online reservations are available for $5, and EZ-Pass holders can use the tag to pay for parking.

RENTAL CARS

Use free AirTrain link to reach rental car counters. Avis, Enterprise, Hertz, and National are located at Station P3. Alamo, Budget, and Dollar are at Station P2.

ALAMO: 973-849-4315 OR 877-222-9075

AVIS: 973-961-4300 OR 800-230-4898

BUDGET: 800-527-0700

DOLLAR: 800-800-4000

HERTZ: 973-621-2000 OR 800-654-3131

NATIONAL: 973-849-2060 OR   888 826-6890

ENTERPRISE: 973-792-0312 OR 800-736-8222

OVERVIEW

PHONE: *800-USA-RAIL (872-7245)*
WEBSITE: *WWW.AMTRAK.COM*
TWITTER: *@AMTRAK*

GENERAL INFORMATION

Amtrak is our national train system, and while it's not particularly punctual or affordable, it will take you to many major northeastern cities in half a day or less. Spending a few hours on Amtrak also makes you want to move to Europe where France is now running trains at 357 mph (as opposed to 35 mph in the US). We exaggerate. But seriously, if you plan a trip at the last minute and miss the requisite advance on buying airline tickets or want to bring liquids with you with checking baggage, you might want to shop Amtrak's fares. Bonus: Amtrak allows you to talk on cell phones in most cars and has plugs for laptop computers at your seat.

Amtrak was created by the federal government in 1971. Today, Amtrak services 500+ stations in 46 states (Alaska, Hawaii, South Dakota, and Wyoming sadly do not have the pleasure of being serviced by Amtrak, as much as Joe Biden would like to commit funding toward a trans-Pacific high-speed link). While not being as advanced as the Eurail system, Amtrak does serve over 30 million passengers a year, employs 20,000 people, still has the same decor it did in the early 1970s, and provides "contract-commuter services" for several state and regional rail lines.

AMTRAK IN NEW YORK

In New York City, Amtrak runs out of Pennsylvania Station, an eyesore currently located underneath Madison Square Garden. We treat the station like our annoying little brother, calling it Penn for short and avoiding it when we can. But don't despair—chances are the city you'll wind up in will have a very nice station, and, if all goes well, so will we, once the front half of the Farley Post Office is converted to a "new" Penn Station. Warning: If you hop in a cab to get to Amtrak, specify that you want to be dropped off at Eighth Avenue and 33rd Street in order to avoid LIRR and Madison Square Garden foot traffic. Don't let the cabbie argue with you, especially if you have luggage. He is just trying to make his life easier.

POPULAR DESTINATIONS

Many New Yorkers use Amtrak to get to Boston, Philadelphia, or Washington DC. Of course, these are the New Yorkers who are traveling on an expense account or fear the Chinatown bus service. Amtrak also runs a line up to Montreal and through western New York state (making stops in Buffalo, Rochester, Albany, etc.) Check Amtrak's website for a complete listing of all Amtrak stations.

GOING TO BOSTON

Amtrak usually runs about two dozen trains daily to Boston. One-way fares cost approximately $70–$200, and the trip, which ends at South Station in downtown Boston, takes about four-and-a-half hours door-to-door. For over $100 one-way you can ride the high speed Acela ("acceleration" and "excellence" combined into one word, though perhaps "expensive" would have been more appropriate) and complete the journey in three to three-and-a-half hours–if there are not track problems.

GOING TO PHILADELPHIA

Dozens of Amtrak trains pass through Philadelphia every day. One-way tickets start from about $50–$55 on a regular Amtrak train; if you're really in a hurry, Acela service starts around $100, which will get you there in an hour or so. The cheapest rail option to Philly is actually to take NJ Transit to Trenton and then hook up with Eastern Pennsylvania's excellent SEPTA service–this will take longer, but will cost you approximately $25. Some commuters take this EVERY day. Thank your lucky stars you're probably not one of them.

GOING TO WASHINGTON DC

(Subtitle: How Much is Your Time Worth?)

Amtrak runs dozens of trains daily to DC and the prices vary dramatically. The cheapest trains cost around $85 one-way and take between three and four hours. The Acela service costs at the cheapest $150 one-way, and delivers you to our nation's capital in less than three hours (sometimes). Worth it? Only you can say. Depending on what time of day you travel, you may be better off taking the cheaper train when the Acela will only save you 30 minutes.

A NOTE ABOUT FARES

While the prices quoted above for Boston, Philly, and DC destinations tend to remain fairly consistent, fare rates to other destinations, such as Cleveland, Chicago, etc., can vary depending on how far in advance you book your seat. For "rail sales" and other discounts, check www.amtrak.com. Military IDs will save you a bundle, so use them if you have them. Occasionally (or rarely), Amtrak frequently offers discounts that can be found on their website–hunt around.

BAGGAGE CHECK (AMTRAK PASSENGERS)

A maximum of two items may be checked up to thirty minutes before departure. Two additional bags may be checked for a fee of $20 each (two carry-on items allowed). No electronic equipment, plastic bags, or paper bags may be checked. See the "Baggage Policy" section of their website for details.

GENERAL INFORMATION

IN NEW YORK STATE CALL: *511*
ALL INQUIRIES (24/7) SAY: *"LONG ISLAND RAIL ROAD"*
FROM OUTSIDE NEW YORK STATE: *877-690-5116*
INTERNATIONAL CALLERS: *212-878-7000*
MTA POLICE: *212-878-1001*
WEBSITE: *WWW.MTA.INFO/LIRR*
TWITTER: *@LIRR*

OVERVIEW

The Long Island Railroad is the busiest railroad in North America. It has eleven lines with 124 stations stretching from Penn Station in midtown Manhattan, to the eastern tip of Long Island, Montauk Point. Over 80 million people ride the LIRR every year. If you are going anywhere on Long Island and you don't have a car, the LIRR is your best bet. Don't be surprised if the feeling of being in a seedy bar creeps over you during evening rush– those middle-aged business men like their beer en route. Despite a recent movement to ban the sale of alcohol on LIRR station platforms and trains, for now, it's still legal to get your buzz on.

If you're not a regular LIRR user, you might find yourself taking the train to Citi Field for a Mets game (Port Washington Branch), Long Beach for some summer surfing (Long Beach Branch), or to Jamaica to transfer to the AirTrain to JFK (tip–the subway is cheaper). For the truly adventurous, take the LIRR all the way out to the Hamptons beach house you are visiting for the weekend (Hamptons Reserve seating is available during the summer for passengers taking eight or more trips). Bring a book as it is a long ride.

FARES AND SCHEDULES

Fares and schedules can be obtained by calling one of the general information lines, depending on your area. They can also be found on the LIRR website. Make sure to buy your ticket before you get on the train at a ticket window or at one of the ticket vending machines in the station. Otherwise it'll cost you an extra $5.75 to $6.50 depending on your destination. As it is a commuter railroad, the LIRR offers weekly and monthly passes, as well as ten-trip packages for on- or off-peak hours. The LIRR's CityTicket program offers discounted one-way tickets for $4 within the five boroughs during weekends.

PETS ON THE LIRR

Trained service animals accompanying passengers with disabilities are permitted on LIRR trains. Other small pets are allowed on trains, but they must be confined to closed, ventilated containers.

BIKES ON THE LIRR

You need a permit ($5) to take your bicycle onto the Long Island Railroad. Pick one up at a ticket window or online at the LIRR website.

METRO-NORTH

GENERAL INFORMATION

IN NEW YORK STATE CALL: *511*
ALL INQUIRIES SAY "*METRO-NORTH RAILROAD*
FROM CONNECTICUT: *877-690-5114*
FROM OUTSIDE NEW YORK STATE: *877-690-5116*
INTERNATIONAL CALLERS: *212-878-7000*
MTA POLICE: *212-878-1001*
WEBSITE: *WWW.MTA.INFO/MNR*
TWITTER: *@METRONORTH*

OVERVIEW

Metro-North is an extremely accessible and efficient railroad with three of its main lines (Hudson, Harlem, and New Haven) originating in Grand Central Station in Manhattan (42nd St & Park Ave). Those three lines east of the Hudson River, along with two lines west of the Hudson River that operate out of Hoboken, NJ (operated by NJ Transit; not shown on map), form the second-largest commuter railroad system in the US. Approximately 250,000 commuters use the tri-state Metro-North service each day for travel between New Jersey, New York, and Connecticut. Metro-North rail lines cover roughly 2,700 square miles of territory. The best thing about Metro-North is that it lands you at Grand Central Station, one of the city's finest pieces of architecture. On weekdays, sneak into the land of platforms via the North Passage, accessible at 47th & 48th Streets. At least for now, it's still legal to have an after work drink on Metro-North. During happy hour (starting somewhere around 3 pm), hit the bar car or buy your booze in advance on the platform at Grand Central. It might make you feel better about being a wage slave. But beware of having too happy of an hour as the bathrooms can be stinky and not all cars have them.

FARES AND SCHEDULES

Fare information is available on Metro-North's extraordinarily detailed website (along with in-depth information on each station, full timetables, and excellent maps) or at Grand Central Station. The cost of a ticket to ride varies depending on your destination so you should probably check the website before setting out. Buy advance tickets on MTA's WebTicket site for the cheapest fares. If you wait until you're on the train to pay, it'll cost you an extra $5.75–$6.50. Monthly and weekly rail passes are also available for commuters. Daily commuters save 50% on fares when they purchase a monthly travel pass.

BIKES ON BOARD

If you're planning on taking your two-wheeler onboard, you'll need to apply for a bicycle permit first. An application form can be found on the Metro-North website at http://mta.info/mnr/html/mnrbikepermit.htm. The $5 lifetime permit fee and application can either be mailed into the MTA, or processed right away at ticket booths and on board trains. Common sense rules for taking bikes on board include: no bikes on escalators, no riding on the platform, and board the train after other passengers have boarded. Unfortunately there are restrictions on bicycles during peak travel times.

ONE-DAY GETAWAYS

Metro-North offers "One-Day Getaway" packages on its website. Packages include reduced rail fare and discounted entry to destinations along MNR lines including Bruce Museum, Dia:Beacon, Hudson River Museum/Andrus Planetarium, Maritime Aquarium at Norwalk, Mohegan Sun Casino, New York Botanical Garden, and Wave Hill. Tickets are available at Metro-North ticket offices or full -service ticket vending machines. The MTA website also suggests one-day hiking and biking excursions.

NJ TRANSIT

GENERAL INFORMATION

ADDRESS: 1 PENN PLZ E NEWARK, NJ 07105

PHONE: 973-275-5555

WEBSITE: WWW.NJTRANSIT.COM

TWITTER: @NJTRANSIT

OVERVIEW

With a service area of over 5,000 square miles, NJ Transit (just "NJ," thank you) is one of the largest transit systems in the country. And yet, sandwiched between New York and Philadelphia, and a feeder into both city's transportation systems, you can't blame NJ Transit for feeling a little slighted. And when you think about it, there's a point there: an incredibly large proportion of those urban workforces are utterly dependent on a commuter system that relies on a handful of underground links with Manhattan and a few bridges into Philly. All of which is to say, let's hear it for NJ Transit, for all they do to get us in and out of two major cities day in and day out, as well as moving folks around the Garden State itself.

That said, are the rails prone to power loss and broken switches? Sure. And did someone or something screw pooches when they or it left much of its rolling stock in a flood plain during Superstorm Sandy? Well, yes. And does the Pascack Valley Line seem to just creep along, which can be problematic when you're trying to make a transfer before reaching the Big Apple? Absolutely. And do you wonder who exactly thought it was a good idea to dub Secaucus Junction "Frank R. Lautenberg Station at Secaucus Junction" long before the Senator passed away? No question. But for all that, the trains are usually clean (and immune to the weirdness that seems to plague the LIRR), and there's nothing better than relaxing on one of their brand spanking new Bombardier MultiLevel Coach cars while your boys wait in traffic at one of the three measly Hudson River automobile crossings. And don't forget NJ Transit's convenient and efficient bus lines connecting areas not served by the train lines.

SECAUCUS JUNCTION STATION

By way of a history lesson, before the three-level hub with the senatorially-laden moniker at Secaucus was built, two major lines crossed but never met, as existential as that sounds. Fourteen years and $450 million later, hundreds of thousands of commuters found relief by being able to connect in Secaucus, without having to travel all the way to Hoboken. That and the super-badass New Jersey Turnpike "Exit 15X" was created from literally nothing. For riders, Secaucus Junction is just an 8-minute ride from Penn Station, and connects ten of NJ Transit's 11 rail lines, while offering service to Newark Airport, downtown Newark, Trenton, and the Jersey Shore.

FARES AND SCHEDULES

Fares and schedules can be obtained at Hoboken, Newark, Penn Station, on NJ Transit's website, or by calling NJ Transit. If you wait to pay until you're on the train and you board from a station that has an available ticket agent or open ticket machine, you'll pay an extra five bucks for the privilege. NJ Transit also offers discounted monthly, weekly, weekend, and ten-trip tickets for regular commuters. Tickets are valid until used and have no expiration date.

PATH GENERAL INFORMATION

PHONE: *800-234-7284*
POLICE/LOST & FOUND: *201-216-6078*
WEBSITE: *WWW.PANYNJ.GOV/PATH*
TWITTER: *@PATHTRAIN*

OVERVIEW

The PATH (Port Authority Trans-Hudson Corp.) is an excellent small rail system that services Newark, Jersey City, Hoboken, and Manhattan. There are a few basic lines that run directly between 33rd Street (Herald Square) in Manhattan & Hoboken, 33rd Street & Jersey City, and Newark & the WTC. Transfers between the lines are available at most stations. The PATH can be quite useful for commuters on the west side of Manhattan when the subway isn't running, say, due to a sick passenger or mysterious police investigation. Additionally, you can catch the PATH to Newark and then either jump in a cheap cab or take New Jersey Transit one stop to Newark Airport.

Check the front or the sides of incoming trains to determine their destination. Don't assume that if a Journal Square train just passed through, the next train is going to Hoboken. Often there will be two Journal Square trains in a row, followed by two Hoboken trains. During the weekend, PATH service can be excruciatingly slow and confusing, and is best only endeavored with a seasoned rider.

FARES & TIMES

The PATH costs $2.50 one-way. Regular riders can purchase 10-trip, 20-trip, and 40-trip SmartLink cards, which reduce the fare per journey to $1.90. The fare for seniors (65+) is $1 per ride. You can also use pay-per-ride MTA MetroCards for easy transition between the PATH and NYC subway. The PATH runs 24/7 (although a modified service operates between 11pm–6am, M–F, and 7:30pm–9 am, Sat, Sun, & holidays).

HUDSON-BERGEN LIGHT RAIL GENERAL INFORMATION

PHONE: *973-275-5555*
WEBSITE: *WWW.NJTRANSIT.COM*
TWITTER: *@NJTRANSIT*

OVERVIEW

Even though it's called the Hudson-Bergen Light Rail system (HBLR, operated by NJ Transit), it actually only serves Hudson county. Bergen County residents are still waiting for their long promised connection. The HBLR has brought about some exciting changes (a.k.a. "gentrification") in Jersey City, though Bayonne remains (for the moment) totally, well...Bayonne. Currently there are 24 stops in the system, including service to Jersey City, Hoboken, Weehawken, and Union City.

FARES & HOURS

The Light Rail is $2.10 per trip; reduced fare is $1.05. Ten-trip tickets are $21, monthly passes cost $64. Unless you have a monthly pass, you need to validate your ticket before boarding at a Ticket Validating Machine (TVM). Once validated, tickets are only valid for 90 minutes, so don't buy too far in advance.

Light rail service operates between 5 am and 1:30 am. Times are approximate, check the website for exact schedules on each line.

BIKES ON BOARD

Bikes are allowed (no permit or fee required) on board during off-peak times—weekdays from 9:30 am to 4 pm and 7 pm to 6 am, and all day Saturday, Sunday, and NJ state holidays. Bicycles have to be accompanied on the low-floor vestibule section of each rail car.

GRAND CENTRAL TERMINAL

GENERAL INFORMATION

NFT MAP: *13*
ADDRESS: *42ND ST & PARK AVE*
GENERAL INFORMATION: *212-340-2583*
LOST AND FOUND: *212-340-2555*
WEBSITE: *WWW.GRANDCENTRALTERMINAL.COM*
TWITTER: *@GRANDCENTRALNYC*
METRO-NORTH: *MTA.INFO/MNR OR @METRONORTH*
MTA SUBWAY STOPS: *4, 5, 6, 7, SHUTTLE TO TIMES SQUARE*
MTA BUS LINES: *M1, M2, M3, M4, M5, M101, M102, M103, M42*
NEWARK AIRPORT EXPRESS: *WWW.NEWARKAIRPORTEXPRESS.COM, 877-8-NEWARK*
JGA/JFK AIRPORT BUS SERVICE: *WWW.NYCAIRPORTER.COM, 718-777-5111 OR 855-269-2247*

OVERVIEW

Grand Central Terminal, designed in the Beaux-Arts style by Warren & Wetmore, is by far the most beautiful of Manhattan's major terminals, and it is considered one of the most stunning terminals in the world. Its convenient location in the heart of Midtown and its refurbishments only add to its appeal. The only downside is that the station will only get you on a train as far north as Dutchess County or as far east as New Haven via Metro-North—in order to head to the Island or Jersey, you'll have to hoof it over to GCT's architecturally ugly stepsister Penn Station.

If you ever find yourself underestimating the importance of the Grand Central renovations (begun in 1996 with continued work and maintenance today), just take a peek at the ceiling toward the Vanderbilt Avenue side—the small patch of black shows how dirty the ceiling was previously (and, believe us, it was really dirty...). In 2013 Grand Central celebrated its 100th anniversary, marked by a comprehensive exhibit in Vanderbilt Hall. The exhibit, worth checking out, survives online at www.gcthistory.com.

Sometime in the next 75 or 100 years, the multi-gazillion-dollar East Side Access project will connect the Long Island Rail Road to Grand Central via the new tunnel under 63rd Street, adding an eight-track terminal and concourse below Grand Central.

AMENITIES & ATTRACTIONS

Diners have any number of choices including Michael Jordan's The Steak House N.Y.C. or Cipriani Dolci for nice views overlooking the main concourse or the food court on the lower level (perfect for commuters or those intent on saving a few bucks). As food courts go, the lower level food court isn't half bad; if you squint, it's like a curated selection of NYC mainstays: gelato from Ciao Bella, cheesecake from Junior's, and Shake Shack for burgers (lower concourse open Monday–Saturday 7 am to 9 pm, Sunday 11 am to 6 pm). After hitting the raw stuff at Oyster Bar, go right outside its entrance to hear a strange audio anomaly: If you and a friend stand in opposite corners and whisper, you'll be able to hear each other clearly.

Alternatively, folks looking to hit the sauce may do so in 1920s grandeur in The Campbell Apartment near the Vanderbilt Avenue entrance, or for a non-edible treat, grab an iPad for your train ride at the shiny Apple Store on the east balcony overlooking the main concourse. One of the more fun spots to shop at in Grand Central is the New York Transit Museum Gallery Annex and Store, a satellite branch of the MTA's excellent Transit Museum in Downtown Brooklyn. The annex features a gallery with changing exhibits and the gift shop has some great gift ideas.

Grand Central Market, located between the east passages of the terminal as you head out toward Lexington Avenue, is a true big-boy market featuring various purveyors of high-quality foodstuffs. Build your own bread-meat-cheese extravaganza here, or take home fresh fish or meat to cook at home later on. Our favorite vendors include Wild Edibles, Dishes at Home and a Midtown branch of the best cheese shop in NYC–Murray's. Market open weekdays 7 am to 9 pm, Saturday 10 am to 7 pm, and Sunday 11 am to 6 pm.

The Municipal Arts Society runs a 75-minute tour of Grand Central guided by MAS docents. Tours depart daily at 12:30 pm. Tickets cost $20 ($15 reduced) at the tour window on the main concourse. Visit www.mas.org/tours for more information. Grand Central also offers a headset audio tour ($8) daily from 9 am to 6 pm, and an app version of the tour ($4.99) via the website for visitors who want to wander on their own (myorpheo. com/official -grand-central -tour).

PENN STATION

GENERAL INFORMATION

NFT MAP: *9*
ADDRESS: *SEVENTH AVE & 33RD ST*
GENERAL INFORMATION (AMTRAK): *800-872-7245*
NJ TRANSIT: *TRACKS 1–12*
AMTRAK: *TRACKS 5–16*
LIRR: *TRACKS 13–21*
MTA SUBWAY STOPS: *1, 2, 3 (SEVENTH AVENUE SIDE) AND A, C, E (EIGHTH AVENUE SIDE)*
NYCT BUS LINES: *M34, M20, M7, M4, Q32*
TRAIN LINES: *LIRR, AMTRAK, NJ TRANSIT*
JGA/JFK AIRPORT BUS SERVICE *WWW.NYCAIRPORTER.COM, 718-777-5111 OR 855-269-2247*
PENN STATION MAP: *WWW.NJTRANSIT.COM/PDF/NYPENN_MAP.PDF*
UNOFFICIAL GUIDE TO NEW YORK PENN STATION: *JASONGIBBS.COM/PENNSTATION*

OVERVIEW

Penn Station, designed by McKim, Mead &; White (New York's greatest Beaux-Arts architectural firm), is a treasure, filled with light and...oh wait, that's the one that was torn down. Penn Station is essentially a basement, complete with well -weathered leather chairs, unidentifiable dust particles, and high-cholesterol snack food. Its claim to fame is that it is the busiest Amtrak station in the country. If the government gods are with us, the plan to convert the eastern half of the Farley Post Office (also designed by McKim, Mead & White) next door to an above-ground, light-filled station will come to fruition. With bureaucracy at hand, we aren't holding our collective breath. Until then, Penn Station will go on servicing 600,000 people per day in the rat's maze under Madison Square Garden.

Penn Station serves Amtrak, the LIRR, and NJ Transit. Amtrak, which is surely the worst national train system of any first-world country, administers the station. How is it that the Europeans have bullet trains and it still takes three or more hours to get from NYC to DC? While we're hoping the new station proposal will come through, will it help the crazed LIRR commuters struggling to squish down stairwells to catch the 6:05 to Ronkonkoma? We can only hope.

Dieters traveling through Penn Station should pre-pack snacks. The fast food joints are just too tempting. Donuts and ice cream and KFC, oh my! Leave yourself time to pick up some magazines and a bottle of water for your train trip. It may turn out to be longer than you think.

The plus side to Penn is that it's easy to get to from just about anywhere in the city via subway or bus. If you are just too ritzy to take the MTA (or you have an abundance of baggage), have your cab driver drop you off anywhere surrounding the station except for Seventh Avenue—it is constantly jammed with tour buses and cabs trying to drop off desperately late passengers.

TEMPORARY PARCEL/ BAGGAGE CHECK

The only facility for storing parcels and baggage in Penn Station is at the Baggage Check on the Amtrak level (to the left of the ticket counter). There are no locker facilities at Penn Station. The Baggage Check is open from 5:15 am until 10 pm and costs $5.50 per item for each 24-hour period.

STATEN ISLAND FERRY

311; WWW.NYC.GOV/STATENISLANDFERRY

The one and only. This free ferry travels between Battery Park and St. George, Staten Island. On weekdays it leaves every 15–30 minutes 5 am–12:30 am and every hour at other times. On Saturday, it leaves every half-hour 6 am–7 pm and every hour at other times. On Sunday, it leaves every half-hour 9 am–7 pm and every hour at other times.

NY WATERWAY

800-53-FERRY; WWW.NYWATERWAY.COM OR @RIDETHEFERRY

The largest ferry service in NY, NYWaterway offers many commuter routes along the Hudson River to and from New Jersey and points north, and a route to Belford in Monmouth County. Their East River Ferry (www.eastriverferry.com, @eastriverferry) shuttles folks between Long Island City, Greenpoint, Williamsburg, and Brooklyn Bridge Park to and from 34th Street and Pier 11 in Manhattan.

NY WATER TAXI

212-742-1969; WWW.NYWATERTAXI.COM OR @NYWATERTAXI

Available mostly for sightseeing, specialty cruises, and charter rides, NY Water Taxi also runs the popular IKEA shuttle to Red Hook.

SEA STREAK

800-BOAT-RIDE (262-8743); WWW.SEASTREAKUSA.COM OR @SEASTREAKFERRY

High-speed catamarans that travel from Atlantic Highlands, NJ to Pier 11/Wall Street in 40 minutes, with connecting service to Midtown at E 35th Street.

CIRCLE LINE

212-563-3200; WWW.CIRCLELINE42.COM OR @CIRCLELINE42NYC

Sightseeing Cruises Circle Line offers many sightseeing tours, including their iconic circle around the island of Manhattan that takes it all in over the course of a 2.5 hour journey. De rigueur for newbies.

SPIRIT OF NEW YORK

866-433-9283; WWW.SPIRITCRUISES.COM

Offers lunch and dinner cruises. Prices start around $50. Leaves from Chelsea Piers, over toward the Statue of Liberty and up the East River to the Williamsburg Bridge. Make a reservation at least one week in advance, but the earlier the better.

LOEB BOATHOUSE

212-517-2233; WWW.THECENTRALPARKBOATHOUSE.COM

You can rent rowboats from April through November at the Lake in Central Park, open seven days a week, weather permitting. Boat rentals cost $15 for the first hour and $3 for every additional 15 minutes (rentals also require a $20 cash deposit). The boathouse is open 10 am–6 pm. Up to four people per boat. No reservations needed.

WORLD YACHT CRUISES

212-630-8100 OR 800-498-4270; WWW.WORLDYACHT.COM OR @WORLDYACHT

These fancy, three-hour dinner cruises start at $105 per person. The cruises depart from Pier 81 (41st Street) and require reservations. The cruise boards at 6 pm, sails at 7 pm, and returns at 10 pm. There's also a Sunday brunch cruise April–October that starts at $50 per person.

PORT AUTHORITY BUS TERMINAL

GENERAL INFORMATION

NFT MAP: 11

ADDRESS: 625 EIGHTH AVE AT 41ST ST

GENERAL INFORMATION: 212-502-2200

WEBSITE: WWW.PANYNJ.GOV/BUS-TERMINALS/PORT-AUTHORI-TY-BUS-TERMINAL.HTML

SUBWAY: A, C, E, 42ND ST/PORT AUTHORITY OR 1, 2, 3, 7, N, R, Q, S TO TIMES SQUARE

NYCT BUS: M42, M34A, M20, M11, M104

NEWARK AIRPORT EXPRESS: 877-8-NEWARK WWW.NEWARKAIRPOR-TEXPRESS.COM,

JGA/JFK AIRPORT BUS SERVICE: WWW.NYCAIRPORTER.COM, 718-777-5111 OR 855-269-2247

OVERVIEW

Devised as a solution to New York City's horrendous bus congestion, the Port Authority Bus Terminal was completed in 1950. The colossal structure consolidated midtown Manhattan's eight separate interstate bus stations (!) into one convenient drop-off and pick-up point. Back in the day the Port Authority held the title of "largest bus terminal in the world," but for now we'll have to be content with merely the biggest depot in the United States. The Port Authority is located on the north and south sides of W 41st Street (b/w Eighth Ave & Ninth Ave) in a neighborhood that real estate agents haven't yet graced with an official name. How about Greyhound Gardens?

There are plenty of things to do should you find that you've got some time to kill here. Send a postcard from the post office, donate blood at the blood bank on the main floor, use the refurbished bathrooms, roll a few strikes and enjoy a cocktail at Frames bowling lounge, chug a couple of decent brews at mini-chain Heartland Brewery, or shop the Greenmarket on Thursdays. There are also many souvenir carts, newsstands, and on-the-go restaurants, as well as a statue of beloved bus driver Ralph Kramden located outside of the south wing. The grungiest area of the terminal is the lower bus level, which is dirty and exhaust-filled, best visited just a few minutes before you need to board your bus.

On Easter Sunday, Christmas Eve, or Thanksgiving, one can see all the angst-ridden sons and daughters of suburban New Jersey parents joyfully waiting in cramped, disgusting corridors for that nauseating bus ride back to Leonia or Morristown or Plainfield or wherever. A fascinating sight.

BUS LINES

ACADEMY: *NORTHEASTERN US AND FLORIDA*

ADIRONDACK: *NEW YORK STATE AND NEARBY CANADIAN DESTINATIONS*

BIEBER: *EASTERN PENNSYLVANIA*

COMMUNITY: *MORRIS AND ESSEX COUNTIES (NJ)*

COMMUNITY LINES: *HUDSON COUNTY (NJ)*

DECAMP: *NORTHERN NEW JERSEY*

GREYHOUND: *US AND CANADA*

LAKELAND: *NORTHERN NEW JERSEY*

MARTZ TRAILWAYS: *NEW YORK, NEW JERSEY, PENNSYLVANIA*

MEGABUS: *US AND CANADA*

NJ TRANSIT: *NEW JERSEY COMMUTER*

OLYMPIA: *NEWARK AIRPORT EXPRESS*

PETER PAN: *MID-ATLANTIC US AND NEW ENGLAND*

ROCKLAND: *ROCKLAND COUNTY (NY) AND NORTHERN NEW JERSEY*

SHORTLINE: *UPSTATE NY, ORANGE, ROCKLAND, SULLIVAN, BERGEN AND PIKE COUNTIES, WOODBURY COMMON*

SUBURBAN: *MERCER, MIDDLESEX, AND SOMERSET COUNTIES (NJ)*

SUSQUEHANNA TRAILWAYS: *SUSQUEHANNA RIVER VALLEY, PA*

TRANS-BRIDGE LINES: *LEHIGH VALLEY, PA*

GWB BUS TERMINAL

GENERAL INFORMATION

NFT MAP: 23
ADDRESS: 4211 BROADWAY AT 178TH ST
PHONE: 800-221-9903 OR 212-564-8484
WEBSITE: WWW.PANYNJ.GOV/BUS-TERMINALS/GEORGE-WASHINGTON-BRIDGE-BUS-STATION.HTML
SUBWAY: A TO 175TH ST OR 1 OR A TO 181ST ST
BUSES: M4, M5, M98, M100, BX3, BX7, BX11, BX13, BX35, BX36

OVERVIEW

The George Washington Bridge Bus Station opened in 1963 to consolidate bus operations in the Washington Heights section of Manhattan. Italian architect Pier Luigi Nervi designed the facility and its striking roof consisting of 26 reinforced concrete triangle sections. The design is a great living example of 1960s architecture, and the reinforced concrete material is typical of Nervi's work. This was his first US project, after designing many well-known structures in Italy including the 1960 Olympic Stadium in Rome.

With easy access to the George Washington Bridge, the station connects Upper Manhattan with Northern New Jersey, and is served by several private carriers along with NJ Transit. A passageway connects to the 175th Street station of the A train (open 5 am to 1 am). Sitting directly atop the Trans-Manhattan Expressway (otherwise known as I-95), the views of the George Washington Bridge are pretty spectacular, and worth checking out even if you're not catching the bus to Hackensack.

For years, the station's 30,000 square feet of retail space sat underutilized, but change is coming slowly. A $183 million rehabilitation is underway to modernize the facility and expand retail opportunities, including a 120,000-square-foot "MarketPlace" (no room for spaces) that will feature a gym, supermarket and Marshall's department store. Part of us hopes it will never lose its "lived-in" charm, but really, any place with pigeons routinely wandering around indoors can never be too sanitized.

BUS COMPANIES

AIR BROOK

(800-800-1990, www.airbrook.com): Casino shuttle to Atlantic City

NEW JERSEY TRANSIT

(973-275-5555, www.njtransit.com): To 60th St, Bergenfield, Bogota, Cliffside Park, Coytesville, Dumont, Edgewater (including Edgewater Commons Mall), Englewood, Englewood Cliffs, West Englewood, Fair Lawn (including the Radburn section), Fairview, Fort Lee, Glen Rock, Guttenberg, Hackensack (including NJ Bus Transfer), Hoboken, North Hackensack (Riverside Square), Irvington, Jersey City, Kearney, Leonia, Maywood, Newark, North Bergen, Paramus (including the Bergen Mall and Garden State Plaza), Paterson (including Broadway Terminal), Ridgewood, Rochelle Park, Teaneck (including Glenpointe and Holy Name Hospital), Union City, Weehawken, and West New York.

ROCKLAND COACHES (COACH USA)

(908-354-3330, www.coachusa.com/rockland): To Alpine, Bergenfield, Central Nyack, Closter, Congers, Coytesville, Cresskill, Demarest, Dumont, Emerson, Englewood, Englewood Cliffs, Fort Lee, Grandview, Harrington Park, Haverstraw, Haworth, Hillsdale, Leonia, Linwood Park, Montvale, Nanuet, New City, New Milford, Northvale, Norwood, Nyack, Old Tappan, Oradell, Palisades, Palisades Park, Park Ridge, Pearl River, Piermont, Rivervale, Rockland Lake, Rockleigh, Sparkill, Spring Valley, Stony Point, Tappan, Tenafly, Upper Nyack, Valley Cottage, West Englewood, Westwood, Woodcliff Lake

SHORTLINE (COACH USA)

(800-631-8405, www.coachusa.com/shortline): Express service to Montgomery, Washingtonville, Monroe, Central Valley and Ridgewood, NJ

BUDGET BUS TRAVEL

OVERVIEW

High-speed rail is efficient, fast, sleek and...decades away. Which is where low-cost, bare-bones intercity bus travel comes in. No, it's not particularly glamorous, especially when you're fumbling with quarters in front of a vending machine at a rest stop along Interstate 91, but it's cheap. Real cheap. Like cheaper than a cab to LaGuardia cheap. Cheaper than a fancy downtown cocktail cheap. Cheaper than an outerborough cocktail cheap. Like $10 cheap. $20 cheap. Even at $30, you're practically saving money sitting quietly on a bus to Boston or DC. No, this is no 300 kilometer-per-hour bullet train. But that *is* a VHS tape of *Look Who's Talking Too*, so what do you want?

There was a moment in time, starting around the late 1990s, when low-cost intercity coach travel was referred to as the "Chinatown Bus." The chartered buses catered to an Asian clientele, traveling between Chinatowns along the Northeast Corridor. The lines had no need for advertising, overhead, or–most important-ly–gates at bus stations. Travelers bought tickets on the sidewalk and boarded buses on street corners. They'd play cheesy movies, subtitled in various Chinese dialects. Soon budget travelers began noticing and it wasn't long before the buses revolution-ized short-haul travel–the fledgling Acela high-speed train was in an entirely differ-ent league, money-wise, and shuttle plane service between Northeastern cities was often not as fast, especially when taking into account post-9/11 security protocols and traffic to and from airports.

The early days of the Chinatown Bus were a hoot. Often trips were perfectly fine. Some-times they seemed a little too efficient; three hours from Boston is great–except on a Chinatown bus. Other times, odds were high that you experienced at least one problem during the course of your trip in-cluding, but not limited to, poor customer service, unmarked bus stops, late depar-tures, less than ideal bus conditions, and loogie-hucking and/or spitting from other passengers. Then there were the cancella-tions without warning, breakdowns, fires, broken bathrooms, fragrant bathrooms or no bathrooms at all, uncoupled luggage, drop-offs on the side of the road near the highway because bus companies didn't have permission to deliver passengers to central transportation hubs, and (alleged) organized crime links. We exaggerate. But only slightly. And still none of that deterred folks from using the buses. Again, the prices were just too good.

Before long, legacy bus carriers like Grey-hound and Trailways began noticing, and rather than trying to beat the Chinatown options, they joined them, creating low-cost carriers like Megabus and BoltBus that mimicked the style and pricing of Chinatown buses. Of course, innovation ruffles feathers, and eventually neighbor-hoods tired of rolling bags clogging up the sidewalks. Concessions ensued, but for the time being a detente exists; the prices are just too good. The free wi-fi isn't too bad either.

After years of accidents, including a par-ticularly gruesome March 2011 accident along I-95 that killed 15 people, the feds began cracking down on the carriers, shut-ting down many, including Fung Wah, one of the original lines. Of the organizations that remained, something miraculous happened: prices have stayed relatively low while oversight and regulation has in-creased. So now at least you can ride with some peace of mind. What were you saying about high-speed what?

BUS COMPANIES

LUCKY STAR BUS TRANSPORTATION
(888-881-0887 or 617-269-5468, www.luckystarbus.com): To Boston 13 times daily 7 am–9 pm. From 55-59 Chrystie St to South Station: one-way $20

WASHINGTON DELUXE
(866-BUS-NY-DC, www.washny.com): To Washington multiple times a day; From 36th St & Seventh Ave. Additional departures from Delancey & Allen Sts, and Empire Blvd and Bedford Ave in Crown Heights, Brooklyn to Dupont Circle and Union Station in DC. Schedule varies by day of the week, so it's recommended that you check the website for info. $26-$35 one-way.

EASTERN TRAVEL
(212-244-6132, www.easternshuttle.com): To Washington DC, Baltimore, Rockville, MD, and Richmond, VA; From Allen St/Canal St and 34th St/Seventh Ave.

YO! BUS
(855-66YOBUS, yobus.com): To Boston and Philadelphia, joint venture of Greyhound and Peter Pan, tickets as low as $10; buses leave from East Broadway and Division St.

VAMOOSE
(212-695-6766, www.vamoosebus.com): To Bethesda, MD, Arlington, VA and Lorton, VA; stops at 30th St and Seventh Ave.

MEGABUS
(us.megabus.com): To destinations across US; departure from 34th St and Eleventh Ave; arrival at 28th St and Seventh Ave.

BOLTBUS
(877-265-8287, www.boltbus.com): To Boston, Philadelphia, Baltimore, DC area; special $1 early fares; stops at 33rd St and Eleventh Ave.

TRIPPERBUS
(877-826-3874, www.tripperbus.com): To Bethesda, MD and Arlington, VA; stops at 31st St and Eighth Ave.

BIKING

GENERAL INFORMATION:

BICYCLE DEFENSE FUND: *WWW.BICYCLEDEFENSEFUND.ORG*

BIKE BLOG NYC: *WWW.BIKEBLOGNYC.COM OR @BIKEBLOGNYC*

BIKE NEW YORK, FIVE BOROUGH BIKETOUR: *WWW.BIKENEWYORK.ORG OR @BIKENEWYORK*

CENTURY ROAD CLUB ASSOCIATION (CRCA): *WWW.CRCA.NET OR @CRCA*

CITIBIKE: *WWW.CITIBIKENYC.COM*

DEPARTMENT OF CITY PLANNING: *WWW.NYC.GOV/HTML/DCP/HTML/ TRANSPORTATION/TD_PROJECTBICYCLE.SHTML*

DEPARTMENT OF PARKS & RECREATION: *WWW.NYCGOVPARKS.ORG*

DEPARTMENT OF TRANSPORTATION: *WWW.NYC.GOV/HTML/DOT/HTML/ BICYCLISTS/BICYCLISTS.SHTML*

FAST & FABULOUS LESBIAN & GAY BIKE CLUB: *WWW.FASTNFAB.ORG*

FIVE BORO BICYCLE CLUB: *WWW.5BBC.ORG OR @5BBC*

LEAGUE OF AMERICAN BICYCLISTS: *WWW.BIKELEAGUE.ORG OR @ BIKELEAGUE*

NEW YORK BICYCLE COALITION: *WWW.NYBC.NET OR @BIKENYBC*

NYC BIKE SHARE: *WWW.CITIBIKENYC.COM OR @CITIBIKENYC*

NEW YORK CYCLE CLUB: *WWW.NYCC.ORG OR @NYCYCLECLUB*

RECYCLE-A-BICYCLE: *WWW.RECYCLEABICYCLE.ORG OR @RAB_NYC*

STREETSBLOG NYC: *WWW.STREETSBLOG.ORG OR @STREETSBLOGNYC*

TIME'S UP! BICYCLE ADVOCACY GROUP: *WWW.TIMES-UP.ORG OR @ NYCTIMESUP*

TRANSPORTATION ALTERNATIVES: *WWW.TRANSALT.ORG OR @TRANSALT*

OVERVIEW

While not for the faint of heart, biking around Manhattan can be one of the most efficient and exhilarating forms of transportation. The advocacy group Transportation Alternatives estimates that over 200,000 New Yorkers hop on a bike each day. Manhattan is relatively flat, and the fitness and environmental advantages of using people power are incontrovertible. However, there are also some downsides, including, but not limited to: psychotic cab drivers, buses, traffic, pedestrians, pavement with potholes, glass, debris, and poor air quality. For years now biking has enjoyed the support of the city: many new miles of bike lanes have been added, and there has been an effort to create well protected lanes whenever possible including in Times Square, Eighth and Ninth Avenues in Chelsea, and Second and Third Avenues in the East Village. These tend to be the safest places to ride, though they often get blocked by parked or standing cars. Central Park is a great place to ride, as is the Greenway along the Hudson River from Battery Park all the way up to the GWB (it's actually a 32-mile loop around the island). East River Park is another nice destination for recreational riding, as well as skating. The most exciting cycling news in recent years is the launch of the Citi Bike bike share program, designed for quick trips around town.

A word about protecting your investment: bikes have to be locked up on the street and are always at risk of being stolen. Unfortunately, bike racks can be hard to come by in NYC, so you may need to get creative on where to park. Always lock them to immovable objects and don't skimp on a cheap bike lock. With over 40,000 bikes a year stolen in NYC, the extra cost for a top-of-the-line bike lock is worth it.

Now that we've got your attention, let's review some of the various rules and regulations pertaining to biking. First, remember that with great power comes great responsibility: bicyclists not only have all the rights of motor vehicles but they are also subject to all the same basic rules, including obeying all traffic signals, signage and pavement markings. Just as you can't drive a car on the sidewalk, neither are you allowed to ride on the sidewalk. And just as you can't drive a car into a park, remember that bicycle riding is prohibited in parks, except along designated bike paths. Some less-known rules: you can use either side of a one-way roadway; deliverymen must wear apparel with the name of their place of business when riding; when riding, you can't wear more than one earphone; feet must be on pedals; and riders must keep hands on the handlebars, and at least one hand when carrying packages. Also keep in mind the rules of equipment: a white headlight and red taillight are mandatory from dusk to dawn, and both bells and reflectors are required. Here's another thing: hand signals are mandatory. Children bring a whole other set of considerations: children under one year are not allowed on bikes, even in a Baby Bjorn; children ages one through five must wear a helmet and sit in an appropriate carrier. Children five through 13 must wear an approved helmet. Oh, and for Pete's sake, don't be a jerk.

CROSSING THE BRIDGES BY BIKE

BROOKLYN BRIDGE

Separate bicycle and pedestrian lanes run down the center of the bridge, with the bicycle lane on the north side and the pedestrian lane on the south. Cyclists should beware of wayfaring tourists taking photographs. The bridge is quite level and, aside from the tourists and planks, fairly easy to traverse.

Brooklyn Access: Stairs to Cadman Plz E and Prospect St, ramp to Johnson & Adams Sts

Manhattan Access: Park Row and Centre St, across from City Hall Park

MANHATTAN BRIDGE

The last of the Brooklyn crossings to be outfitted with decent pedestrian and bike paths, the Manhattan Bridge bike and pedestrian paths are on separate sides of the bridge. The walking path is on the south side, and the bike path is on the north side of the bridge. The major drawback to walking across the Manhattan Bridge is that you have to climb a steep set of stairs on the Brooklyn side (not the best conditions for lugging around a stroller or suitcase). Fortunately, the bike path on the north side of the bridge is ramped on both approaches. However, be careful on Jay Street when accessing the bridge in Brooklyn due to the dangerous, fast-moving traffic.

Brooklyn Access: Jay St & Sands St

Manhattan Access: Bike Lane–Canal St & Forsyth St. Pedestrian Lane–Bowery, just south of Canal St

WILLIAMSBURG BRIDGE

The Williamsburg Bridge has the widest pedestrian/bike path of the three bridges to Brooklyn. The path on the north side, shared by cyclists and pedestrians, is 12 feet wide. The southern path, at eight feet wide, is also shared by bikers and walkers. Now that both sides of the bridge are always open to pedestrians and bikes, this is one of the best ways to get to and from Brooklyn. As a bonus fitness feature, the steep gradient on both the Manhattan and Brooklyn sides of the bridge gives bikers and pedestrians a good workout.

Brooklyn Access: North Entrance–Driggs Ave, right by the Washington Plz

South Entrance–Bedford Ave b/w S 5th & S 6th Sts

Manhattan Access: Delancey St & Clinton St/Suffolk St

GEORGE WASHINGTON BRIDGE

Bikers get marginalized by the pedestrians on this crossway to New Jersey. The north walkway is for pedestrians only, and the south side is shared by pedestrians and bikers. Cyclists had to fight to keep their right to even bike on this one walkway, as city officials wanted to institute a "walk your bike across" rule to avoid bicycle/pedestrian accidents during construction. The bikers won the battle but are warned to "exercise extra caution" when passing pedestrians.

Manhattan Access: W 178th St & Fort Washington Ave

New Jersey Access: Hudson Ter in Fort Lee

ROBERT F. KENNEDY BRIDGE

Biking is officially prohibited on this two-mile span that connects the Bronx, Queens, and Manhattan. Unofficially, people ride between the boroughs and over to Wards Island all the time. The bike path is quite narrow, compared to the paths on other bridges, and the lighting at night is mediocre at best. The tight path sees less pedestrian/cycling traffic than other bridges, which, paired with the insufficient lighting, gives the span a rather ominous feeling after dark. If you're worried about safety, or keen on obeying the laws, the 103rd Street footbridge provides an alternative way to reach Wards Island sans car. This pedestrian pass is open only during the warmer months, and then only during daylight hours.

Bronx Access: 133rd St & Cypress Ave

Manhattan Access: Ramps–124/126th Sts & First Ave Stairs–Second Ave and 124/126 Sts

Queens Access: 26th St & Hoyt Ave (beware of extremely steep stairs).

ED KOCH QUEENSBORO BRIDGE

The north outer roadway of the Ed Koch Queensboro Bridge is open exclusively to bikers, 24/7, except for the day of the New York Marathon. More than 2,500 cyclists and pedestrians per day traverse the bridge. Bikers complain about safety issues on the Manhattan side of the bridge: With no direct connection from Manhattan onto the bridge's West Side, bikers are forced into an awkward five-block detour to get to Second Avenue, where they can finally access the bridge.

Manhattan Entrance: 60th St, b/w First Ave & Second Ave

Queens Entrance: Queens Plz & Crescent St

CITI BIKE BIKE SHARE

The membership-only Citi Bike bike sharing program began in 2013. Designed for short jaunts around town, annual memberships cost $95 and entitle the user to unlimited trips of up to 45 minutes. One-day and 7-day "Access Passes" for unlimited trips up to 30 minutes are available for $9.95 and $25, respectively. Trips exceeding the time limit incur steep overage charges; much like ZipCar, the program is not intended to function as a bike rental. At the program's outset, stations were limited to Manhattan south of 60th Street and a small swath of Brooklyn between Brooklyn Heights and Bedford-Stuyvesant, with plans to eventually expand to other neighborhoods. The bikes themselves are functional three-speed machines, with easily adjustable seats, bells and LED safety lights, and multiple logos of main sponsor Citibank, which pledged more than $40 million to start the program. For more information visit citibikenyc.com.

BIKES AND MASS TRANSIT

You can take your bike on trains and some buses—just make sure it's not during rush hour and you are courteous to other passengers. The subway requires you to carry your bike down staircases, use the service gate instead of the turnstile, and board at the very front or back end of the train. To ride the commuter railroads with your bike, you may need to purchase a bike permit. For appropriate contact information, see transportation pages.

AMTRAK: *TRAIN WITH BAGGAGE CAR REQUIRED*

LIRR: *$5 PERMIT REQUIRED*

METRO-NORTH: *$5 PERMIT REQUIRED*

NJ TRANSIT: *NO PERMIT REQUIRED*

PATH: *NO PERMIT REQUIRED*

NEW YORK WATER TAXI: *AS SPACE ALLOWS; NO FEE OR PERMIT REQUIRED*

NY WATERWAY: *$1.25 SURCHARGE*

STATEN ISLAND FERRY: *ENTER AT LOWER LEVEL*

BUS COMPANIES: *CALL INDIVIDUAL COMPANIES*

CHELSEA PIERS

GENERAL INFORMATION

NFT MAP: *8*
ADDRESS: *23RD ST & HUDSON RIVER PARK*
PHONE: *212-336-6666*
WEBSITE: *WWW.CHELSEAPIERS.COM*
TWITTER: *@CHELSEAPIERSNYC*

OVERVIEW

Opened in 1910 as a popular port for trans-Atlantic ships, Chelsea Piers found itself neglected and deteriorating by the 1960s. In 1992, Roland W. Betts (fraternity brother of George W. Bush) began the plan to renovate and refurbish the piers as a gargantuan 28-acre sports and entertainment center. In 1995, Chelsea Piers re-opened its doors to the public at a final cost of $120 million—all private money. The only help from the state was a very generous 49-year lease. By 1998, Chelsea Piers was the third most popular attraction in New York City.

HOW TO GET THERE

Unless you live in Chelsea, it's a real pain to get to the Piers. The closest subway is the C or E to 23rd Street and Eighth Avenue, and then it's still a three-avenue block hike there. If you're lucky, you can hop a M23 bus on 23rd Street and expedite the last leg of your journey. L train commuters should get off at the Eighth Avenue stop and take the M14D bus across to the West Side Highway where you'll be dropped off at 18th Street. There are two Citi Bike stations near Chelsea Piers: 22nd Street and 10th Avenue and 18th Street and 11th Avenue.

If you drive, entering from the south can be a little tricky. It's pretty well signed, so keep your eyes peeled. Basically you exit right at Eleventh Avenue and 22nd Street, turn left onto 24th Street, and then make a left onto the West Side Highway. Enter Chelsea Piers the same way you would if you were approaching from the north. Parking costs $16 for the first hour, $21 for two, $25 for three on up to $60 for eight ($10 for each additional hour thereafter). Street parking in the West 20s is an excellent alternative in the evenings after 6 pm.

FACILITIES

Chelsea Piers is amazing. There are swimming pools, ice skating rinks, a bowling alley, spa, restaurants, shops, batting cages–you name it. So, what's the catch? Well, it's gonna cost ya. Like Manhattan rents, only investment bankers can afford this place.

CHELSEA BREWING COMPANY

212-336-6440 or www.chelseabrewingco.com. Microbrewery and restaurant. Try the amber ale, wings, nachos, and cheesy fries–all excellent.

THE GOLF CLUB AT CHELSEA PIERS

212-336-6400. Aside from potentially long wait times, the 250-yard driving range with 52 heated stalls and automated ball -feed (no buckets or bending over!) is pretty awesome. $25 buys you 90 balls (peak) or 147 balls (off-peak). If you don't bring your own, club hire is $4/one club, $6/two, $7/three, or $12/ten. Before 6 pm on weekdays, you can whack all the balls you want for $25 between 6:30 and 9 am.

BOWLMOR

212-835-2695 or www.bowlmor.com. Schmancy 40-lane bowling alley equipped with video games, bar, and private eight-lanc bowling suite.

'WICHCRAFT

212-780-0577 or wichcraftnyc.com. Handcrafted sandwiches, soups, salads, and sweets.

PAUL LABRECQUE SALON & SPA

212-988-7186. Hair, skin, nails, and massage services to get you ready for the court, pitch, or pool.

THE SPORTS CENTER

212-336-6000. A very expensive monster health club with a 10,000-square-foot climbing wall, a quarter-mile track, a swimming pool, and enough fitness equipment for a small army in training. If you have to ask how much the membership is, you can't afford it.

SKY RINK

212-336-6100. Two 24/7 ice rinks mainly used for classes, training, and bar mitzvahs.

PIER SIXTY & THE LIGHTHOUSE

212-336-6144 or piersixty.com. 10,000-square-foot event space for private gatherings catered by Abigail Kirsch.

THE FIELD HOUSE

212-336-6500. The Field House is an 80,000-square-foot building with a 23-foot climbing wall, a gymnastics training center, four batting cages, two basketball courts, and two indoor soccer fields.

SPIRIT CRUISE

866-433-9283 or www.spiritofnewyork.com. Ships run out of Chelsea Piers. Dinner cruises start at around $80/person, and if you're having a big function, you can rent the entire boat.

GOLF

Unfortunately, but not surprisingly, there are no golf courses on the island of Manhattan. Thankfully, there are two driving ranges where you can at least smack the ball around until you can get to a real course, as well as a golf simulator at Chelsea Piers that lets you play a full round "at" various popular courses (Pebble Beach, St. Andrews, etc.). NYC has a number of private and public courses throughout the outer boroughs and Westchester; however, they don't even come close to satisfying the area's huge demand for courses.

NAME	ADDRESS	PHONE	BLURBS
CHELSEA PIERS GOLF SIMULATOR	PIER 59	212-336-6400	PROBABLY THE BEST WAY TO GO. LESS FRUSTRATING.
CLEARVIEW GOLF COURSE	202-12 WILLETS POINT BLVD	718-229-2570	PAR 70, 18-HOLES. ONE OF NYC'S FINEST PUBLIC COURSES.
DOUGLASTON GOLF COURSE	63-20 MARATHON PKWY	718-224-6566	PAR 67, 18-HOLES
FOREST PARK GOLF COURSE	101 FOREST PARK DR	718-296-0999	PAR 70, 18-HOLES
LA TOURETTE GOLF COURSE	1001 RICHMOND HILL RD	718-351-1889	18 HOLES, PAR 72
MOSHOLU GOLF COURSE	3700 JEROME AVE	718-655-9164	9 HOLES, PAR 30
PELHAM/SPLIT ROCK GOLF COURSE	870 SHORE RD	718-885-1258	$31 M-F; $38 WEEKENDS. TWILIGHT RATE (AFTER 4 PM) $16
SILVER LAKE GOLF COURSE	915 VICTORY BLVD	918-442-4653	18 HOLES, PAR 69
SOUTH SHORE GOLF COURSE	200 HUGUENOT AVE	718-984-0101	18 HOLES, PAR 72
VAN CORTLANDT GOLF COURSE	BAILEY AVE & VAN CORTLANDT PARK S	718-543-4595	18 HOLES, PAR 70

SWIMMING

For swimming pools in Manhattan, you pretty much have two options: pay exorbitant gym fees or health club fees in order to use the private swimming facilities, or wait until the summer to share the city's free outdoor pools with openly urinating summer camp attendees. OK, so it's not that bad! Some YMCAs and YWCAs have nice indoor pools, and their fees are reasonable. And several of the same New York public recreation centers that have outdoor pools (and some that do not) have indoor pools for year-round swimming. Though plenty of kids use the pools, there are dedicated adult swim hours in the mornings, at lunch time, and in the evenings (pee-free if you get there early). Just don't forget to follow each pool's admittance ritual, strange as it may seem–the locker room attendants generally rule with an iron fist. And if you can wait the obligatory 30 minutes, there's an authentic local food court near the standout public pool in Red Hook (155 Bay St, Brooklyn).

Then there's the Hudson. Yes, we're serious. There are about eight races in the Hudson each year, and the water quality is tested before each race. New York City also has some great beaches for swimming, including Coney Island, Manhattan Beach, and the Rockaways. If you prefer your swimming area enclosed, check out the pool options in Manhattan.

NAME	STREET	PHONE
92ND STREET Y	1395 LEXINGTON AVE	212-415-5700
ASPHALT GREEN	555 E 90TH ST	212-369-8890
ASSER LEVY RECREATION CENTER	E 23RD ST & ASSER LEVY PL	212-447-2020
HARLEM YMCA	180 W 135TH ST	212-912-2100
JACKIE ROBINSON POOL	85 BRADHURST AVE	212-234-9607
JOHN JAY	E 77TH ST & CHEROKEE PL	212-794-6566
LASKER POOL	W 110TH ST & LENOX AVE	212-534-7639
LENOX HILL NEIGHBORHOOD HOUSE	331 E 70TH ST	212-744-5022
MARCUS GARVEY	18 MT MORRIS PARK W	212-410-2818
RECREATION CENTER 54	348 E 54TH ST	212-754-5411
RECREATION CENTER 59	533 W 59TH ST	212-397-3159
RIVERBANK STATE PARK	679 RIVERSIDE DR	212-694-3600
THOMAS JEFFERSON PARK	2180 1ST AVE	212-860-1383
TOMPKINS SQUARE MINI POOL	500 E 9TH ST	212-387-6784
TONY DAPOLITO RECREATION CENTER	1 CLARKSON ST	212-242-5228
VANDERBILT YMCA	224 E 47TH ST	212-912-2500

TENNIS

GENERAL INFORMATION

PARKS PERMIT OFFICE: 212-360-8131

WEBSITE: WWW.NYCGOVPARKS.ORG/PERMITS/TENNIS-PERMITS

PERMIT LOCATIONS (MANHATTAN): THE ARSENAL, 830 FIFTH AVE & 64TH ST; PARAGON SPORTING GOODS STORE, 867 BROADWAY & 18TH ST

OVERVIEW

There are more tennis courts on the island of Manhattan than you might think, although getting to them may be a bit more than you bargained for. Most of the public courts in Manhattan are either smack in the middle of Central Park or are on the edges of the city—such as Hudson River Park (Map 5), East River Park and Riverside Park (Map 16). These courts in particular can make for some pretty windy playing conditions.

The Parks tennis season starts on the first Saturday of April and ends on the Sunday before Thanksgiving. Permits are good for use until the end of the season at all public courts in all boroughs, and are good for one hour of singles or two hours of doubles play. Fees are: Adults (18–61 yrs), $200; Juniors (17 yrs and under), $10; Senior Citizen (62 yrs and over), $20; Single-play tickets $15. Permits can be acquired in person at the Parks Department headquarters Central Park or Paragon Sporting Goods or online via the Parks website or by mail (applications can be found online). Renewals are accepted in person, by mail or via the website, except if originally purchased at Paragon.

GETTING A PERMIT

NAME	ADDRESS	PHONE	BLURBS
CENTRAL PARK TENNIS CENTER	W 93RD ST NEAR WEST DR	212-280-0205	26 FAST-DRY COURTS, 4 HARDCOURTS, LESSONS
DICK SAVITT TENNIS CENTER	575 W 218TH ST	212-942-7100	PRIVATE, 6 RUBBER COURTS
EAST RIVER PARK	EAST RIVER PARK AT BROOME ST	212-533-0656	THE PARK THE FDR DRIVE BUILT. 12 HARDCOURTS, LESSONS
FORT WASHINGTON PARK	W 170TH ST & HAVEN AVE	212-304-2322	10 HARDCOURTS, LESSONS
FREDERICK JOHNSON PLAYGROUND	W 151ST ST & 7TH AVE	212-234-9609	8 HARDCOURTS, LESSONS
INWOOD HILL PARK	SEAMAN AVE & W 207TH ST	212-304-2381	9 HARDCOURTS, LESSONS
MANHATTAN PLAZA RACQUET CLUB	450 W 43RD ST	212-594-0554	PRIVATE, 5 CUSHIONED HARDCOURTS
MIDTOWN TENNIS CLUB	341 8TH AVE	212-989-8572	PRIVATE, 8 HAR-TRU COURTS
ONE UN NEW YORK	1 UNITED NATIONS PLAZA	212-702-5016	PRIVATE, 1 HARDCOURT
RIVERBANK STATE PARK	679 RIVERSIDE DR	212-694-3600	SUMMER MONTHS4 HARDCOURTS
RIVERSIDE PARK	W 96TH ST & RIVERSIDE DR	212-978-0277	10 CLAY COURTS
ROCKEFELLER UNIVERSITY	1230 YORK AVE	212-327-8000	1 HARDCOURT
ROOSEVELT ISLAND RACQUET CLUB	281 MAIN ST	212-935-0250	PRIVATE, 12 HAR-TRU COURTS
SPORTIME AT RANDALL'S ISLAND	RANDALLS ISLAND PARK	212-427-6150	PUBLIC/PRIVATE, LESSONS 5 INDOOR HARDCOURTS, 5 INDOOR/OUTDOOR HARDCOURTS, 10 INDOOR/OUTDOOR CLAY COURTS
SUTTON EAST TENNIS CLUB	488 E 60TH ST	212-751-3452	PRIVATE, 8 HAR-TRU COURTS
THE RIVER CLUB	447 E 52ND ST	212-751-0100	PRIVATE, 2 HAR-TRU COURTS
TOWER TENNIS COURTS	1725 YORK AVE	212-860-2464	PRIVATE, 2 HARDCOURTS
TOWN TENNIS CLUB	430 E 56TH ST	212-752-4059	PRIVATE, 2 HARDCOURTS
VANDERBILT TENNIS CLUB	15 VANDERBILT AVE	212-599-6500	PRIVATE, 2 HARDCOURTS

BOWLING

If you want to go bowling in Manhattan, you have four solid options. Keep in mind that there's just about no way to bowl cheaply, so if you're struggling to keep a positive balance in your bank account, you may want to find another activity or head out to New Jersey.

Frames (Map 12): you can pay per game or per lane. Connected to the Port Authority (remember this in case you have a long wait for a bus), Frames has 30 lanes, a full bar and pub menu, and two game-rooms, with a new dance floor and lounge on the way. You can even make online reservations. At Chelsea Piers, you'll find ***Bowlmor (Map 8)***. The high-end bowling alley (formerly 300) offers 40 lanes. Not cheap but they do feature all -you-can-bowl specials on slow nights.

The original ***Bowlmor Lanes (Map 6)*** in the Village also runs a Monday night "Night Strike" special where $25 per person provides shoes and all the games you can bowl—assuming you can handle the sometimes long wait (not such a big deal since they offer free pool upstairs along with not-so-free cocktails in the lounge).

Finally, for the world's ultimate (hipster) bowling experience, head to ***The Gutter (Map 29)*** in Brooklyn—the borough's first new bowling alley in over fifty years. It's like a Stroh's ad from the 1980s (except the beer is fancier). It doesn't get any better than bowling on beautiful, old-school lanes and drinking tasty microbrews with your buddies. But The Gutter now has some serious competition, as sprawling ***Brooklyn Bowl (Map 29)*** has opened two blocks away. Featuring food by Blue Ribbon and live bands many nights, it's already become another great bowling option—and again, far better than anything in Manhattan.

NAME	ADDRESS	PHONE	BLURBS
BOWLMOR	PIER 60	212-835-2695	VIP BOWLING ON CHELSEA PIERS.
BOWLMOR	110 UNIVERSITY PL	212-255-8188	BRIGHT, LOUD, EXPENSIVE, AND SOMETIMES REALLY FUN.
BOWLMOR	222 W 44TH ST	212-680-0012	FIFTY LANES AND SEVEN THEMED ROOMS OF AWESOME.
FRAMES	550 9TH AVE	212-268-6909	BOWL BEFORE YOU GET ON THE BUS TO BRIDGEWATER.
LUCKY STRIKE LANES	624 W 42ND ST	646-829-0170	AMERICA'S OTHER, DRUNKER PASTIME—WITH A LOUNGE AND DRESS CODE.

BILLIARDS

Whether you're looking for a new hobby or need a new atmosphere in which to booze (that isn't your 300 sq. ft. apartment), a good pool -hall is a great way to get the job done. Or perhaps you simply enjoy a hearty game of 8-ball, and it's as simple as that; in any case, an eclectic mix of options dot the island of Manhattan.

Fat Cat (Map 5) is a great option if you're looking for a chill setting–located underground in a dim basement, it holds 20 tables and offers an hourly rate of $5.50–$6.50 (not to mention the cheap beer). For those of you who tire of shiny balls and green felt, there are multiple Scrabble, checkers, and chess stations scattered about–and if that's not enough, there are nightly jazz and comedy performances in the performance room.

If you're uptown, head to *Eastside Billiards (Map 17)*, where in addition to the 16 tables, you can also play ping-pong. Or ditch your friends and wander into the attached video game arcade, the largest of its kind outside of Times Square (so they say). On the other hand, if you don't have any friends to begin with, think about signing up for one of the East Side seasonal pool leagues–where you not only get to compete and socialize, but receive additional discounts. Last but not least is *Amsterdam Billiards Club (Map 6)*–Manhattan's swankiest billiards parlor. With its mahogany bar, multiple fireplaces, and extensive wine list, the club is best suited for corporate events and private parties (for 20 to 500 people). It also boasts the largest co-ed league in the country and offers lessons for all skill levels. So what are you waiting for? Turn off the latest CSI spin-off (or whatever crap you're watching), get off the couch, and give yourself a real challenge– play some pool!

NAME	ADDRESS	PHONE	BLURBS
AMSTERDAM BILLIARDS CLUB	110 E 11TH ST	212-995-0333	EXPENSIVE AND MORE POSH THAN MOST POOL HALLS.
EASTSIDE BILLIARDS	163 E 86TH ST	212-831-7665	GO FOR THE POOL, NOT THE ATMOSPHERE.
FAT CAT	75 CHRISTOPHER ST	212-675-6056	LAID BACK VIBE. PLUS PING PONG AND JAZZ!
POST BILLIARDS CAFÉ	154 POST AVE	212-569-1840	WHEN YOU NEED TO SHOOT POOL WAY WAY UPTOWN.
SOCIETY BILLIARDS + BAR	10 E 21ST ST	212-420-1000	WELL -APPOINTED, CLASSY POOL HALL.
TROPICAL 128	128 ELIZABETH ST	212-925-8219	CHALLENGE THE CHINATOWN CHAMPIONS. POLYNESIAN THEME, BILLIARDS, AND LOTS OF DUDES.

PHOTO : DAN DELUCA

BARCLAYS CENTER

GENERAL INFORMATION

ADDRESS: 620 ATLANTIC AVENUE, BROOKLYN NY 11217
WEBSITE: BARCLAYSCENTER.COM
TWITTER: @BARCLAYSCENTER
NETS: WWW.NBA.COM/NETS OR @BROOKLYNNETS
TICKETS: 877-77-BKTIX

OVERVIEW

Barclays Center, the new home for the Brooklyn Nets, opened in 2012 as part of the controversial $4.9 billion Atlantic Yards redevelopment project that decked over LIRR tracks and focused everyone's attention on controversial eminent domain issues, for a while there at least, until Barbra, Jay-Z, and Deron Williams redirected it again.

In the end, expectations were lowered just enough (after Gehry's insanely expensive master plan was ditched) to make the final product look kind of cool: the brown weathered steel exterior evokes the site's industrial past and pays slight tribute to the brownstone materials in the surrounding neighborhoods. In addition, the height is not overwhelming; the structure almost fits snugly into the Flatbush Avenue streetscape. The triangular public space at the intersection of Flatbush and Atlantic is visually appealing: the new subway entrance features a living planted roof and the arena's exterior structure, along with its oculus sky opening (don't worry, we had to look up that word, too) and mesmerizing LED screen is—yikes—almost kind of elegant. As arenas go, it's pretty nice looking. And it's about 59 times more appealing looking than the Atlantic Center Mall.

The Brooklyn Nets began play at the arena for the 2012–13 season after playing in New Jersey since 1977, and the NHL's New York Islanders will begin play at Barclays Center for the 2015-16 season. The arena has hosted college basketball almost since it opened, including the Barclays Center Classic, an early season eight-team tournament. For those who don't dig basketball, the concerts (accommodating 19,000 fans) have been big time: Barbra Streisand, Jay-Z (part owner of the Nets), Billy Joel, not to mention the MTV Video Music Awards and Rock 'n Roll Hall of Fame ceremonies.

HOW TO GET THERE–DRIVING

Parking is so limited that Barclays Center practically demands that you use public transport, but if you must, you can reserve a spot at the center (should there be any available, being a suiteholder helps), find a nearby garage, or scour for street parking (try Fort Greene instead of Park Slope).

HOW TO GET THERE– MASS TRANSIT

Part of the draw of Barclays Center is its proximity to Brooklyn's largest transportation hub. The 2, 3, 4, 5, B, D, N, Q and R trains all service the arena, and you can also take the to Lafayette Avenue or the to Fulton Street. The LIRR stops at Atlantic Terminal, just across the street from the arena. In addition, eleven bus lines stop right outside or nearby.

HOW TO GET TICKETS

To avoid exorbitant Ticketmaster charges, the American Express Box Office (yes, even the freakin' box office has naming rights attached to it) is open Monday–Saturday 12 pm–6 pm (Saturday 4 pm). Despite being a box office, they will not sell tickets to events on the first day tickets are offered to the public.

METLIFE STADIUM

GENERAL INFORMATION

ADDRESS: *ONE METLIFE STADIUM DR, EAST RUTHERFORD, NJ 07073*
PHONE: *201-559-1500*
WEBSITE: *WWW.METLIFESTADIUM.COM OR @MLSTADIUM*
GIANTS: *WWW.GIANTS.COM OR @GIANTS*
JETS: *WWW.NEWYORKJETS.COM OR @NYJETS*
BOX OFFICE: *201-559-1300*
TICKETMASTER: *WWW.TICKETMASTER.COM OR 800-745-3000*

OVERVIEW

The $1.6 billion MetLife Stadium is a state-of-the-art facility that hosts 20 NFL games a season—the most of any NFL stadium—as well as the biggest of big name concerts. In February 2014 it became the first cold-weather outdoor stadium to host a Super Bowl (though interestingly it wasn't the coldest temperature ever for a Super Bowl game). The stadium is home to both the New York Jets and New York Giants; the changeover from week to week to give the facility home team touches is fascinating in and of itself. Even the team shop switches from one to another. So that $1.6 billion is put to good use. Did we mention that New Jersey taxpayers are still paying off bonds from the old Giants Stadium, which was demolished in 2010?

HOW TO GET THERE—DRIVING

MetLife Stadium is only five miles from the Lincoln Tunnel (closer to Midtown than Citi Field), but leave early if you want to get to the game on time—remember that the Giants and the Jets are a) sold out for every game and b) have tons of fans from both Long Island and the five boroughs. You can take the Lincoln Tunnel to Route 3W to Route 120 N, or you can try either the Holland Tunnel to the New Jersey Turnpike N to Exit 16W, or the George Washington Bridge to the New Jersey Turnpike S to Exit 16W. Accessing the stadium from Exit 16W allows direct access to parking areas. Parking costs $30 for most events except NFL games where all cars must have pre-paid parking permits only.

HOW TO GET THERE— MASS TRANSIT

On game days NJ Transit now runs trains directly to the stadium (Meadowlands Sports Complex) from Secaucus Junction for events over 50,000 (people, that is). Round-trip tickets are $4.50 and travel time is 10 minutes. Train service begins three hours before the start of a major event or football game. After events, trains will depart frequently from the Meadowlands for up to two hours. Metro-North runs trains directly to Secaucus Junction for selected games.

HOW TO GET TICKETS

In general, scalpers and friends are the only options for Jets and the Giants games. Try the resale sites if you're dying to attend a game. The box office is open Monday–Friday 11 am to 5 pm.

MADISON SQUARE GARDEN

GENERAL INFORMATION

NFT MAP: *9*
ADDRESS: *4 PENNSYLVANIA PLZ NEW YORK, NY 10001*
PHONE: *212-465-6741*
WEBSITE: *WWW.THEGARDEN.COM OR @THEGARDEN*
KNICKS: *WWW.NBA.COM/KNICKS OR @NYKNICKS*
LIBERTY: *WWW.NYLIBERTY.COM OR @NYLIBERTY*
RANGERS: *RANGERS.NHL.COM OR @NYRANGERS*
TICKETMASTER: *WWW.TICKETMASTER.COM OR 800-745-3000*

OVERVIEW

Once resembling the Doge's Palace in Venice (c.1900), the since-relocated Altoid 'tween Seventh and Eighth Avenues atop Penn Station remains one of the legendary venues in sport, becoming so almost solely by way of the sport of boxing. Now, for good and ill, "The World's Most Famous Arena" houses the NBA's Knicks (catch Spike Lee and various supermodels courtside), NHL's Rangers, The Liberty of the WNBA, St. John's University's Red Storm, as well as concerts, tennis tournaments, dog shows, political conventions, and, for those of you with 2+ years of graduate school, monster truck rallies and "professional" wrestling. There's also The Theater at Madison Square Garden for more intimate shows. Check out MSG's website for a full calendar of events. A $1 billion (!) renovation completed in 2013 upgraded nearly everything and added two bridges running parallel to the floor that provide a unique view from way, way high above.

HOW TO GET THERE— MASS TRANSIT

MSG is right above Penn Station, which makes getting there very easy. You can take the A, C, E and 1, 2, 3 lines to 34th Street and Penn Station, or the N, Q, R, B, D and PATH lines to 34th Street and 6th Avenue. The Long Island Rail Road also runs right into Penn Station.

HOW TO GET TICKETS

Box Office open Monday–Saturday 10 am–6 pm. Try Ticketmaster or the resale sites for single-game seats for the Knicks and the Rangers. The ubiquitous ticket scalpers surrounding the Garden are a good last resort for when your rich out-of-town friends breeze in to see a game. Liberty tickets (and tickets for other events) are usually available through Ticketmaster. First day of concert ticket sales are via Ticketmaster only.

CITI FIELD

GENERAL INFORMATION

ADDRESS: 123-01 ROOSEVELT AVE, FLUSHING NY, 11368

CITI FIELD BOX OFFICE: 718-507-TIXX

WEBSITE: WWW.METS.COM

TWITTER: @METS

METS CLUBHOUSE SHOPS: 11 W 42ND ST & ROOSEVELT FIELD MALL, GARDEN CITY, LI

OVERVIEW

Shea Stadium, the Mets longtime former home, is all but a very distant memory, except for some rousing Billy Joel concerts toward the end there that they sometimes replay on PBS late at night. And although most find Citi Field appealing enough, its debut coincided with the worldwide economic downturn and a particularly brutal period in the Mets history—connected in more ways than you'd think.

All of that aside, Citi Field is actually a pretty nice ballpark. Fans enter through The Jackie Robinson Rotunda, getting a little lesson on civil rights as they read the inspiring quotes etched in the façade and pose for pictures next to Robert Indiana's sculpture of the number 42. The food options are strong, from Danny Meyer's Shake Shack (beware multi-inning lines) to the Italian sandwiches courtesy Mama's of Corona. Beer options rise above the typical Crud Light—head to the outfield beyond the scoreboard for expanded tap and bottle options.

So much about Citi Field seems to be a response to the old Shea Stadium. Where the old sprawling multi-use facility sometimes seemed cavernous, Citi Field strives for an intimate experience—the only problem is that sightlines are often blocked, even in the high roller seats behind the dugouts. Speaking of which, tickets are expensive—after all, they have to pay for the privately financed $800 million-plus stadium somehow—but the resale market is robust and the Mets tier ticket prices so that a weeknight game against a lousy team can be a pretty good deal (even if you have no view of the left field corner). Oh, and a bit of advice: steer clear of section 538—yes, the seats are cheap, but that out-of-town scoreboard works hard to block your view from the upper reaches.

HOW TO GET TICKETS

You can order Mets tickets by phone through the Mets' box office, on the internet through the Mets' website, or at the Mets Clubhouse Shops (11 West 42nd St, the Manhattan Mall, and Roosevelt Field Mall in Garden City). StubHub (www.stubhub.com) is a good option to scoop up unwanted tickets at reduced prices and there are StubHub kiosks located just outside the entrance to Citi Field.

HOW TO GET THERE— MASS TRANSIT

The 7 train runs straight to Citi Field, and the MTA frequently offers special express trains that make limited stops between Citi Field and Times Square, making it by far the easiest way to get to the stadium. The E, F, M and R trains connect with the 7 at 74th Street-Roosevelt Avenue. The other option from Midtown is the Port Washington LIRR from Penn Station, which stops at Citi Field on game days. Seastreak (seastreakusa.com/mets.aspx or 800-BOATRIDE) runs ferries from Highlands, NJ for selected games; see website for details.

YANKEE STADIUM

GENERAL INFORMATION

ADDRESS: 1 E 161ST ST, BRONX NY 10451
TELEPHONE: 718-293-4300
WEBSITE: WWW.YANKEES.COM
TWITTER: @YANKEES

OVERVIEW

When a city or a team builds a new stadium they usually take the opportunity to come in with something bold and fresh. When the Yankees opened their new stadium in 2009 after 85 years in the old place, it was striking how similar it looked to the old version. And that was by design: after all, as they say, if it ain't broke, spend $1.5 billion to basically replicate it across the street. Architecturally, the exterior and the iconic frieze at the top of the upper decks are just about exactly the same. That said, there are some key changes—the concourses are wide and airy, the concessions are better (the Lobel's Sliced Steak Sandwich Cart is far and away our favorite), that 59-by-101-foot HD LED scoreboard is boffo-redonkulous, and the open-plan lower level allows you to catch a glimpse of the action from the area behind the expensive seats. That's the good. The not so good includes but is not limited to: seats cost more and seem farther away from the field of play, the place doesn't get as loud anymore, there is a stupid wire that runs across your field of vision on the first and third base lines from the upper levels, you have to pay extra to get into the schmancy outfield bar, you can't get into other places without a fancy seat, half the fancy seats go unused so there is all this empty space where all the best seats are, there are major unconscionable blind spots in the bleachers where that schmancy outfield bar juts out—we could go on. One thing that's the same: you still can't bring a bag into the place, which is just asinine if you're coming from work.

But if you've never done it, make sure you check out Monument Park at least once. A sort hall of fame for Yankees players, Monument Park sits just beyond the center field wall. The bronze plaques immortalize the great players—and there have been many of them over the years—who made the franchise one of the most successful in all of sports. Monument Park is open until 45 minutes before the start of a game. Follow signs from the main entrance.

HOW TO GET THERE— MASS TRANSIT

Getting to the stadium by subway is easy. The 4 and D and the B (on weekdays) all run express to the stadium, and you can easily hook up with those lines at several junctions in Manhattan. A dedicated Metro-North station (Yankees–E 153rd Street) brings folks from Grand Central on the Hudson line in under 15 minutes. Seastreak (seastreakusa.com/yankees.aspx or 800-BOATRIDE) runs ferries from Highlands, NJ for selected games; see website for details.

HOW TO GET TICKETS

You can purchase tickets by phone through Ticketmaster, at the box office or the Yankee store, or online through either Ticketmaster or the Yankees website. StubHub is a good option to grab unwanted tickets, especially when the team is underperforming. And of course the illegal scalpers who are all over the damned place.

MEDIA

TELEVISION

1	NY1	(Time Warner Cable 24-Hour News) www.ny1.com
1	FiOS1	(Verizon FiOS 24-Hour News) www.fios1news.com
2	WCBS	(CBS) newyork.cbslocal.com
4	WNBC	(NBC) www.nbcnewyork.com
5	WNYW	(FOX) www.myfoxny.com
7	WABC	(ABC) abclocal.go.com/wabc
9	WWOR	(My9) www.my9nj.com
11	WPIX	(PIX11/CW) pix11.com
12	News12	(Cablevision 24-Hour News) www.news12.com
13	WNET	(PBS) www.thirteen.org
21	WLIW	(PBS–Long Island) www.wliw.org
25	WNYE	(NYCTV/NYC Media) www.nyc.gov/media
31	WPXN	(Ion) iontelevision.com
41	WXTV	(Univision) nuevayork.univision.com
47	WNJU	(Telemundo) www.telemundo47.com
48	WRNN	(RNN) www.rnntv.com
49	WEDW	(PBS–Connecticut) www.cpbn.org
55	WLNY	(CBS Affiliate) newyork.cbslocal.com/station/wlny
63	WMBC	(Ethnic/Religious) www.wmbctv.com

AM STATIONS

570	WMCA	Religious
620	WSNR	Russian
660	WFAN	Sports Talk and Giants/Devils/Nets/Yankees
710	WOR	Talk/New York Mets
770	WABC	Conservative Talk
820	WNYC	Public Radio; NPR Affiliate
880	WCBS	News
930	WPAT	Multi-Cultural (NJ)
970	WNYM	Salem Radio Network; Talk & College Sports
1010	WINS	News
1050	WEPN	ESPN Deportes; Spanish Language Sports Talk & Jets/Mets
1100	WHLI	Easy Listening/Standards
1130	WBBR	Bloomberg Radio
1160	WVNJ	Talk and Brokered Programming
1190	WLIB	Gospel
1230	WFAS	News/Talk/Iona Basketball
1240	WGBB	Mandarin Chinese Language
1280	WADO	Spanish Language Talk/Sports/Sports Broadcasts
1330	WWRV	Spanish Language Christian
1380	WKDM	Chinese and Spanish Language Brokered Programming
1430	WNSW	Spanish Language Christian
1460	WVOX	Variety; Westchester Focus
1480	WZRC	Cantonese Chinese Language
1520	WTHE	Gospel
1530	WJDM	Spanish Language Christian
1560	WQEW	Radio Disney
1600	WWRL	Spanish Language
1660	WWRU	Korean Language

FM STATIONS

88.1	WCWP	College (LIU-Post)
88.3	WBGO	Jazz (NJ)
88.7	WRHU	College (Hofstra University)
88.9	WSIA	College (College of Staten Island)
89.1	WFDU	College (Fairleigh Dickinson University)
89.1	WNYU	College (NYU)
89.5	WSOU	College/Rock (Seton Hall University)
89.9	WKCR	College/Jazz (Columbia University)
90.3	WKRB	College (Kingsborough Community College)
90.3	WHCR	College (City College of New York)
90.3	WHPC	College (Nassau Community College)
90.7	WFUV	Adult Alternative (Fordham University)
91.1	WFMU	Free-form! (NJ)
91.5	WNYE	NYC Radio
92.3	WNOW	Top 40
92.7	WQBU	Spanish Language
93.1	WPAT	Spanish Language

93.5	WVIP	Caribbean
93.9	WNYC	Public Radio; NPR Affiliate
94.7	WNSH	Country
95.5	WPLJ	Hot Adult Contemporary
96.3	WXNY	Spanish Language
96.7	WKLV	Contemporary Christian
97.1	WQHT	Hot 97; Mainstream Urban
97.9	WSKQ	La Mega; Spanish Language
98.3	WKJY	Adult Contemporary
98.7	WEPN	ESPN New York; Sports Talk and New York Jets
99.5	WBAI	Listener Supported Variety
100.3	WHTZ	(Z-100) Top 40 Contemporary Hit Radio
100.7	WHUD	Adult Contemporary
101.1	WCBS	Oldies
101.9	WFAN	Sports Talk and Giants/Devils/Nets/Yankees
102.7	WWFS	Hot Adult Contemporary
103.5	WKTU	Rhythmic Contemporary
103.9	WFAS	Adult Contemporary
104.3	WAXQ	Classic Rock
105.1	WWPR	Power Urban Contemporary
105.5	WDHA	Rock (NJ)
105.9	WQXR	Classical
106.7	WLTW	Adult Contemporary
107.1	WXPK	Adult Alternative
107.5	WBLS	Urban Adult Contemporary

PRINT MEDIA

AM New York (240 W 35th St, 9th Floor, 646-293-9499, www.amny.com): Free daily; pick it up at the subway but please dispose of properly so as to prevent track fires.

Brooklyn Paper (1 Metrotech Ctr, Ste 1001, 718-260-2500, brooklynpaper.com): Brooklyn's hometown weekly with in-depth brunch and kickball coverage.

Daily News (4 New York Plaza, 212-210-2100, www.nydailynews.com): Daily tabloid; rival of the Post. Good sports.

El Diario (1 Metrotech Ctr, 18th Floor, Brooklyn, 212-807-4600, www.eldiariony.com): Daily; America's oldest Spanish-language newspaper.

The L Magazine (1 Metrotech Ctr, 18th Floor, Ste B, Brooklyn, 718-596-3462, www.thelmagazine.com): Free bi-weekly with arts and events focus.

Metro New York (120 Broadway, 6th Flr, 212-457-7790, www.metro.us/newyork): Free daily; pick it up at the subway but please dispose of properly so as to prevent track fires.

Newsday (235 Pinelawn Rd, Melville, 800-639-7329, www.newsday.com): Daily based in Long Island.

New York Magazine (75 Varick St, 212-508-0700, nymag.com): New York City-focused news, arts, culture bi-weekly with emphasis on cloying trend pieces.

New York Review of Books (435 Hudson St, 3rd Floor, 212-757-8070, www.nybooks.com): Bi-weekly intellectual lit review.

New York Observer (321 W 44th St, 6th Floor, 212-755-2400, observer.com): Weekly that seeks influence by focusing on rich people problems.

New York Post (1211 Avenue of the Americas, 212-930-8000, nypost.com): Daily tabloid with infuriating and irresistible coverage and iconic headlines.

The New York Times (620 Eighth Ave, 212-556-1234, nytimes.com): Daily; former "Grey Lady," now with Clairol treatments.

The New Yorker (4 Times Square, 212-286-5400, www.newyorker.com): Weekly with intellectualish analysis; often subscribed, seldom finished.

Staten Island Advance (950 Fingerboard Rd, Staten Island, 718-981-1234, www.silive.com/advance): Richmond County's hometown daily; pronounce it "ADD-vance" to sound in-the-know.

Time Out New York (475 Tenth Ave, 12th Fl, 646-432-3000, www.timeout.com/newyork): Comprehensive weekly guide to goings-on in the city with crazy-making "Top 5, 10, 15, 20" lists.

The Village Voice (80 Maiden Ln, Ste 2105, 212-475-3333, www.villagevoice.com): Ur alternative weekly trying to rehab from skanky ad addiction.

Wall Street Journal (1211 Avenue of the Americas, 212-416-2000, www.wsj.com): Financial news with expanded local coverage.

CALENDAR OF EVENTS

JANUARY

Winter Antiques Show: Park Ave Armory at 67th St; Selections from all over the country.

Three Kings Day Parade: El Museo del Barrio; Features a cast of hundreds from all over the city dressed as kings or animals—camels, sheep, and donkeys (early Jan).

New York Boat Show: Jacob Javits Convention Center; Don't go expecting a test drive (early Jan).

Lunar New Year: Chinatown; Features dragons, performers, and parades.

NYC Winter Jazzfest: Greenwich Village; A full weekend of jazz at multiple Village venues.

FEBRUARY

Empire State Building Run-Up: Empire State Building; Run until the 86th floor (0.2 miles) or heart seizure.

Westminster Dog Show: Madison Square Garden; Fancy canines who know more about grooming than most of you deadbeats.

Fashion Week: Lincoln Center; Twice yearly week-long celeb-studded event.

MARCH

The Art Show: Park Ave Armory at 67th St; Art fair organized by Art Dealers Association of America to benefit charity.

St Patrick's Day Parade: Fifth Avenue; Hoochless LIRR holiday, gays need not apply (March 17).

Orchid Show: New York Botanical Garden; Yearly festival with changing themes.

Whitney Biennial: Whitney Museum; Whitney's most important American art, every other year (March–June).

Greek Independence Day Parade: Fifth Avenue; Floats and bands representing area Greek Orthodox churches and Greek federations and organizations (Late March).

The Armory Show: West Side Piers; Brilliant best-of-galleries show.

New Directors/New Films: MoMA/Lincoln Center; Film festival featuring new films by emerging directors.

Pier Antique Show: Pier 94; Look at old things you can't afford.

APRIL

Macy's Flower Show: Broadway and 34th St; Flowers and leather-clad vixens. Okay, just flowers really.

Easter Parade: Fifth Avenue; Starts at 11 am, get there early with your Easter bonnet (Easter Sunday).

New York Antiquarian Book Fair: Park Ave Armory at 67th St; Dealers exhibiting rare books, maps, manuscripts, illuminated manuscripts, and various ephemera.

New York International Auto Show: Jacob Javits Convention Center; Traffic jam.

Tribeca Film Festival: Various Lower Manhattan locations; Festival includes film screenings, panels, lectures, discussion groups, and concerts.

Affordable Art Fair: Midtown; Prices from $100 to no more than $10,000; worth a look if you're buying.

New York City Ballet Spring Season: Lincoln Center; Features new and classical ballet (April–June).

MAY

Outsider Art Fair: Chelsea; Art in many forms of media from an international set.

The Great Five Boro Bike Tour: The single worst day of the year to use the BQE (first Sunday in May).

Ninth Avenue International Food Festival: Ninth Ave from 42nd to 57th Sts.

Fleet Week: USS Intrepid; Around Memorial Day weekend—Hello, Sailor!

New York AIDS Walk: Central Park; 10K walk whose proceeds go toward finding a cure.

Lower East Side Festival of the Arts: Theater for the New City, 155 First Ave; Celebrating Beatniks and Pop Art (last weekend in May).

Cherry Blossom Festival: Brooklyn Botanic Garden; Flowering trees and Japanese cultural events (late April–early May).

Martin Luther King, Jr/369th Regiment Parade: Fifth Avenue; Celebration of equal rights (third Sunday in May).

JUNE

Puerto Rican Day Parade: Fifth Avenue; Puerto Rican pride (second Sunday in June).

Metropolitan Opera Summer Recital Series: Various locations throughout five boroughs; Free performances through June and July.

Museum Mile Festival: Fifth Avenue; Free admission and block party from 82nd–105th Sts.

NYC Pride: March from Midtown to Christopher St; Commemorates the 1969 Stonewall riots (last Sunday in June).

Blue Note Jazz Festival: Various locations; All kinds of jazz.

Mermaid Parade: Coney Island; Showcase of sea-creatures and freaks/celebration of Coney Island.

Feast of St Anthony of Padua: Little Italy; Patron saint of expectant mothers, Portugal, seekers of lost articles, shipwrecks, Tigua Indians, and travel hostesses, among other things (Saturday before summer solstice).

Central Park SummerStage: Central Park; Free concerts, but get there very, VERY early. (June–August).

Bryant Park Summer Film Festival: Sixth Ave at 42nd St; Free films Monday evenings (June–August).

Midsummer Night Swing: Lincoln Center; Live performances with free dance lessons (June–July).

Big Apple Barbecue Block Party: Madison Sq Park; Endless smoked meats from country's top smokers.

American Crafts Festival: Lincoln Center; Celebrating quilts and such.

Village Voice 4Knots Music Festival: South Street Seaport; Free outdoor show featuring renowned and emerging indie artists.

Howl Festival: Tompkins Square Park; Spirit of Alan Ginsberg lives on in multiday East Village festival.

JULY

Macy's Fireworks Display: East River; Independence Day's literal highlight (July 4).

Washington Square Music Festival: W 4th St at LaGuardia Pl; Open-air concert Tuesdays in July.

New York Philharmonic Concerts in the Parks: Various locations throughout five boroughs; Varied programs.

Summergarden: MoMA; Free classical concerts July Sundays in sculpture garden.

Celebrate Brooklyn!: Prospect Park Bandshell; Nine weeks of free outdoor film, music, dance, and theater events (July–August).

Mostly Mozart: Lincoln Center; The name says it all (July–August).

Shakespeare in the Park: Delacorte Theater in Central Park; Every summer two free outsized outside plays with boldface names bring long lunch hour lines for evening shows.

PS1 Warm Up: MoMA PS1, Long Island City; Sweaty DJ-dance-installations every Saturday afternoon (late June–Labor Day).

AUGUST

Harlem Week: Harlem; Music and community events last all month long.

Hong Kong Dragon Boat Festival: Flushing-Meadows Park Lake, Queens; Wimpy canoes need not apply.

New York International Fringe Festival: Various locations; 200 companies, 16 days, more than 20 venues, 1,200 performances—and your friends expect you to show up to all of them.

US Open: USTA National Tennis Center, Flushing; Final Grand Slam event of the year (August–September).

Lincoln Center Out of Doors: Lincoln Center; Free outdoor performances throughout the month.

SEPTEMBER

West Indian American Day Carnival: Eastern Parkway from Utica to Grand Army Plaza, Brooklyn; Children's parade on Saturday, adult's parade on Labor Day (Labor Day Weekend).

Richmond County Fair: Historic Richmondtown, Staten Island; Best agricultural competitions (Labor Day).

Fashion Week: Lincoln Center; Twice yearly week-long celeb-studded event.

Feast of San Gennaro: Little Italy; Plenty of greasy street food.

Atlantic Antic: Brooklyn Heights; Multicultural street fair.

DUMBO Art Festival: DUMBO, Brooklyn; Hundreds of artists exhibiting in front of stunning bridge-skyline backdrop.

OCTOBER

New York Film Festival: Lincoln Center; Features film premieres (early October).

Autumn Crafts Festival: Lincoln Center; Celebrating quilts and such.

Columbus Day Parade: Fifth Avenue; Celebrating the second person to discover America (Columbus Day).

Halloween Parade: West Village; Brings a new meaning to costumed event (October 31).

Halloween Dog Parade: East Village; Cute dogs, terrible puns.Blessing of the Animals: St John the Divine, Morningside Heights; Where to take your gecko.

Big Apple Circus: Lincoln Center; Step right up (October–January)!

Hispanic Day Parade: Fifth Ave b/w 44th and 86th Sts; A celebration of Latin America's rich heritage (mid-October).

Open House NY: Various locations, all boroughs; Insider access to architecture and design landmarks (early October).

NY Comic Con: Jacob Javits Center; Comic enthusiasts convene at the nerd mecca.

NOVEMBER

New York City Marathon: Verrazano Bridge to Central Park; 26 miles of NYC air (first Sunday of November).

Veteran's Day Parade: Fifth Ave from 26th St to 56th St; Opening service at Eternal Light Memorial in Madison Square Park.

Macy's Thanksgiving Day Parade: Central Park West at 77th St to Macy's in Herald Square; Giant balloons with Santa bringing up the rear.

The Nutcracker Suite: Lincoln Center; Balanchine's ballet is a Christmas tradition (November–December).

Christmas Spectacular: Radio City Music Hall; Rockettes' mesmerizing legs steal show from Santa and little people (November–January).

Origami Christmas Tree: Museum of Natural History; Hopefully not decorated with candles (Nov–Jan).

Pier Antique Show: Pier 94; Look at old things you can't afford.

DECEMBER

Christmas Tree Lighting Ceremony: Rockefeller Center; Most enchanting spot in the city, if you don't mind sharing it with about a million others.

Menorah Lighting: Fifth Avenue & 59th St; Just the world's biggest menorah, that's what.

John Lennon Anniversary Vigil: Strawberry Fields, Central Park; Every December 8 crowds gather to remember the singer/songwriter on the anniversary of his death.

Holiday Window Displays: Saks Fifth Avenue, Macy's, Lord & Taylor, etc.; A New York tradition.

Alvin Ailey American Dance Theater: New York City Center; Winter season lasts all month long.

Messiah Sing-In: Lincoln Center; For once—just this once—it's OK to sing along. Don't blow it.

New Year's Eve Ball Drop: Times Square; Welcome the new year with a freezing mob (December 31). New Year's Eve Fireworks: Central Park; Hot cider and food available (December 31).

New Year's Eve Midnight Run: Central Park; Never too soon to start with the resolutions (four miles).

USEFUL PHONE NUMBERS

EMERGENCIES: *911*

GENERAL CITY INFORMATION: *311*

MTA HOTLINE: *511*

CITY BOARD OF ELECTIONS: *VOTE.NYC.NY.US OR 212-487-5400*

CON EDISON: *800-752-6633*

TIME WARNER CABLE: *212-358-0900 (MANHATTAN); 718-358-0900 (QUEENS/ BROOKLYN); 718-816-8686 (STATEN ISLAND)*

CABLEVISION: *718-860-3514*

VERIZON: *800-837-4966*

BATHROOMS

When nature calls, New York can make your life excruciatingly difficult. The city-sponsored public bathroom offerings, including dodgy subway restrooms and the sporadic experimentation with self-cleaning super porta-potties, leave a lot to be desired. Your best bet, especially in an emergency, remains bathrooms in stores and other buildings that are open to the public.

The three most popular bathroom choices for needy New Yorkers (and visitors) are Barnes & Noble, Starbucks, and any kind of fast food chain. Barnes & Noble bathrooms are essentially open to everyone (as long as you're willing to walk past countless shelves of books during your navigation to the restrooms). They're usually clean enough, but sometimes you'll find yourself waiting in line during the evening and weekends. Although Starbucks bathrooms are more prevalent, they tend to be more closely guarded (in some places you have to ask for a key) and not as clean as you'd like. Fast food restrooms are similarly unhygienic, but easy to use inconspicuously without needing to purchase anything.

For a nice interactive map of bathrooms in NYC (including hours and even ratings), try the Bathroom Diaries at www.thebathroomdiaries.com or–if you have a smart phone–any of a number of apps designed to help you avoid a ticket for peeing in the street. If you're busting to go and there's no Barnes & Noble, Starbucks, or fast food joint in sight, consider the following options:

Public buildings: Libraries, train stations (Grand Central, Penn Station) and shopping areas (e.g., South Street Seaport, World Financial Center, Manhattan Mall, The Shops at Columbus Circle).

Department stores: Macy's, Bloomingdale's, Saks, etc.

Other stores: Old Navy, Bed Bath & Beyond, FAO Schwarz, The Strand, etc.

Supermarkets: Whole Foods is a sure bet; with garden-variety Pathmark, Food Emporium, D'Agostino, Gristedes, Key Food, etc. you'll probably have to ask, because those are usually way in the back among the employee lockers.

Diners: In every neighborhood, and usually busy enough so that if you simply stride in and head towards the back (since that's where the bathroom is most of the time anyway) WITHOUT stopping, they probably won't notice. Works for us, usually.

Bars: Good option at night when most other places are closed; head straight back; can get raunchy toward closing time.

Parks: Nothing beats a stainless steel "mirror" and a transient bathing in the sink. That said, things aren't always what they used to be–newly renovated parks sometimes have very nice facilities and the public-private Bryant Park bathroom is among the nicest in Midtown (and stocked with fresh flowers, to boot).

Hotels: Midtown hotels are basically public buildings, for all intents and purposes; lobbies are also good for a quick rest.

Times Square Visitors Center: 1560 Broadway.

Subways: At ends of lines, in major transit hubs and some stops between; raunchy, not for the timid.

WEBSITES

thebowenyboys.blogspot.com or @BoweryBoys: NYC history.

ny.curbed.com or @CurbedNY: For those who obsess over building permits.

www.eatingintranslation.com or @EIT: One guy eats his away through NYC.

ny.eater.com or @EaterNY: Restaurant gossip galore.

www.forgotten-ny.com or @ForgottenNY: Fascinating look at the relics of New York's past.

www.gothamgazette.com or @GothamGazette: NYC policy and politics website.

www.gothamist.com or @Gothamist: Blog detailing various daily news and goings-on in the city.

newyork.craigslist.org: Classified site that single-handedly put print media out of business.

www.notfortourists.com or @notfortourists: The ultimate NYC website.

www.nyc.gov or @nyc311: New York City government resources.

www.nyc-grid.com or @paulsahner: Photo blog of NYC, block by block.

www.nycgo.com or @nycgo: The official NYC tourism site. www.overheardinnewyork.com: Repository of great overheard snippets.

www.scoutingny.com or @nycscout: The city from point of view of a film scout.

www.theskint.com or @theskint: Free and cheap worthwhile events listed daily.

www.vanishingnewyork.blogspot.com or @jeremoss: Chronicling lost or nearly lost old-timey time spots.

ESSENTIAL NEW YORK SONGS

"Sidewalks of New York"–Various, written by James Blake and Charles Lawlor, 1894

"Give My Regards to Broadway"–Various, written by George Cohan, 190

"I'll Take Manhattan"–Various, written by Rodgers and Hart, 1925

"Puttin' on the Ritz"–Various, written by Irving Berlin, 1929

"42nd Street"–Various, written by Al Dubin and Harry Warren, 1932

"Take the A Train"–Duke Ellington, 1940

"Autumn in New York"–Frank Sinatra, 1947

"Spanish Harlem"–Ben E. King, 1961

"Car 54 Where Are You?"–Nat Hiken and John Strauss, 1961

"On Broadway"–Various, written by Weil/Mann/Leiber/Stoller, 1962

"Talkin' New York"–Bob Dylan, 1962

"Up on the Roof"–The Drifters, 1963

"59th Street Bridge Song"–Simon and Garfunkel, 1966

"I'm Waiting for My Man"–Velvet Underground, 1967

"Brooklyn Roads"–Neil Diamond, 1968

"Crosstown Traffic"–Jimi Hendrix, 1969

"Personality Crisis"–The New York Dolls, 1973

"New York State of Mind"–Billy Joel, 1976

"53rd and 3rd"–The Ramones, 1977

"Shattered"–Rolling Stones, 1978

"New York, New York"–Frank Sinatra, 1979

"Life During Wartime"–Talking Heads, 1979

"New York New York"–Grandmaster Flash and the Furious 5, 1984

"No Sleep Til Brooklyn"–Beastie Boys, 1987

"Christmas in Hollis"–Run-D.M.C., 1987

"New York"–U2, 2000

"I've Got New York"–The 6ths, 2000

"New York, New York"–Ryan Adams, 2001

"The Empty Page"–Sonic Youth, 2002

"New York"–Ja Rule f. Fat Joe, Jadakiss, 2004

"Empire State of Mind"–Jay-Z, 2009

ESSENTIAL NEW YORK MOVIES

The Crowd (1928)

42nd Street (1933)

King Kong (1933)

Pride of the Yankees (1942)

Arsenic and Old Lace (1944)

Miracle on 34th Street (1947)

On the Town (1949)

On the Waterfront (1954)

The Blackboard Jungle (1955)

An Affair to Remember (1957)

The Apartment (1960)

Breakfast at Tiffany's (1961)

West Side Story (1961)

Barefoot in the Park (1967)

John & Mary (1969)

Midnight Cowboy (1969)

French Connection (1970)

The Out of Towners (1970)

Shaft (1971)

Across 110th Street (1972)

Mean Streets (1973)

Serpico (1973)

Godfather II (1974)

The Taking of Pelham One Two Three (1974)

Dog Day Afternoon (1975)

Taxi Driver (1976)

Saturday Night Fever (1977)

Superman (1978)

Manhattan (1979)

The Warriors (1979)

Fame (1980)

Escape From New York (1981)

Nighthawks (1981)

Ghostbusters (1984)

The Muppets Take Manhattan (1984)

After Hours (1985)

Crocodile Dundee (1986)

Wall Street (1987)

Moonstruck (1987)

Big (1988)

Bright Lights, Big City (1988)

Working Girl (1988)

Do the Right Thing (1989)

Last Exit to Brooklyn (1989)

When Harry Met Sally (1989)

A Bronx Tale (1993)

Kids (1995)

Men in Black (1997)

Bringing Out the Dead (1999)

The Royal Tenenbaums (2001)

Gangs of New York (2002)

Spider-Man (2002)

25th Hour (2003)

The Interpreter (2005)

Inside Man (2006)

The Devil Wears Prada (2006)

American Gangster (2007)

Enchanted (2007)

Sex and the City (2008)

New York I Love You (2009)

Whatever Works (2009)

The Wolf of Wall Street (2013)

ESSENTIAL NEW YORK BOOKS

A Tree Grows in Brooklyn by Betty Smith; coming-of-age story set in the slums of Brooklyn.

The Alienist by Caleb Carr; great portrait of late-19th century New York complete with serial killer, detective, and Teddy Roosevelt.

The BonFire of the Vanities by Tom Wolfe; money, class, and politics undo a wealthy bond trader.

Bright Lights, Big City by Jay McInerney; 1980s yuppie and the temptations of the city.

Catcher in the Rye by J. D. Salinger; classic portrayal of teenage angst.

The Death and Life of Great American Cities by Jane Jacobs; influential exposition on what matters in making cities work.

The Encyclopedia of New York City by Kenneth T. Jackson, ed.; huge and definitive reference work.

Gotham: A History of New York City to 1898 by Edwin G. Burrows and Mike Wallace; authoritative history of New York.

The Epic of New York City by Edward Robb Ellis; super-readable chapter-by-chapter compendium of hits and highlights of NYC history.

The Fuck-Up by Arthur Nersesian; scraping by in the East Village of the '80s.

Here is New York by E. B. White; reflections on the city.

House of Mirth by Edith Wharton; climbing the social ladder in upper crust, late 19th-century NY.

Knickerbocker's History of New York by Washington Irving; very early (1809) whimsical "history" of NY.

Manchild in the Promised Land by Claude Brown; autobiographical tale of growing up in Harlem.

The Power Broker by Robert Caro; lengthy biography of 20th century municipal titan Robert Moses, you'll never look at the city the same way after reading it.

The Recognitions by William Gaddis; ever thought New Yorkers were phony? They are.

Washington Square by Henry James; love and marriage in upper-middle-class 1880s NY.

The Cricket in Times Square by George Selden; classic children's book.

This Is New York by Miroslav Sasek; charming children's book from 1960; great gift idea.

PHOTO : WALLY GOBETZ

NEW YORK TIMELINE

a timeline of significant events in New York history (by no means complete)

1524: Giovanni de Verrazano enters the New York harbor.

1609: Henry Hudson explores what is now called the Hudson River.

1626: The Dutch purchase Manhattan and New Amsterdam is founded.

1647: Peter Stuyvesant becomes Director General of New Amsterdam.

1664: The British capture the colony and rename it "New York."

1754: King's College/Columbia founded.

1776: British drive colonial army from New York and hold it for the duration of the war.

1776: Fire destroys a third of the city.

1789: Washington takes the Oath of Office as the first President of the United States.

1801: Alexander Hamilton founds the New-York Evening Post, still published today as the New York Post.

1811: The Commissioners Plan dictates a grid plan for the streets of New York.

1812: City Hall completed.

1825: Completion of the Erie Canal connects New York City commerce to the Great Lakes.

1835: New York Herald publishes its first edition.

1835: Great Fire destroys 600 buildings and kills 30 New Yorkers.

1854: First Tammany Hall-supported mayor Fernando Woods elected.

1859: Central Park opens.

1863: The Draft Riots terrorize New York for three days.

1868: Prospect Park opens.

1871: Thomas Nast cartoons and New York Times exposes lead to the end of the Tweed Ring.

1880: The population of Manhattan reaches over 1 million.

1883: Brooklyn Bridge opens.

1886: The Statue of Liberty is dedicated, inspires first ticker tape parade.

1888: The Blizzard of '88 incapacitates the city for two weeks.

1892: Ellis Island opens; 16 million immigrants will pass through in the next 32 years.

1897: Steeplechase Park opens, first large amusement park in Coney Island.

1898: The City of Greater New York is founded when the five boroughs are merged.

1904: General Slocum disaster kills 1,021.

1904: The subway opens.

1906: First New Year's celebration in Times Square.

1911: Triangle Shirtwaist Fire kills 146, impels work safety movement.

1920: A TNT-packed horse cart explodes on Wall Street, killing 30; the crime goes unsolved.

1923: The Yankees win their first World Championship.

1929: Stock market crashes, signaling the beginning of the Great Depression.

1929: The Chrysler Building is completed.

1930: The Empire State Building is built, then tallest in the world.

1927: The Holland Tunnel opens, making it the world's longest underwater tunnel.

1931: The George Washington Bridge is completed.

1933: Fiorello LaGuardia elected mayor.

1934: Robert Moses becomes Parks Commissioner.

1939: The city's first airport, LaGuardia, opens.

1950: United Nations opens.

1955: Dodgers win the World Series; they move to LA two years later.

1963: Pennsylvania Station is demolished to the dismay of many; preservation efforts gain steam.

1964: The Verrazano-Narrows Bridge is built, at the time the world's longest suspension bridge.

1965: Malcolm X assassinated in the Audubon Ballroom.

1965: Blackout strands hundreds of thousands during rush hour.

1969: The Stonewall Rebellion marks beginning of the gay rights movement.

1969: The Miracle Mets win the World Series.

1970: Knicks win their first championship.

1970: First New York City Marathon takes place.

1971: World Trade Center opens.

1975: Ford to City: Drop Dead.

1977: Thousands arrested for various mischief during a city-wide blackout.

1981: First NYC AIDS death begins a decade of tragedy.

1977: Ed Koch elected mayor to the first of three terms.

1987: Black Monday–stock market plunges.

1993: Giuliani elected mayor.

1993: A bomb explodes in the parking garage of the World Trade Center, killing 5.

1994: Rangers win the Stanley Cup after a 40-year drought.

2000: NFT publishes its first edition.

2001: The World Trade Center is destroyed in a terrorist attack; New Yorkers vow to rebuild.

2003: Blackout becomes best party in NYC history.

2003: Tokens are no longer accepted in subway turnstiles.

2006: Ground is broken on the WTC memorial.

2007: Construction begins (again) on the Second Avenue subway line.

2009: Bloomberg purchases a third term.

2012: 1 WTC is once again tallest in NYC.

2012: Superstorm Sandy ravages Zone A, altering New Yorkers' relationship with the waterfront.

2013: Bill de Blasio wins the mayoral election, co-starring his photogenic family.

2014: NYC hosts Super Bowl XLVIII, first outdoor cold-weather city game in history.

HOSPITALS

If you have to get to a hospital (especially in an emergency), it's best to go to the closest one. However, as a quick reference, the following is a list of the largest hospitals by neighborhood, complete with the name of its corresponding map. But no matter which hospital you drag yourself into, for heaven's sake make sure you have your insurance card.

LOWER MANHATTAN
NewYork-Presbyterian/Lower Manhattan Hospital (William & Beekman Sts, just south of the Brooklyn Bridge; Map 3)

EAST VILLAGE
Beth Israel Medical Center (14th St & Broadway/Union Square; Map 10)

MURRAY HILL
Bellevue Hospital Center (First Ave & 27th St; Map 10); NYU Langone Medical Center (First Ave & 31st St; Map 10)

HELL'S KITCHEN/UPPER WEST SIDE
St Luke's Roosevelt Hospital (Tenth Ave & 58th St; Map 11)

EAST SIDE
NewYork-Presbyterian (York Ave & 68th St; Map 15); Lenox Hill Hospital (Lexington Ave & 77th St; Map 15); Mt Sinai Medical Center (Madison Ave & 101st St; Map 17)

COLUMBIA/MORNINGSIDE HEIGHTS
St Luke's Hospital Center (Amsterdam Ave & 114th St; Map 18)

FARTHER UPTOWN
Columbia Presbyterian Medical Center (168th St & Broadway; Map 23)

If you have a condition that isn't immediately life threatening, certain hospitals in New York specialize and excel in specific areas of medicine:

CANCER:
Memorial Sloan-Kettering

BIRTHING CENTER/LABOR & DELIVERY:
St Luke's Roosevelt

DIGESTIVE DISORDERS:
Mt Sinai

DENTISTRY:
NYU College of Dentistry

EAR, NOSE, AND THROAT:
Mt Sinai

EYES:
New York Eye and Ear Infirmary

GERIATRICS:
Mt Sinai, NewYork-Presbyterian

HEART:
NewYork-Presbyterian

HORMONAL DISORDERS:
 NewYork-Presbyterian

KIDNEY DISEASE:
NewYork-Presbyterian

MENTAL HEALTH:
Bellevue

NEUROLOGY:
NewYork-Presbyterian, NYU Medical Center

ORTHOPEDICS:
Hospital for Special Surgery, NewYork-Presbyterian

PEDIATRICS:
Children's Hospital of NewYork-Presbyterian

PSYCHIATRY:
NewYork-Presbyterian, NYU Medical Center

RHEUMATOLOGY:
Hospital for Special Surgery, Hospital for Joint Diseases Orthopedic Institute, NYU Medical Center

LIBRARIES

Beginner's mistake: Walk into the "main branch" of the New York Public Library at Bryant Park, and ask how to check out books. Trust us; it's happened. Recognizable for its reclining stone lions, Patience and Fortitude, the famous building is a research library with non-circulating materials that you can peruse only in the iconic reading room. In 2008, the Children's Center, a circulating children's library, moved to this location and now you can check out kids books here, too. If you want to read War and Peace or 50 Shades of Da Vinci Pray Love, it's best to go to your local branch (there are 80 of them spread out through Manhattan, The Bronx and Staten Island). Note: Holds take a very long time to fill, at least a week to a week and a half. If the book you need is only a 20-minute subway ride away, and you need the book now, invest the time and the subway fare.

The **main branch of the New York Public Library** (Map 12) (renamed the Schwarzman Building in 2008, for billionaire donor Stephen A. Schwarzman) is one of Manhattan's architectural treasures. Designed by Carrère and Hastings and opened to the public in 1911, the building was one of the Beaux-Arts firm's most famous commissions. The main branch has several special collections and services, such as the Humanities and Social Sciences Library, the Map Division, Exhibition galleries, and divisions dedicated to various ethnic groups. The main branch contains 88 miles of shelves and has more than 10,000 current periodicals from almost 150 countries. Research libraries require an ACCESS card, which you can apply for at the library and which allows you to request materials in any of the reading rooms. Card sign-up can be slow, so be patient, and it never hurts to bring along multiple kinds of ID, or a piece of mail if you're a new NYC resident.

If it's reference material you're after, there are specialized research libraries to help: **The Schomburg Center for Research in Black Culture** (Map 22) is the nation's foremost source on African-American history. The **Library for the Performing Arts** (Map 14) contains the Theatre on Film and Tape Archive, featuring taped performances of many Broadway shows. There's also the **Andrew Heiskell Braille and Talking Book Library** (Map 9), designed to be barrier-free. The library contains large collections of special format materials and audio equipment for listening to recorded books and magazines. You can check out the full system online at www.nypl.org.

LGBT

Very few places, anywhere, rival New York when it comes to quality gay living. Gay men can get almost anything they want, any time of day, with many businesses catering specifically to gay clientele. Bars remain the backbone of the social scene: some, like *Industry* (Map 11), focus on a chic atmosphere, while places like *The Phoenix* (Map 7) and *9th Avenue Saloon* (Map 11) are friendly dive bars. You can sing your face off on karaoke nights at *Pieces* (Map 5) or *XES Lounge* (Map 9), get into trouble at *The Cock* (Map 6), and dance with the locals at *The Ritz* (Map 11) or with bridge-and-tunnel types at *XL* (Map 11).

There are more lesbian bars and parties than ever in New York City, so all you have to do is decide what night, which neighborhood and how you'll snag a girl! Although you'll find quality drinks, music, and women at *Henrietta Hudson* (Map 5), the notorious and intolerable bathroom line might discourage those lesbians who actually have a bladder. *Lovergirl* (www. lovergirlnyc.com) puts on Saturday night dance parties while *Cubbyhole* (Map 5) promises a homey atmosphere and friendly crowd. In Brooklyn, chill on the patio at *Ginger's* (Map 33).

WEBSITES

NEWYORK.GAYCITIES.COM
New York section of comprehensive LGBT-focused travel site.

WWW.GAYELLOWPAGES.COM
Gayellow Pages for gay/lesbian-owned and gay/lesbian-friendly businesses in the US and Canada.

PUBLICATIONS

GAY CITY NEWS
Bi-weekly newspaper for lesbian and gay New Yorkers including current local and national news items (www.gaycitynews. com or @GayCityNews).

GET OUT!
Weekly with emphasis on goings on about town (getoutmag.com or @GetOutMag).

NEXT MAGAZINE
Weekly magazine that includes frisky nightlife listings, film reviews, feature articles, and more (www.nextmagazine.com or @NextMagazineNY).

BOOKSHOPS

BLUESTOCKINGS
Lesbian/radical bookstore and activist center with regular readings and a fair-trade cafe (172 Allen St, 212-777-6028, www. bluestockings.com or @bluestockings).

HEALTH CENTERS AND SUPPORT ORGANIZATIONS

CALLEN-LORDE COMMUNITY HEALTH CENTER
Health care and services for the LGBT community (356 W 18th St, 212-271-7200, www. callen-lorde.org or @CallenLorde).

GMHC
Founded in 1981, Gay Men's Health Crisis is dedicated to AIDS awareness and support for those living with HIV (446 W 33rd St, 212-367-1000, www.gmhc.org or @GMHC).

THE LESBIAN, GAY, BISEXUAL & TRANSGENDER COMMUNITY CENTER
The largest LGBT multi-service organization on the East Coast (208 W 13th, 212-620-7310, www.gaycenter.org).

GLBT NATIONAL HELP CENTER
Switchboard for referrals, advice, and counseling (888-843-4564, www.glnh.org or @glbtNatlHelpCtr).

IDENTITY HOUSE
Offers LGBTQ peer counseling services, short-term therapy and/or referrals, groups, and workshops (208 W 13th St, 212-243-8181, www.identityhouse.org).

LAMBDA LEGAL
Legal foundation securing civil rights for the entire LGBT population (120 Wall St, 19th Flr, 212 809-8585, www.lambdalegal. org, @LambdaLegal).

NATIONAL GAY & LESBIAN TASK FORCE
National organization building LGBT political power and de-marginalizing LGBT issues (80 Maiden Ln, Ste 1504, 212-604-9830, www.thetaskforce.org or @TheTaskForce).

NEW YORK CITY ANTI-VIOLENCE PROJECT
24-hour crisis support line for violence against LGTBH communities (212-714-1141, www.avp.org or @antiviolence).

PFLAG
Parents, Families, and Friends of Lesbians and Gays working together to raise awareness of LGBT youth and adults (130 E 25th St, Ste M1, 646-240-4288, www.pflagnyc. org or @pflagnyc).

IMMIGRATION EQUALITY
Advocates for changing US policy on immigration of permanent partners (40 Exchange Pl, Ste 1300, 212-714-2904, immigrationequality.org or @IEquality).

GLAAD (GAY AND LESBIAN ALLIANCE AGAINST DEFAMATION)
The are the folks who go to bat for you in the media (104 W 29th St, 4th Flr, 212-629-3322, www.glaad.org or @glaad).

OUTDANCING @ STEPPING OUT STUDIOS
The first LGBT partner dance program in the US (37 W 26th St, 9th Flr, 646-742-9400, www.steppingoutstudios.com).

LGBT CONNECTIONS NIGHT AT LEO BAR:
Each third Friday of the month, Asia Society partners with various LGBT professional organizations; free exhibition tours included (725 Park Ave, 212-327-9352, www.asiasociety.org).

POSITIVE ALLIANCE
Organizes weekly Friday social mixer and party for HIV+ gay men, their friends and supporters at The Ritz (369 W 46th St, 2nd Flr); also provides regular email newsletter with links to resources and news updates (@PozAlliance).

ANNUAL EVENTS

PRIDE WEEK
Usually the last full week in June (212-807-7433, www.nycpride.org or @NYCPride).

NEWFEST
NY's Premier LGBT Film Festival: Showcase of international gay and lesbian films, July (646-290-8136, newfest.org or @NewFestNYC).

DOG RUNS

It's good to be a dog in New York. NYC's pooches are among the world's most pampered: they celebrate birthdays, don expensive sweaters, and prance down Fifth Avenue in weather-appropriate gear. Even for those of us who can't afford to dress our pups in Burberry raincoats, there are ways to spoil our canine companions. NYC is full of dog runs–both formal and informal–scattered throughout the city's parks and neighborhood community spaces. Good thing too, as the fine for having a dog off-leash can run upward of $100, and park officials are vigilant. While the city takes no active role in the management of the dog runs, it provides space to the community groups who do. These community groups are always eager for help (volunteer time or financial contributions) and many post volunteer information on park bulletin boards. It can take many years and several thousand dollars to build a dog run in New York. NYC boasts dozens of dog runs, but that doesn't seem like very many when you consider that there are more than a million pooches in the five boroughs. Each dog run is different. It's good to know, for example, that Riverside Park at 87th Street has a fountain and hose to keep dogs cool in the summer. Formal runs are probably the safest bet for pets, as most are enclosed and maintained. For safety reasons, choke or pronged collars are forbidden, and identification and rabies tags should remain on the flat collar. Most runs prohibit dogs in heat, aggressive dogs, and dogs without up-to-date shots. For more information about dog runs in city parks, see www.nycgovparks.org/facilities/dogareas.

There are no dog runs in Central Park, but before 9 am the park is full of people walking their dogs off-leash. While this is a strict no-no the rest of the day (and punishable by hefty fines), park officials tolerate the practice as long as dogs maintain a low profile, and are leashed immediately at 9 am. Check out www.centralparknyc.org for more info and check in with Central Park Paws, an initiative of the Central Park Conservancy to connect with dog owners about responsible ways to enjoy the park.

While there are too many dog runs to create a complete list, these are some of the best-established ones.

P.S. 234
(300 Greenwich St at Chambers St, Map 2): Private run/membership required.

FISH BRIDGE PARK
(Dover and Pearl Sts, Map 3): Concrete-surfaced run; features water hose, wading pool, and lock box with newspapers.

COLEMAN OVAL PARK
(Pike & Monroe Sts, Map 4): Under the Manhattan Bridge.

WEST VILLAGE D.O.G. RUN
(Little W 12th St between Washington St & 10th Ave, www.wvdog.org, Map 5): Features benches, water hose, and drink bowl; membership required.

WASHINGTON SQUARE PARK
(MacDougal St at W 4th St, Map 6): Located in the south part of the park, this is a large, gravel -surfaced run with many spectators; popular and gets very crowded, but is well -maintained nonetheless.

MERCER-HOUSTON DOG RUN
(Mercer St at Houston St, mercerhoustondogrun.org, Map 6): Private run with a membership; benefits include running water and a plastic wading pool for your dog to splash in.

UNION SQUARE
(Broadway at 15th St, Map 6): Crushed stone surface.

TOMPKINS SQUARE PARK
(Avenue B at 10th St, www.tompkinssquaredogrun.com, Map 7): NYC's first dog run opened in 1990; this community-centered run offers lots of shade, benches, and running water–but be aware: toys, frisbees, balls, and dogs in heat are prohibited.

THOMAS SMITH TRIANGLE
(11th Ave at 23rd St, Map 8): Concrete-surfaced run.

CHELSEA WATERSIDE PARK
(11th Ave at 22nd St, Map 8)

MADISON SQUARE PARK
(Madison Ave at 25th St, Map 10): Medium-sized run with gravel surface and plenty of trees.

DEWITT CLINTON PARK
(11th Ave at 52nd & 54th Sts, Map 11): Two small concrete-surfaced runs.

ASTRO'S HELL'S KITCHEN NEIGHBORHOOD DOG RUN
(W 39th St at 10th Ave, astrosdogrun. org, Map 11): A private dog run featuring chairs, umbrellas, fenced garden, and woodchip surface.

EAST RIVER ESPLANADE
(East River at 63rd St, Map 13): Concrete dog run by the river.

PETER DETMOLD PARK
(Beekman Pl at 51st St, Map 13): Large well -maintained run with cement and dirt surfaces and many trees.

ROBERT MOSES PARK
(First Ave and 42nd St, Map 13): Concrete surface.

THEODORE ROOSEVELT PARK
(Central Park W at W 81st St, Map 14): Gravel surface.

RIVERSIDE PARK
(Riverside Dr at 72nd St, Map 14)

CARL SCHURZ PARK
(East End Ave at 85th-86th Sts, Map 15, 17): Medium-sized enclosed run with pebbled surface and separate space for small dogs; this run has benches and shady trees, and running water is available in the bathrooms.

RIVERSIDE PARK
(Riverside Dr at 87th St, Map 16): Medium-sized run with gravel surface.

RIVERSIDE PARK
(Riverside Dr at 105th-106th Sts, Map 16): Medium-sized run with gravel surface.

MORNINGSIDE PARK
(Morningside Ave b/w 114th & 119th Sts, Map 18)

THOMAS JEFFERSON PARK
(E 112th St at First Ave, Map 20): Wood chip surface.

J. HOOD WRIGHT PARK
(Haven Ave at W 173rd St, Map 23): An enclosed dirt-surfaced run.

FORT TRYON PARK/SIR WILLIAM'S DOG RUN
(Margaret Corbin Dr, Washington Heights, Map 24)

INWOOD HILL DOG RUN
(Dyckman St and Payson Ave, Map 25): Gravel surface.

KOWSKY PLAZA DOG RUN
(Gateway Plaza, Battery Park City): Located near the marina, this area has small hills for your dog to run on, as well as a small fountain and bathing pool.

BATTERY PARK CITY
(Along River Ter between Park Pl W and Murray St): Concrete surfaced run with a view of the river.

HOTELS

If you're reading this you're probably not a tourist, and if you're not a tourist you probably don't need a hotel. However, chances are good that at some point your obnoxious friend or relative from out of state will suddenly come a-knockin', bearing news of their long-awaited arrival to the big city. "So I thought I'd stay at your place," they will suggest casually, displaying their complete ignorance of the number of square feet in an average New York apartment–and simultaneously realizing your greatest fear of playing host to someone you greatly dislike. Or there's the possibility that your place is infested with mice, bed bugs, or pigeons and you need to escape, pronto. Or maybe you're just looking for a romantic (or slightly less than romantic) getaway without leaving the city. Whatever the case, be assured that there is a seemingly endless array of possibilities to suit all your overnight desires and needs.

Obviously, your options run from dirt cheap (well, by New York standards) to disgustingly, offensively expensive. For those with tons of extra cash, either call us or check out some of the elite luxury chains– *The Ritz Carlton* (cheaper to stay at the one in *Battery Park* than *Central Park* (Map 12), The *Four Seasons* (Map 12) at E 57th St, *The W* at *Union Square* (Map 10), *Times Square* (Map 12), *E 39th St* (Map 10), and *Lexington Ave at 49th St* (Map 13), *Le Parker Meridien* (Map 12), The Peninsula (Map 12), *The St. Regis* (Map 12), and *The Mandarin-Oriental* (Map 11)

Those hotels that are more unique to Manhattan include: *The Lowell* (Map 15), a fortress of pretentiousness nestled beside Central Park, which successfully captures the feel of a snobby, high-class gentleman's club. For a similar feeling, only with a heavy dose of Renaissance Italy and a design dating back to 1882, check into The *New York Palace* (Map 12). If you prefer more modern surroundings, the swank-tastic *Bryant Park Hotel* (Map 12) (once the landmark Radiator building before it was transformed) is a favorite amongst entertainment and fashion industry folks. Similarly, The *Regency* (Map 15), nicknamed "Hollywood East" in the 1960s, is a must for all celeb-stalkers hangers-on alike. Meanwhile, The *Algonquin* (Map 12) offers complimentary delivery of the New Yorker, as if to suggest that they cater to a more literary crowd (maybe in the 1920s, but whether or not that's the case today is up for debate). If you're feeling fabulous, there's *The Muse Hotel* (Map 12), located in the heart of Times Square, mere steps away from the bright lights of Broadway.

If you're more comfortable with the old-money folks (or if you're a nostalgic member of the nouveau-riche), check out the apartment-size rooms at **The Carlyle** (Map 15). Be a bit easier on your wallet and get a room at **The Excelsior Hotel** (Map 14)—it may be a tad less indulgent, but get over it, you're still right on Central Park. Yet more affordable and not an ounce less attractive is **The Hudson** (Map 11), a chic boutique hotel from Ian Schrager. Then there's **The Shoreham**(Map 12), which offers complimentary champagne at the front desk (so it's definitely worth a shot to pose as a guest) in addition to a fantastically retro bar, that looks like it's straight out of A Clockwork Orange. If you are gay or have a gay relative or friend coming to visit, consider **The Out NYC** (Map 11), a sleek resort hotel catering to a LGBT clientele that bills itself as New York's first "straight-friendly" hotel. Last but certainly not least, one can always stay at the world-famous **Waldorf Astoria** (Map 13), where unrivaled service and a lavish renovation more than justify the cost of staying (at least for the 1% and those who edging close to that elite coterie).

There are additional high-end options downtown, perfect for nights of drunken bar-hopping or cool European friends with deep but chic pockets. The sexier of these hotels include: The **Hotel Gansevoort** (Map 5), a sleek tower of luxury, located steps away from the Meatpacking District—New York's very own version of Miami Beach! Nearby, you'll find **The Maritime Hotel** (Map 8), which does a great impression of a cruise ship, replete with porthole-shaped windows and La Bottega, an Italian restaurant with a massive outdoor patio that feels like the deck of a Carnival liner. In trendy SoHo, you'll find **The Mercer Hotel** (Map 6), **60 Thompson** (Map 6), and **The So-Ho Grand** (Map 2) (there's also its sister, **The Tribeca Grand** (Map 2), farther south)—which vary ever-so-slightly in degrees of coolness, depending on your demands. A little ways north, next to Gramercy Park, you'll find **The Inn at Irving Place** (Map 10)—things are a tad less modern at this upscale bed and breakfast (it consists of two restored 19th-century townhouses), but the Cibar Lounge, the rock and fashion royalty, and the lack of any visible signage outside are sure to validate your inner yearning to hip. Speaking of which, there are a few new boutique hotels on the Bowery to make all your rock star dreams come true. **The Bowery Hotel** (Map 6) was the first to make its mark on this former stretch of skid row. The Lobby Bar is worth checking out even if you

can't afford a room. Up the street the semi-sleek **Cooper Square Hotel** (Map 6) is competing for models and I-Bankers expense accounts. Check out how they squeezed the fancy hotel in between two existing tenement buildings. And not too far away is the super fancy **Crosby Street Hotel** (Map 6), another of those cool hotels we'll never be able to afford. One thing we can afford is a stroll down the High Line to crane our necks at the exhibitionists who often can be spotted cavorting in the floor-to-ceiling windows of **The Standard** (Map 5) which, er, straddles the airborne park. Guests are reminded by staff that their rooms will be highly visible and they should be careful, which of course prompts many to be careful to show off as much as they can for onlookers.

But speaking of money and thrills we can't afford, let's get real—most of us can't begin to afford such luxuries as those outlined above. We live in a city where pay is kinda flat (or at least flatter than expenses), there's a rent affordability crisis unlike anything in NYC history, and the only reason you really need a hotel is because as much as you might love Aunt Edna from Des Moines and want to spend time with her during her fortnight in the city,

you don't want to step on her as she sleeps on the floor of your studio apartment when you stumble home after last call. For these real-world occasions, rest assured there are a few hotels in the city where real people can actually afford to stay. Some of these include **The Gershwin Hotel** (Map 9), **Herald Square Hotel** (Map 9), **The Hotel at Times Square** (Map 12), **Red Roof Inn** (Map 9), **Second Home on Second Avenue** (Map 6), and **The Chelsea Savoy** (Map 9)—all solid, safe choices.

More mid-range options include: **Hotel Thirty Thirty** (Map 9), **The Abingdon Guest House** (Map 5), **The Roger Williams Hotel** (Map 9), **Portland Square Hotel** (Map 12), **Comfort Inn** (Map 9), **Clarion Hotel** (Map 10), and **The New Yorker Hotel** (Map 8).

Whatever you do, never book your family, friends, or self into a hotel that you don't know or haven't scouted, no matter how appealing the cost—if it seems too good to be true, it may well be. Some of the lowest-priced "hotels" in town appear on some leading hotel booking sites, and they can be really scary. Some are in unsavory neighborhoods, or are in old buildings and barely qualify as hotels. You may arrive and find that someone's suitcases are already

in your room, or that there's no heat or hot water, or that the room feels more like a homeless shelter than a hotel. (Yup, this actually happens. Even to seasoned New Yorkers like us, when we get too enamored of a would-be bargain.) And let's not mention the bedbug threat. Suffice it to say, always always always go with a brand you trust, or check it out beforehand in person or online. That's the only way to be sure you or your out-of-town visitors won't end up with the most unwelcome kind of New York story.

No matter what range of hotel you are looking to book, and for whatever reason, note that rates are generally highest during the holiday season and the summer, and lowest during the off season. Other specific events, like Fashion Week or the UN General Assembly, can cause the price of hotel rooms to increase markedly. Regardless of time of year, sometimes you'll get a better deal if you book well in advance, and sometimes you can score an awesome find by booking at the very last minute on a site like Hotwire. com or checking a site for rooms in private apartments like Airbnb.com. And sometimes you're just out of luck–rates are ballpark and they are subject to change up until you have the reservation. If you find yourself in a bind and you need to get a room for yourself or someone else, also try some of the other aggregator sites: Hotels.com, Priceline, Hotwire, Travelocity, Kayak, Expedia, or even individual company websites. You can also call a hotel directly to ask if they have any specials. Be aware that not all hotels have a star rating and sometimes those that do aren't accurate. The quoted rates will give you an idea of the quality being offered. The bottom line is, like most things in New York, while you have plenty of options, few of them are cheap–but with serendipity and creativity, you may be the lucky one who gets the bargain.

NIGHTLIFE

If you ever get bored in New York City, you have only yourself to blame. When it comes to nightlife in particular, the only difficulty you'll have is in choosing amongst the seemingly infinite options for entertainment. You can just head out with your NFT and see where you end up, because many bars and venues open early and close late (can you say 4am?!). If you need a little more guidance, New York's top weeklies–The Village Voice and Time Out New York–offer tons of listings and round-ups of goings on about town, as do websites such as Flavorpill (www.flavorpill.com), Brooklyn Vegan (www.brooklynvegan.com), and Oh My Rockness (www.ohmyrockness.com). A favorite for usually cheap and off-beat picks is The Skint (www.theskint.com). For those of you who require more than your typical night out, NonsenseNYC (www.nonsensenyc.com) is an e-mail newsletter with a ton of dance parties, interactive art shows, guerrilla theater and other unusual events. Just a quick word of caution: don't forget to pace yourselves.

DIVE BARS

There is no shortage of dumps in this city, so we've done our best to single out the darkest and the dirtiest. The oldest on our list is, of course, **McSorley's Old Ale House** (Map 6), which has been in operation 1854 and looks like it's straight out of *Gangs of New York*. Best experienced during the day and avoided like the plague on evenings and weekends, it's worth checking out the place where Abe Lincoln drank and soaking in all that old-school barroom atmosphere. A popular choice among our staff is the oh-so-derelict **Milano's** (Map 6). Tucked away on swiftly gentrifying Houston Street, it's been a boozy refuge since 1880. In the East Village Lucy has been a fixture behind the bar at **Lucy's** (Map 7) for over three decades. Other downtown favorites include Chinatown karaoke gem **Winnie's** (Map 3), **Nancy Whiskey** (Map 2), **Puffy's Tavern** (Map 2), **Blue & Gold** (Map 6) and **Mona's** (Map 7). In Midtown, **Jimmy's Corner** (Map 12) is the ultimate escape from Times Square tourist swarms, and the classic **Subway Inn** (Map 15) remains a lone holdout amid office towers and Bloomingdale's shoppers. Near Port Authority keep New York City real by giving **Holland Bar** (Map 11) a few bucks in exchange for a beer. Uptown, we like **Reif's Tavern** (Map 17), **Dublin House** (Map 14), **1020 Bar** (Map 18) and **Ding Dong Lounge** (Map 16). On the other side of the East River, check out **Turkey's Nest** (Map 29) and **Greenpoint Tavern** (Map 29) in Williamsburg and the Red Hook classic **Sunny's** (Map 32). Finally, we offer drunken shout outs to true dives that are gone but never forgotten: Mars Bar, Max Fish, Holiday Cocktail Lounge, Milady's and so many more. If you're new to the city, Google them and see all the grime and grit you missed out on...

GREAT BEER SELECTIONS

It's a marvelous time to be a beer geek in New York City. The number of watering holes with mind-boggling craft beer lists grows every year, so we'll do your liver a favor and suggest a few of the best. If you're braving a bar crawl in Greenwich Village, heavily trodden **Peculier Pub** (Map 6) and **Blind Tiger Ale House** (Map 5) offer large and diverse selections, and **Vol de Nuit** (Map 5) has a huge list of Belgian beers. Going several steps further with the Trappist schtick, the East Village's **Burp Castle** (Map 6) has a fine array of Belgians, but use your inside voice or you'll be soundly shushed. Nearby **Jimmy's 43** (Map 6) and **d.b.a.** (Map 7) are our neighborhood favorites where beer is concerned, and over in Alphabet City, **Zum Schneider** (Map 7) offers a slew of unique choice to wash down its German fare. In the Lower East Side, **Spitzer's Corner** (Map 4) is worth checking out early on a week night (good luck on a weekend). Beer shop **Good Beer** (Map 7) is a great place to order a flight of four beers or a growler to go, **Top Hops** (Map 4) offers a great selection of bottles and drafts, as well as a standing bar area, and **Randolph Beer** (Map 3) shines with—surprise, surprise—a great brew list. In Midtown your best bets are **Rattle n' Hum** (Map 9) or **Ginger Man** (Map 9), which has an absolutely amazing selection with over 100 bottles and 60 taps. Chelsea has **Pony Bar** (Map 11) and **Valhalla** (Map 11) to get your hops fix. Our Uptown favorite is **Earl's Beer & Cheese** (Map 17), which has a small space but excellent beer list.

If you're seeking good beer in Brooklyn, make Wiliamsburg your first stop. In fact, just head to cozy, Belgian-focused **Spuyten Duyvil** (Map 29), which has over 100 bottles and a rotating cask ale. From there, **Barcade** (Map 29) achieves an awesome synergy between its classic '80s arcade games and stellar beer list—our only complaint is that we can't drink and play Dig Dug at the same time. If you're a real beer nerd, you must go sipping at **Torst** (Map 28), a sleek Danish-inspired taproom with incredible beers on draft. In Carroll Gardens, **Bar Great Harry** (Map 32) is not only a great hangout, but it also has tons of fine beers to sample.

OUTDOOR SPACES

Outdoor space is a precious commodity in NYC, so couple it with booze and you've got the perfect destination for cooped-up city dwellers when the weather turns warm. Actually, you can find New Yorkers stubbornly holding court at outdoor venues in all sorts of weather short of electrical storms and sub-freezing temperatures, and they'll only retreat from those conditions when chased indoors by the staff. Although entry to many of the finest outdoor drinking dens requires supermodel looks or celebrity status, or at the very least a staggering tolerance for douchebags, there are plenty of options for the mere mortals among us. For example, the **Vu Bar** (Map 9) at the top of La Quinta Inn in Koreatown is a low-key establishment that'll let you in no matter what you wear or who you hang out with. For a little fancier but still accessible night out in the open air, try **Bookmarks** (Map 12), the rooftop bar in the Library Hotel. For drinks with a view, check out **Berry Park** (Map 29) in Williamsburg, which looks out across the river toward Manhattan, or if you're hip enough to get in, glide up to **The Ides at Wythe Hotel** (Map 29) for a perfect Instagram skyline moment.

Our favorite places to enjoy a drink outside are in the many back patios that turn the darkest, funkiest watering holes into bona fide oases, no matter how small and concrete-laden they may be. Beer lovers congregate in the backyards at **d.b.a.** (Map 7) in the East Village and **Spuyten Duyvil** (Map 29) in Williamsburg, and the aptly named **Gowanus Yacht Club** (Map 32) remains our Carroll Gardens favorite. More outdoor drinking can be had at **Sweet & Vicious** (Map 6) for frozen margaritas in the Lower East Side, **The Park** (Map 8) in Chelsea, **The Heights Bar & Grill** (Map 18) in Morningside Heights, **The Gate** (Map 33) in Park Slope, and **Union Pool** (Map 29) in Williamsburg. In Long Island City, there's an excellent beer garden called **Studio Square** (Map 27). Speaking of beer gardens, there's a seeming resurgence of these all -but-disappeared drinking venues, once popular with the central European immigrant set. Predictably packed results can be found at **La Birreria** (Map 9) or **Spritzenhaus** (Map 29). But if you can only visit one, make it the 100-year-old **Bohemian Hall & Beer Garden** (Map 26) in Astoria. Snag a picnic table in the massive outdoor area with a gang of friends, and knock back frosty pitchers of pilsner just like they did in the old days (polka dancing optional).

BEST JUKEBOX

Personal taste factors heavily in this category of course, but here is a condensed list of NFT picks. For Manhattan: **Ace Bar** (Map 7) (indie rock/punk), **Hi-Fi** (Map 7) (a huge and diverse selection), **7B (Horseshoe Bar)** (Map 7) (rock all the way), **WCOU Radio (Tile Bar)** (Map 7) (eclectic), **The Magician** (Map 4) (eclectic), **Rudy's Bar & Grill** (Map 11) (blues), **Welcome to the Johnsons** (Map 4) (indie rock/punk). For Brooklyn: **Boat Bar** (Map 32) (Carroll Gardens–indie rock), the **Brooklyn Social Club** (Map 32) (Carroll Gardens–country/soul) and **The Levee** (Map 29) (Williamsburg–good all around).

DJS AND DANCING

New York's old cabaret laws make it tough to find free dance spots, but they do exist (albeit often with the velvet rope scenario that may deter the impatient). On the weekends, entry into the swankier clubs doesn't come without paying your dues in long lines and pricey cover charges. That's not our style. You'll find us dancing and hanging out at **Santos Party House** (Map 3) as well as **Le Poisson Rouge** (Map 6). In and around Williamsburg, we suggest checking out the lively dance scenes at **Bembe** (Map 29) or **Glasslands** (Map 29). Or combine shaking your best move with a few frames at **Brooklyn Bowl** (Map 29) that has frequent late-night DJ sets by the likes of Questlove.

FANCY COCKTAILS

In recent years mixology has practically become a religion in New York, and its temples of worship are conveniently clustered in the East Village. For starters, head to **Death & Company** (Map 7), tell the knowledgeable servers what you like in a drink, and prepare to be converted. If wait lists aren't your thing (and there often is one) **The Summit Bar** (Map 7), **Elsa** (Map 7), **Louis 649** (Map 7), and bitters-focus **Amor y Amargo** (Map 7) are all solid options nearby. **Mayahuel** (Map 6), located among 6th Street's Indian restaurants is practically a crash course in all things tequila and mezcal. If hardly-secret speakeasies are your thing, **PDT** (Map 7) is accessible through a telephone booth in deep-fried-dog haven Crif Dogs (reservations recommended). In the West Village, **Employees Only** (Map 5) is located behind psychic's shop. And speaking of the West Village, be sure to check out **Little Branch** (Map 5) for live jazz and some of the strongest mixed drinks we've ever had the pleasure of meeting. **The Dead Rabbit** (Map 1) has brought a mixologist den to Wall Street in a historic building from the 1800's. Farther uptown, **Rye House** (Map 9) is our preferred after-work headquarters. In Midtown, the classy **The Campbell Apartment** (Map 13), tucked inside Grand Central Terminal, is a must – especially if someone else is paying. **The Penrose** (Map 15) adds a touch of cocktail class to the Upper East Side. And for the blazer/cocktail dress set, there are your opulent hotel bars, such as **Rose Bar** (Map 10) inside the Gramercy Park Hotel, **King Cole Bar** (Map 12) inside the St. Regis Hotel, or **Bemelmans Bar** (Map 15) inside the Caryle Hotel. We're banking on our beverages to ease the pain of that tab.

Considering all the options in Manhattan, it's probably no surprise that Brooklyn has many bars offering just-as-high caliber cocktails, minus some of the crowds. Don't believe us? Head to **Dram** (Map 29), **Hotel Delmano** (Map 29), **Maison Premiere** (Map 29) or **Huckleberry Bar** (Map 29) in Williamsburg, or venture a little further east to **Ba'sik** (Map 29) or **The Richardson** (Map 29). **Clover Club** (Map 32) is our favorite for mixed drinks in Cobble Hill, while **Hanson Dry** (Map 31) keeps Fort Greene residents buzzing with stellar drinks.

If you find yourself in Long Island City, Queens be sure to check out **Dutch Kills** (Map 27) and marvel at that custom-crafted ice that won't water down your drink no matter how slowly you savor it.

WINE BARS

With a name like **Terroir** (Map 3) has some funky wines and a friendly atmosphere despite the self-described "elitist wine bar" label. If it's date night, cozy up in the West Village at **Vin Sur Vingt** (Map 5) for a glass of Bordeaux. Go rustic -chic in at **Black Mountain Wine House** (Map 32) with a working fireplace and country lodge experience. In Brooklyn of course.

MUSIC–OVERVIEW

New York caters to a wide array of tastes in everything, and music is no exception. From the indie rock venues of Brooklyn to the history-steeped jazz clubs in Greenwich Village to amateur night at the Apollo, your musical thirst can be quenched in every possible way.

JAZZ, FOLK AND COUNTRY

There are plenty of places to see jazz in the city, starting off with classic joints such as the *Village Vanguard* (Map 5) and *Birdland* (Map 11). There's also the "Jazz at Lincoln Center" complex in the Time Warner Center on Columbus Circle which has three rooms: the 1,000-plus-seat, designed-for-jazz Rose Theater, the Allen Room, an amphitheater with a great view of the park, and the nightclub-esque Dizzy's Club Coca Cola. For a smaller (and cheaper) jazz experience, try *Jazz Gallery* (Map 9) or *Arthur's Tavern* (Map 5) which always has a no cover charge policy. *The Nuyorican Poets Café* (Map 7) has frequent jazz performances. In Brooklyn, one of your best bets is the small back room at Park Slope's *Barbes* (Map 33). Easily one of the best weekly jazz experiences is the Mingus Big Band's residency at *The Jazz Standard* (Map 10). If you've never done it, do it–it's a truly great and unpredictable band that even surly Mr. Mingus (might) have been proud of. For folk & country, try Rodeo Bar (Map 10), *Hank's Saloon* (Map 33), *Parkside Lounge* (Map 7) or *Jalopy* (Map 32).

ROCK AND POP

In case you've just moved back to NYC from, say, ten years in Mumbai, the rock scene is now firmly entrenched in Brooklyn. However, Manhattan's *Bowery Ballroom* (Map 6) remains the top live venue, with excellent sound and a good layout. Other notable spots this side of the East River include *Santos Party House* (Map 3), *Webster Hall* (Map 6), and the *Highline Ballroom* (Map 8). *Irving Plaza* (Map 10), *Terminal 5* (Map 11), and *Hammerstein Ballroom* (Map 8) aren't our favorites, but are worthwhile for the occasional top-notch acts. The best remaining small club in Manhattan is *Mercury Lounge* (Map 7), which gets great bands right before they're ready to move up to Bowery Ballroom. As far as the rest of the Lower East Side, it helps if you like your clubs to be punky basements (*Cake Shop*, Map 4) or former bodegas (*Arlene's Grocery*, Map 4). *Fat Baby* (Map 4), and *Fontana's* (Map 3) all offer plenty of goings-on south of Houston Street as well.

When it comes to new talent, it's really the clubs in Brooklyn that shine. If you know your way around Bowery Ballroom, you'll feel right at home at Brooklyn's premiere venue, *Music Hall of Williamsburg* (Map 29). Then there's *Glasslands Gallery* (Map 29), *Trash Bar* (Map 29), *Cameo Gallery* (Map 29), *Pete's Candy Store* (Map 29), *Brooklyn Bowl* (Map 29)...basically, the rocking never stops in Map 29. Maybe we'll even forgive *The Knitting Factory* (Map 29) for leaving Manhattan to move here. In Greenpoint, check out the *Warsaw* (Map 28) in the Polish National Home. We also love the *The Bell House* (Map 33) in Gowanus, *Brooklyn Masonic Temple* (Map 31) in Fort Greene and *Union Hall* (Map 33) in Park Slope.

EXPERIMENTAL

A number of venues in New York provide a place for experimental music to get exposure. *Experimental Intermedia* (Map 3) is fully dedicated to showcasing the avant-garde. John Zorn's performance space, *The Stone* (Map 7), takes an experimental approach in the venue's concept as well as its music, with a different artist acting as curator for an entire month and artists taking in 100% of the proceeds. *The Kitchen* (Map 8) features experimental music in addition to film, dance, and other art forms. *Le Poisson Rouge* (Map 6) has brought an exciting mix of different sounds back to the heart of Greenwich Village, and is one of our favorite spots. In Brooklyn, the experimental scene is cranking away, especially at *Issue Project Room's* (Map 30) space in Downtown Brooklyn, *Glasslands Gallery* (Map 29) in Williamsburg, and *Jalopy* (Map 32) in Carroll Gardens.

EVERYTHING ELSE

A few places run the gamut of musical genres; folksy artists one night, hot Latin tango the next, and a slew of comedy, spoken word, and other acts. *Joe's Pub* (Map 6) presents an excellent variety of popular styles and often hosts celebrated international musicians. Keep an eye on *BAMCafé* (Map 31) for a variety of great performers. For cabaret or piano bar, try *Don't Tell Mama* (Map 11), *Duplex* (Map 5), or *Brandy's* (Map 15). For a more plush experience, try the *Café Carlyle* (Map 15). But for top cabaret talent at affordable prices, go directly to *The Metropolitan Room* (Map 9). If you're seeking some R&B or soul, check out the *Apollo Theater* (Map 19), though they mostly get "oldies" acts. The Apollo's Amateur Night on Wednesday is your chance to see some up-and-comers. The *Pyramid Club* (Map 7) has open mic MC'ing nights. *Barbes* (Map 33) in Park Slope hosts a wide palette of "world music" (for lack of a better term), including Latin American, European, and traditional US styles, plus more experimental fare. For more sounds of the south, *SOB's* (Map 5) has live South American music and dancing and should definitely be experienced at least once. *Nublu* (Map 7) is always reliable for a fun and sweaty night, especially on Wednesdays when they feature Brazilian bands and DJs. For African music, check out *Barbes* (Map 33) on Wednesday nights with the Mandingo Ambassadors. And oh yeah–then there's all that classical music stuff, at places like *Carnegie Hall* (Map 12) and *Lincoln Center* (Map 14)–maybe you've heard of them?

RESTAURANTS

Sure, eating out in New York can be a competitive sport, sometimes a contact sport. However, once you're equipped with enough information about New York's 25,000 restaurant choices, the rewards are limitless, and we can confirm that this is one of the best damn towns on Earth to eat in. Certainly you could take advantage of the city's gourmet grocery stores and make fabulous meals at home, but compare your Citarella grocery bill to the check at Westville and you'll be eating out more often. But not to worry, we can always help you find the perfect place. Whether you're looking for a restaurant with a rare 28 from Zagat, or you refuse to let that D health rating get between you and good food (re: Kosher delis and Chinatown basements), you'll never have to settle.

EATING OLD

Since New York City is a perpetual culinary hotspot featuring tons of celebrity chefs (and Top Chef contestants who packed their knives and went), it's easy to get wrapped up in trendy food that looks more like a Rorschach test than dinner. Some experimental restaurants are remarkably on the cutting edge, but when you're not in the mood for aerated olive-chocolate foie gras (Wylie Dufresne, we're looking at you), you can rely on the Big Apple's longstanding heavyweights. They've relaxed the tie and jacket rule, but you can still rub elbows with the who's who at the posh *21 Club* (circa 1929, Map 12); dine on New American cuisine at the 200-plus-year-old *Bridge Café*, the oldest business in the city, older than Chase Manhattan (circa 1794, Map 1); slurp fresh-shucked oysters and enjoy amazing desserts under the vaulted, tiled ceiling at Grand Central Station's *Oyster Bar* (circa 1913, Map 13); sample more oysters and one of the best burgers in existence at the venerable Midtown watering hole *P.J. Clarke's* (circa 1884, Map 13); order the sturgeon scrambled with eggs, onions, and a bialy on the side at *Barney Greengrass* (circa 1908, Map 16); feast like old-world royalty at *The Russian Tea Room* (circa 1927, Map 12); or expand your culinary horizons with calf's spleen and cheese on a roll at *Ferdinando's Focacceria* (circa 1904, Map 32).

EATING CHEAP

New York has always had options for us broke folks, and the economic collapse (still hanging on, isn't it?) didn't hurt those options either. At **Shake Shack** (Map 9, 11, 14, 17, Battery Park City), you can still grab a Shack Burger for under $5 or a Shack Stack (twice the goods) for under $10. Ethnic food has always been a great friend to eaters on a budget. For the city's most succulent soup dumplings, head to **Shanghai Café** (Map 3). For brilliant Middle Eastern go to **Hummus Place** (Map 7), **Gazala Place** (Map 11), or **Taïm** (Map 5) for some of the best falafel on the planet. For Mexican check out the taquería at The Corner a.k.a. **La Esquina** (Map 6) or head out to Bushwick's factory-restaurant **Tortillería Los Hermanos**. The Indian lunch buffet at **Tiffin Wallah** (Map 10) is less than ten bucks and veggie friendly to boot. **Papaya King** (Map 17) has kept hot dog lovers grinning since 1932. For a gigantic plate of Puerto Rican food under ten dollars, sit at the counter of **La Taza De Oro** (Map 8). For a cheap breakfast that even celebs appreciate, **La Bonbonniere** (Map 5) can't be beat. And many of us can't survive a day without the staples of NYC Jewish eats: bagels and knishes. For bagels, go with perennial winner **Ess-a-Bagel** (Map 10, 13) or try our favorites: **Kossar's Bialys** (Map 4), **Absolute Bagels** (Map 16), or the original **Tal Bagels** (Map 13, 16, 17). For knishes, nothing beats the **Yonah Schimmel Knish Bakery** (Map 6). Since the NFT office began in Chinatown and we're always broke (free advice: don't go into publishing), we are certified experts on eating cheap in this part of town. At **Nice Green Bo** (Map 3) get the scallion pancakes, at **Food Shing/Food Sing 88** (Map 3) get the beef noodle soup, at **Fuleen** (Map 3) get the shrimp with chili sauce, and for Malaysian order the stingray (!) at **Sanur** (Map 3).

EATING HIP

Eating hip usually involves the food of the moment (kale chips and artisanal popsicles), beautiful people (who couldn't possibly eat another bite of that amuse-bouche), and some kind of exclusivity (unpublished phone numbers and hidden entrances). Although, with this little hiccup in our economic stability, even the hippest places have had to let the dirty, burger-eating plebeians through their doors. That being said, the ultimate in cool dining is, of course, **Rao's** (Map 20)—or so we hear. But unless you're the Mayor, the Governor, or Woody Allen, you probably won't be getting a reservation anytime soon. If you can find the unmarked basement door of **Bobo** (Map 5), you'll really impress your date. Head east to try the always crowded, no-reservations eatery **Freemans** (Map 6), which hides itself at the end of an alleyway; do not miss the pork chops. For fans of Japanese izakayas, nothing is quite as fun as an evening at **En Brasserie** (Map 5). Its gourmet menu brilliantly fuses homemade miso with duck, cod, tofu, and anything else you can think of. And the low lighting will make anyone look good. **Zenkichi** (Map 29) also has killer Japanese, and yes, it's behind a camouflaged front door, but both the food an ambiance are stellar, and it's a great date spot. David Chang's restaurant mini-empire is still on people's radars, so try **Momofuku Ko** (Map 6). If the lines are too long at the Momofukus or you don't have friends that can afford to score a table at **The Spotted Pig** (Map 5), try **Kuma Inn** (Map 4) on the Lower East Side. The small plates like Chinese sausage with Thai chili-lime sauce and pork wasabi dumplings are brilliant, it's BYO sake, and there's no secret phone number. If you don't mind waiting and your date isn't a vegetarian, grab a cocktail in the lobby of the slick Ace Hotel and get ready for a dinner you won't soon forget at **The Breslin** (Map 9).

EATING LATE

Some say New York never sleeps, and some (ahem, Madrid) insist that it does, but like any big city it depends on the neighborhood, so let us help you locate some options. *Kang Suh's* (Map 9) Korean barbecue runs all night, as well as the Turkish kebab spot *Bereket* (Map 4), and a host of classic diners like *Odessa* (Map 7) and *Waverly Restaurant* (Map 5). *Veselka* (Map 6) is the place for late-night Ukrainian soul food. You'll find cabbies chowing down past 3 am at *Lahore Deli* (Map 6), *Big Arc Chicken* (Map 7), or *99 Cents Fresh Pizza* (Map 11, 13). *French Roast* (Map 5, 14) serves good croque-monsieurs 24 hours, and that dessert you declined earlier in the evening. If you're near Chinatown at 3 a.m, let the wonton soup and barbecue duck at *Great NY Noodletown* (Map 3) soak up all that beer. And, of course, *Blue Ribbon* (Map 6) is still one of the best places to eat after midnight.

EATING PIZZA

We don't care what Chicago says; we do pizza best! The coal oven spots top most lists: *Grimaldi's* (Map 30), *Lombardi's* (Map 6), *Luzzo's* (Map 7), *John's Pizzeria* (Map 5), and the original *Patsy's* (Map 20) in East Harlem. The coal oven enjoys extra cachet because it's illegal now, except in the aforementioned eateries where they were already in operation. However, the regular brick oven joints, such as *Franny's* (Map 33), *Keste* (Map 5), Co (Map 8) and *Lucali* (Map 32) are no slouches. For an upscale pie, try the exquisite creations at Mario Batali's *Otto* (Map 6). Trying to find something edible near Wall Street? Check out *Adrienne's* (Map 1) delicious rectangle pies on Stone Street, or walk up to TriBeCa for a luscious Brussels-sprout-bacon-caramelized-onion pie at *Saluggi's* (Map 2). For a classic Village scene complete with live jazz, check out *Arturo's* (Map 6) on Houston Street. The outer boroughs seriously represent here: Louie & Ernie's in The Bronx, *Tufino* in Queens (Map 26), Denino's on Staten Island, and, of course, Roberta's and Di Fara in Brooklyn. Pizza by the slice practically deserves its own category, but the highlights include *Patsy's* (Map 20, definitely the best slice in the city), *Artichoke Basille's Pizza* (Map 6, get the grandma slice), *Farinella* (Map 15, very unique), and *Joe's* (Map 5, classic NY Style).

EATING ETHNIC

Spin a globe, blindly stick your finger onto a spot, and chances are you can find that cuisine on offer in New York. And an outstanding offering it will be. To wit:

ARGENTINE:
Buenos Aires (Map 7)

AUSTRIAN:
Edi & The Wolf (Map 7)

AUSTRALIAN:
Tuck Shop (Map 6) and The Thirsty Koala (Map 26)

CHINESE:
Joe's Shanghai (Map 3), Old Sichuan (Map 3) and Szechuan Gourmet (Map 9)

CUBAN:
Café Habana (Map 6)

DOMINICAN:
El Malecon (Map 16) and El Castillo de Jagua (Map 4)

EGYPTIAN:
Kabab Café (Map 26)

ETHIOPIAN:
Ghenet (Map 33) and Zoma (Map 19)

GERMAN:
Heidelberg (Map 15), Zum Schneider (Map 7) and Hallo Berlin (Map 11)

GREEK:
Kefi (Map 14), Periyali (Map 9) and Pylos (Map 7)

INDIAN:
Dawat (Map 13), Banjara (Map 7) and Indian Tandoor Oven (Map 15)

ITALIAN:
Babbo (Map 6), Felidia (Map 13), Il Giglio (Map 2), Sfoglia (Map 17), Al Di La (Map 33), I Trulli (Map 10) and countless others

JAPANESE:
Nobu (Map 2), Takahachi (Map 7), Ki Sushi (Map 32) and about 40 others

JEWISH:
Sammy's Roumanian (Map 6) and B&H Dairy (Map 6)

KOREAN:
Kang Suh (Map 9), Seoul Garden (Map 9) and Dok Suni (Map 7)

MALAYSIAN:
New Malaysia (Map 3)

MEXICAN:
Alma (Map 32) and Mexico 2000 (Map 29)

NEW ZEALAND:
Nelson Blue (Map 1)

PAKISTANI:
Pakistan Tea House (Map 2) and Haandi (Map 10)

POLISH:
Christina's (Map 28) and Lomzynianka (Map 28)

RUSSIAN:
The Russian Vodka Room (Map 12) and Russian Samovar (Map 12)

SCANDINAVIAN:
Aquavit (Map 13) and Smörgås Chef (Map 1)

SOUTH AFRICAN:
Madiba (Map 31)

SOUTHERN AMERICAN:
Sylvia's (Map 19) and Cheryl's Global Soul (Map 33)

SPANISH:
Socarrat (Map 9) and Tia Pol (Map 8)

SRI LANKAN:
Sigiri (Map 7)

THAI:
Pongsri Thai (Map 3) and Sripraphai (Queens)

TURKISH:
Turkish Kitchen (Map 10)

EATING MEAT

New York is home to arguably the world's best steakhouse, **Peter Luger** (Map 29), but it's competitive at the top, and clawing at Luger's heels are: **Mark Joseph Steakhouse** (Map 1) and classics like **Sparks** (Map 13), **Palm** (Map 13), **Smith & Wollensky** (Map 13) and the **Strip House** (Map 6). For the Brazilian-style "all you can eat meat fest," **Churrascaria Plataforma** (Map 11) does the trick. As for hamburgers, the rankings provide material for eternal debate: **Corner Bistro** (Map 5, 26), **Burger Joint** at Le Parker Meridien (Map 12), **J.G. Melon** (Map 15) and **Bonnie's Grill** (Map 33), to name a few. **Royale** (Map 7) compliments the perfect patty with stellar fixins for a song, and **Korzo Haus** (Map 7) serves a succulent ground beef patty wrapped in Hungarian fried bread, topped with Central European goodies. Texans and Missourians alike can agree that New York has some damn good BBQ, even if we sometimes recruit our BBQ talent from down South: **Daisy May's** (Map 11), **Hill Country** (Map 9), **Dinosaur Bar-B-Que** (Map 18) and **Blue Smoke** (Map 10, Battery Park City) in Manhattan, and **Fette Sau** (Map 29) and **The Smoke Joint** (Map 31) in Brooklyn.

EATING VEGGIE

You could live your whole life here, never eat a shred of meat, and feast like a king every day (and probably live longer). Try the quality Indian fare at **Pongal** (Map 10), and, for high-end eats, **Franchia** (Map 10), **Candle 79** (Map 15), **Dirt Candy** (Map 7), and **GoBo** (Map 5). For those on a budget, try **Atlas Café** (Map 7) for a quick bite and **Angelica Kitchen** (Map 6) for something a step up. For a delicious macrobiotic meal including dessert, **Souen** (Map 5, 6) has yet to disappoint. For adventurous veggie heads, nothing beats **HanGawi** (Map 9), consistently voted one of the best vegetarian and Korean restaurants in the city.

OUR FAVORITE RESTAURANTS

Consensus on this subject is always difficult, but with a group of New Yorkers opinionated enough to produce the NFT, we have to at least try and duke it out. We've historically granted the accolade to **Blue Ribbon** (Map 6): it's open 'til 4 a.m., it's where the chefs of other restaurants go, it's got fondue, beef marrow, fried chicken, great liquor, a great vibe and great service. And it will always have that special place in our hearts and stomachs, but we also have to give a shout out to a few others: **Alma** (Map 32), an out-of-the-way rooftop Mexican restaurant with stunning views and equally good tamales, mole, margaritas, and ambiance, **Sigiri** (Map 7), a spicy Sri Lankan gem that's BYOB to boot; **Babbo** (Map 6), because it's Babbo (call at least one month ahead); **Arturo's** (Map 6), a classic, old-school pizza joint with live jazz, Greenwich Village locals and amazing coal -fired pizza and **Kuma Inn** (Map 4), a hard-to-find Asian tapas restaurant that's cool and hip but also affordable, laid-back and mind-blowingly delicious.

For a price, you can buy anything here: a live octopus, a bag of Icelandic moss, a vintage accordion, a rolling ladder, a slap bracelet, a 3D printer, a Ferrari, a dozen cronut holes, that thing you jam into an orange to suck the juice out, anything you want. Even print books! While we occasionally lament the presence of chain stores, we'll challenge anyone to find a better city for shopping.

CLOTHING & ACCESSORIES

The Upper East Side is a classic destination for high fashion. Madison Avenue is the main artery in the 50s, 60s, and 70s, rounded out by Fifth Avenue and 57th Street. In this neighborhood you'll find **Chanel** (Map 12), **Burberry** (Map 12), **Tiffany & Co** (Map 12), and other names of that ilk. For department stores, start with the original **Bloomingdale's** (Map 15), which is close to these titans: **Saks Fifth Avenue** (Map 12), **Henri Bendel** (Map 12), **Barneys** (Map 15), and **Bergdorf Goodman** (Map 12) if money's no object. We assume it is an object, so check out their intricate window displays for free; they're especially good around the holidays.

That being said, there are some bargains on the Upper East Side, too. **Bis Designer Resale** (Map 15) sells gently worn items from the likes of Hermes and Gucci at a fraction of the original price. **Housing Works Thrift Shop** (Map 15) typically has a great selection, and proceeds serve those affected by AIDS and homelessness. If you can deal with the crush of midtown tourists, look for sales at **Macy's** (Map 9), or try **Century 21** (Map 1, 14).

These days, "vintage clothing" can mean "cute throwback" or "real period costume." The cute throwback t-shirts are at **Yellow Rat Bastard** (Map 6), but serious applicants should investigate **What Goes Around Comes Around** (Map 2). Our favorites overall: **Tokio 7** (Map 6) in the East Village, **INA** (Map 6) in NoHo, **Edith Machinist** (Map 4) on the Lower East Side, **Monk Vintage** (Map 29) in Williamsburg, and for the especially fashion-forward, **Eva Gentry Consignment** (Map 32) in Boerum Hill. Devotees should attend the next Manhattan Vintage Clothing Show, where over 90 dealers sell their finery from the last century.

SoHo looks more and more like an outdoor mall, but it's still a great place to shop because of the variety and uber-high concentration. Beyond **Uniqlo** (Map 6) and **H&M** (Map 6), there are countless huge names like **Marc Jacobs** (Map 6), **Balenciaga** (Map 6), and **Anna Sui** (Map 6).

The West Village (and the Meatpacking District therein) is the spot for small, high-end boutiques. Some are a little more accessible like **Castor & Pollux** (Map 5), and then others have $2,000 jeans. You can check out chic designs at **Stella McCartney** (Map 5), **Alexander McQueen** (Map 5), and department store **Jeffrey** (Map 5), lampooned for its snobbery on *Saturday Night Live* (back when SNL kicked ass).

FLEA MARKETS & BAZAARS

For a classic, grungy, sprawling flea market, try **The Annex Markets** (Map 11) on 39th Street between Ninth and Tenth Avenues or **GreenFlea Market** (Map 14) on Columbus between 76th and 77th Streets. The more fashionable **Brooklyn Flea** (Map 31) dominates Fort Greene, Williamsburg, and Park Slope on the weekends with hundreds of hip vendors offering all things handcrafted: wood furniture, picture frames, sock monkeys, gold leaf necklaces, those rings made out of typewriter keys, you get the idea. **Artists & Fleas** (Map 8, 29) has a similar artsy feel in Williamsburg and inside Chelsea Market. **The Brooklyn Night Bazaar** (Map 28) in Greenpoint takes that model and adds food carts, booze, and live music, open Friday and Saturday nights until 1 a.m. **The Market NYC** (Map 6) on Bleecker Street between Thompson and Sullivan in Nolita features a refreshing group of young, local designers and their clothes, jewelry, collectibles, and other artwork.

FURNITURE

Done with IKEA and curb shopping on trash night? Get your credit card(s) ready for the stuff you can't afford at **West Elm** (Map 30), **Room & Board** (Map 6), and **BoConcept** (Map 6). Have even more money to spend? Check out **ligne Roset** (Map 10) and the Meatpacking District's brilliant **Vitra** (Map 5). If vintage is your thing, head straight to Williamsburg's **Two Jakes** (Map 29) or check out a smaller shop like Fort Greene's **Yu Interiors** (Map 31). Regular folks seeking solid pieces should look no further than the quality wood furniture at **Gothic Cabinet Craft** (Map 28) or **Scott Jordan Furniture** (Map 5).

SPORTS & OUTDOORS

Paragon Sporting Goods (Map 9) by Union Square isn't cheap, but it's a landmark and it's been there since 1908. **City Sports** (Map 1, 12) and **Modell's** (Map 1, 3, 6, 9) offer a broad range of affordable sports clothing, shoes, and athletic equipment. For cold weather and mountain gear, head to **Tent & Trails** (Map 2), where you can also rent sleeping bags, tents, and packs.

HOUSEWARES & HOME DESIGN

You'll lose hours of your life eyeing the exotic furnishings in **ABC Carpet & Home** (Map 9) just off Union Square. For those with shallower pockets, there's **Gracious Home** (Map 8, 14, 15) and any of **Muji's** four Manhattan locations (Map 3, 8, 9, 12). For paint, window dressings, and other home improvement supplies, try **Janovic** (Map 11, 16) or Crest Hardware in Williamsburg. Prepare for sensory overload if you take on the 35 showrooms at the **A&D Building** (Map 13). Showrooms are open to the public, unlike at some smaller design shops nearby, which require business cards upon entry.

The adorable dinnerware at **Fishs Eddy** (Map 9) is a great alternative to mega-chains like Pottery Barn. **Zabar's** (Map 14) often-ignored second floor is a longtime favorite among the city's cooks. In Brooklyn, we love browsing for new toys and tools at **The Brooklyn Kitchen** (Map 29) and **A Cook's Companion** (Map 32). Downtown, small but sublime **Global Table** (Map 6) has excellent, reasonably priced housewares, and **Lancelotti** (Map 7) is stuffed with colorful accessories. The Asian kitchen wares at Pearl River are unparalleled for cuteness and affordability.

FOOD

Three revered emporiums make the Upper West Side a culinary heaven: **Fairway** (Map 14, 15, 18, 32), **Citarella** (Map 5, 14, 15), and **Zabar's** (Map 14)—and then the Zabar's offshoot **Eli's Vinegar Factory** (Map 17) graces the Upper East Side. The much more affordable **Trader Joe's** (Map 6, 9, 32) is steadily multiplying, but the lines, the lines. **Essex Street Market** (Map 4) on the Lower East Side is a beloved institution filled with amazing meat, fish, produce, and cheese. **Grand Central Market** (Map 13) is equally good, located right in the eponymous station. **Chelsea Market** (Map 8), housed in a National Biscuit Company factory complex, has excellent restaurants, bakeries, and food vendors (spoiler: it's not really a market).

For farm-to-table, the biggest player is the **Union Square Greenmarket** (Map 9), which operates year-round on Mondays, Wednesdays, Fridays, and Saturdays, packed with talented chefs. **The Grand Army Plaza Greenmarket** (Map 33) in Brooklyn is also excellent and less claustrophobic than Union Square.

And now, imported foods. When it comes to Italian, Arthur Avenue in the Bronx is famed for its bakeries, butchers, and grocers, and don't forget Graham Avenue in East Williamsburg. The more centrally located **Di Palo Fine Foods** (Map 3) has regional Italian goodies and acclaimed fresh ricotta. Friendly **Despana** (Map 3) will satisfy all your Spanish desires, including $100-a-pound jamon iberico. **Sahadi's** (Map 32) has an impressive range of Middle Eastern specialties, and make time to visit their neighbors on Atlantic Avenue. For Indian and pan-Asian spices, teas, and groceries, try **Kalustyan's** (Map 10). **New York Mart** (Map 3) is a solid one-stop for Chinese goods, and not just dehydrated scallops! There's even a destination for anglophiles, **Myers of Keswick** (Map 5), and **Aussies, Tuck Shop** (Map 6).

Cheese mongers? Among the best are **Murray's** (Map 5) in the West Village, **Lamarca Cheese Shop** (Map 10) in Gramercy, small but powerful **Stinky** (Map 32) in Carroll Gardens, and **Bedford Cheese Shop** (Map 29) in Williamsburg. If you're low on cash, **East Village Cheese** (Map 6) is your go-to. They don't give out free samples and the line is always long, but it's one of the cheapest options in Manhattan by far. Then you'll need bread to go with your cheese, of course. Our favorites are **Sullivan Street Bakery** (Map 11), **Grandaisy Bakery** (Map 2, 14), and **Amy's Bread** (Map 8, 11). For prosciutto to accompany the bread and cheese, hit **Faicco's Pork Store** (Map 5), **Emily's Pork Store** (Map 29), **G Esposito & Sons** (Map 32), or **Choice Greene** (Map 31).

Coffee is absolutely everywhere, so maybe there's no point in trying to pick a favorite, but we do enjoy the beans at **Porto Rico** (Map 4, 5, 6), or **Colombe** (Map 2, 6) for an excellent step up. Tea drinkers (yes, there are many in this coffee-fueled town!) should consult the knowledgeable staff at **McNulty** (Map 5), or connoisseurs can head to the exquisite **Bellocq** (Map 28). For something harder, **Astor Wines & Spirits** (Map 6) is always reliable and affordable, but **BQE Wine & Liquors** can be even cheaper (Map 29).

ART SUPPLIES

You can't put a bird on it 'til you stock up on paint! Check out **Blick Art Materials** (Map 6), convenient to both NYU and Cooper Union. You can find the best selection of paper at **New York Central Art Supply** (Map 6) on Third Avenue. **SoHo Art Materials** (Map 2) on Wooster Street is a small, traditional shop that sells super premium paints and brushes for fine artists. Don't forget to check out both **Sam Flax** (Map 13) and **A.I. Friedman** (Map 9) for graphic design supplies and portfolios. **Lee's Art Shop** (Map 12) is a fabulous resource; how it has survived midtown rents is anyone's guess. As for Williamsburg, **Artist & Craftsman** (Map 29) is a good bet for supplies.

BOOKS

These beloved shops and their adorable cats are disappearing faster than anything else in the city, but thank goodness **The Strand** (Map 6) is still here with 18 miles of new and used books, and those tantalizing $2 carts outside. Right down the street is the smaller **Alabaster Bookshop** (Map 6), then **Spoonbill & Sugartown** (Map 29) in Williamsburg is full of art and design books, and **Unnameable Books** (Map 33) in Prospect Heights is fun for browsing. **Idlewild** (Map 9, 29, 32) is mecca for travel guides and travel literature. The gift shop at the **Lower East Side Tenement Museum** (Map 4) is a great place to start digging into NYC history, as is **Freebird Books** (Map 32) above Red Hook.

MUSICAL INSTRUMENTS & ACCESSORIES

Unfortunately, 48th Street is no longer Music Row, but **Roberto's Winds** (Map 12) still chugs along over on 46th. Our favorites for gigging rock bands include **Matt Umanov Guitars** (Map 5) for guitars and amps, **Rogue Music** (Map 9) for keyboards, and **Ludlow Guitars** (Map 4) for guitars and basses. Go see the jumble of world instruments hanging from the ceiling at **Music Inn** (Map 6), which is among the last of a dying breed. Accordionists, and accordionists only, head to **Main Squeeze** (Map 4). Classical violinists and other civilized types should visit **Strings and Other Things** (Map 14).

MUSIC FOR LISTENING

CDs and cassettes are scarce these days, but vinyl is still supremely cool. We always love hip **Other Music** (Map 6) and avant-garde **Downtown Music** (Map 3). If you're into trolling through used bins, head to Bleecker Street's **Rebel Rebel** (Map 5) and **Bleecker Street Records** (Map 5). Or head to one of North Brooklyn's many options, like **Earwax** (Map 29), **Academy Annex** (Map 29), **Rough Trade** (Map 29), or **Permanent Records** (Map 28).

ELECTRONICS

If you can't remember what a regular 2D printer is (and why should you?), go straight to the 3D photo booth at the **MakerBot Store** (Map 7). **B&H** (Map 8) is the top destination for professionals and amateurs when it comes to photography, audio, and video, plus they have a decent selection of computers. Note that the hectic megastore is run by Orthodox Jews who strictly observe the Sabbath and holidays, so always check the hours online before heading over. For photographic equipment especially, remember the holy trinity of B&H, **Adorama** (Map 9), and **K&M Camera** (Map 3). B&H is the mothership, Adorama's great if you're nearby, and K&M is the only one open on Saturdays. Remember to flash that student ID if you've got it, as some art stores offer a discount. Audiophiles are wonderfully served by **Stereo Exchange** (Map 6) and the jaw-dropping **Sound by Singer** (Map 9). For all things Mac, try **Tekserve** (Map 9), the (other) Apple specialists.

WEIRD & BIZARRE

First on the list is **Brooklyn Superhero Supply** (Map 33), where your anti-gravity elixir and gold lame sidekick cape are waiting. **Evolution** (Map 6) is mandatory for those with a dark side; think macabre biological jewelry, preserved scorpions, and bat skeletons. Equally bewitching is **Enchantments** (Map 7), your incense-filled emporium for motherwort, frankincense tears, and all things wicca. Scribes and pen nerds, report to **City Hall's Fountain Pen Hospital** (Map 3). And then you'll need the ultimate accessory for your library, so call the **Putnam Rolling Ladder Company** (Map 6). Antique button collectors, check out the Upper East Side's **Tender Buttons** (Map 15). **Western Spirit** (Map 2) is the city's only wild west themed store, selling not just Texan kitsch, but Lucchese boots and turquoise bolo ties. If you need authentic NYC memorabilia, whether it's a lucky NYPD horseshoe or a real taxi cab medallion, go directly to the **New York City Store** (Map 3). Full disclosure, that medallion isn't actually usable–those can sell for over a million bucks.

SHOPPING DISTRICTS

In the age of internet shopping, these districts are fading out, so see them while you can. The Garment District (25th to 40th Streets, Fifth to Ninth Avenues) has fabrics, buttons, zippers, ribbons, sequins, and doo-dads of all sorts. The Diamond District (47th Street between Fifth and Sixth Avenues) is the world's largest market for the precious stone. The Flower District (28th Street between 6th and 7th Avenues) is right above the Perfume District (Broadway in the 20s and 30s). Bowery below Houston is chock full of restaurant supply stores, and Bowery below Delancey is the Lighting District.

ART GALLERIES

OVERVIEW

If you want to see cutting-edge art, go to New York City's galleries. There are more than 500 galleries in the city, with artwork created in every conceivable medium (and of varying quality) on display. SoHo, Chelsea, DUMBO, and Williamsburg are the hot spots for gallery goers, but there are also many famous (and often more traditional) galleries and auction houses uptown, including **Christie's** (Map 12) and **Sotheby's** (Map 15). With so much to choose from, there's almost always something that's at least provocative, if not actually good.

The scene at the upscale galleries is sometimes intimidating, especially if you look like you are on a budget. If you aren't interested in buying, they aren't interested in you being there. Some bigger galleries require appointments. Cut your teeth at smaller galleries; they aren't as scary. Also, put your name on the mailing lists. You'll get invites to openings so crowded that no one will try to pressure you into buying (and there's free wine). The Armory Show (www.thearmoryshow.com), an annual show of new art, is also a great way to see what the galleries have to offer without intimidation.

SOHO AREA

It wasn't so long ago that there were hundreds of art galleries in SoHo. Now it has practically become an outdoor mall. However, there are still some permanent artworks in gallery spaces, such as Walter De Maria's excellent **The Broken Kilometer** (Map 6) (a Dia-sponsored space at 393 West Broadway), and his sublime **New York Earth Room** (Map 6). A short jaunt down to TriBeCa will land you in LaMonte Young's awesome aural experience Dream House at the **MELA Foundation** (Map 2). On the Lower East Side check out **Canada** (Map 3) for fun openings and **Envoy Gallery** (Map 6 for cutting edge photography and celebrity sightings.

CHELSEA

The commercialization of SoHo in the late 90s helped make Chelsea the center of the city's gallery scene. Our recommendation is to hit at least two streets–W 24th and W 22nd Streets, both between 10th and 11th Avenue. Also, check out the famous "artist's" bookstore **Printed Matter** (Map 8). Finally, poke your head into the **Starrett-Lehigh Building** (Map 8), not only for the art but also for the great pillars, windows, and converted freight elevators.

BROOKLYN

While the concentration of galleries in Brooklyn is nowhere near the same as in Chelsea, added together, there are well over a hundred in the borough now, with the three biggest areas being in DUMBO, Williamsburg, and Bushwick. Look for great events like Bushwick Open Studios and the DUMBO Arts Festival to get yourself oriented to Brooklyn's ever-growing art scene.

Multiplexes abound in NYC, though of course you should brace yourself for far steeper ticket and concession prices than in the rest of the country (with the possible exception of LA). Dinner and a movie turns out to be a rather exorbitant affair, but hey, we don't live in the Big Apple because it's cheap. And whether you're looking for the latest box office hit, or a classic from the French New Wave, there's a theater to meet your needs.

If you're after a first-run Hollywood blockbuster, we highly recommend the **AMC Loews Kips Bay** (Map 10) in Murray Hill. It has spacious theaters with large screens, big sound, comfortable seats, plenty of aisle room, and most importantly, fewer people! **The AMC Loews Village** (Map 6) is gargantuan, too, but movies there sell out hours or days in advance on the weekends. An IMAX theater and a cheesy '30s movie palace decorating theme make **AMC Loews Lincoln Square** (Map 14) a great place to catch a huge film, and its ideal location offers loads of after-movie options. Another great choice is the **Regal Battery Park 16** (Battery Park City), but it's starting to get just as crowded as the Union Square location.

For independent or foreign films, the **Landmark Sunshine** (Map 6) has surpassed the **Angelika** (Map 6) as the superior downtown movie house. Don't get us wrong–the Angelika still presents great movies, but the tiny screens and constant subway rumble can sometimes make you wish you'd waited for the DVD. **The IFC Center** (Map 5) always shows great indie flicks.

If you're looking for revivals, check the listings at the **Film Forum** (Map 5), **BAM Rose Cinemas** (Map 31), and the **MoMA** (Map 12). Regular attendance at those three venues can provide an excellent education in cinema history. For the truly adventurous, there's **Anthology Film Archives** (Map 6), which plays a repertory of forgotten classics, obscure international hits, and experimental American shorts. Finally, up in Harlem the tiny but terrific **Maysles Cinema** (Map 19) shows truly brilliant indie movies focusing on New York City. This may be the most unique movie going experience in Manhattan.

The most decadent and enjoyable movie experiences can be found at the theaters that feel the most "New York." Sadly, the Beekman Theatre immortalized in Woody Allen's Annie Hall was demolished in 2005 to make room for a new ward for Sloan-Kettering (it's hard to argue with a cancer hospital, but film buffs can't help but wish they'd found another space for their expansion). **Clearview's Ziegfeld** (Map 12) on 54th Street is a vestige from a time long past when movie theaters were real works of art. This space is so posh with its gilding and red velvet, you'll feel like you're crossing the Atlantic on an expensive ocean liner. **The Paris Theatre** (Map 12) on 58th Street is one of our favorites in the city–it has the best balcony, hands down!

BROOKLYN

Seeing a movie in Brooklyn a significantly better experience these days. Our favorite is the jewel -box twin **Heights Cinema** (Map 30). Also check out indie/blockbuster mashup **Cobble Hill Cinemas** (Map 32), **BAM Rose Cinemas** (Map 31), and food/drink **Nitehawk Cinemas** in Williamsburg (Map 29).

MUSEUMS

Make a resolution: Go to at least one museum in New York City every month. There are over 100 museums in the five boroughs, from the **Metropolitan Museum of Art** (Map 15) to the **Dyckman Farmhouse Museum** (Map 25), an 18th-century relic in upper Manhattan. Many of these museums have special programs and lectures that are open to the public, as well as children's events and summer festivals. When you've found your favorite museums, look into membership. Benefits include free admission, guest passes, party invites, and a discount at the gift shop.

The famous Museum Mile comprises nine world-class museums along Fifth Avenue between 82nd Street and 105th Street, including the **Met** (Map 15), and Frank Lloyd Wright's architectural masterpiece, the **Guggenheim** (Map 17). **El Museo del Barrio** (Map 17), devoted to early Latin American art, **The Museum of the City of New York** (Map 17), the **Cooper-Hewitt National Design Museum** (Map 17) (housed in the Andrew Carnegie's Mansion), and the **Jewish Museum** (Map 17) are also along the mile. A few blocks off the stretch is **The Whitney Museum of American Art** (Map 15), which showcases contemporary American artists and features the celebrated Biennial in even-numbered years.

See medieval European art at **The Cloisters** (Map 25) (also a famous picnic spot), exhibitions of up and coming African-American artists at the **Studio Museum in Harlem** (Map 19), and **PS1** (Map 27) for contemporary art. Take the kids to the Brooklyn Children's Museum or the **Children's Museum of Manhattan** (Map 14). **The Lower East Side Tenement Museum** (Map 4) and the **Ellis Island Immigration Museum** (Map 1) will take you back to your roots, and the treasures of the Orient are on display at the **Asia Society** (Map 15). Couch potatoes can meet their maker at the **The Paley Center for Media** (Map 12), which features a massive collection of tens of thousands of television and radio programs and advertisements for your viewing pleasure. **The Brooklyn Museum** (Map 33) supplements its wide-ranging permanent collection with edgy exhibitions, performances, and other special events.

Just about every museum in the city is worth a visit. Other favorites include the **New Museum of Contemporary Art** (Map 6) (in its spiffy building on The Bowery), the **New-York Historical Society** (Map 14) (which focuses its exhibits on the birth of the city), the **New York Transit Museum** (Map 30), the **Morgan Library** (Map 9) (with copies of Gutenberg's Bible on display), the **Museum of the Moving Image** (Map 26), **The Museum of Sex** (Map 9), and the **Queens Museum of Art** (check out the panorama of New York City). **The National September 11 Memorial Museum** (Map 1) aims to tell the definitive story of that day, relating the huge implications thereof, at the very spot it happened. Finally, the **Museum of Arts and Design** (Map 12), on the southern edge of Columbus Circle, is a bold redesign of Edward Durrell Stone's quirky masterpiece for Huntington Hartford; the excellent permanent collection and diverting exhibitions, plus working artists-in-residence and a small lovely museum store, make the museum a must-see.

BOOKSTORES

The New York City book scene has taken a sharp decline in terms of diversity in recent years, with many excellent bookshops all going the way of the dodo. The remaining independent stores are now the last outposts before everything interesting or alternative disappears altogether. And some of NYC's richest cultural neighborhoods—such as the East Village and the Lower East Side—don't have enough bookstores to even come close to properly serving their populations. So we thought we'd take this opportunity to list some of our favorite remaining shops...

GENERAL NEW/USED

The Strand (Map 6) on Broadway, the largest and arguably most popular independent bookstore in town, boasts staggering range and depth in its offerings (and often the best prices around to boot). Whether you're interested in art tomes, rare first editions, foreign language texts, non-fiction works, or the latest bestseller, it's impossible to be disappointed. In SoHo, **McNally Jackson** (Map 6) might just be our favorite bookstore after The Strand. **St. Mark's Bookshop** (Map 6) anchors the border between the NYU crowd and the East Village hipster contingent and features an excellent selection of literary journals. Argosy Book Store (Map 13) on 59th Street is still a top destination for antiquarian books. With four locations around the city, the punchy **Shakespeare & Company** (Maps 6, 10, 15) is a local chain that somehow manages to maintain an aura of independence. In the West Village, **Three Lives and Co.** (Map 5) should be your destination. The **Barnes & Noble** (Map 9) in Union Square is their signature store and has a great feel. **The Housing Works Used Book Cafe** (Map 6) has a vintage coffeehouse feel and

is one of our favorite bookstores—all of the profits go to help homeless New Yorkers living with HIV/AIDS.

SMALL/USED

Fortunately there are still a lot of used bookstores tucked away all over the city. **Mercer Street Books** (Map 6) serves NYU and **East Village Books** (Map 7) takes care of the East Village, while on the Upper East Side both **Corner Bookstore** (Map 17) and **Crawford Doyle** (Map 15) keep it old-school. In Brooklyn, check out **Unnameable Books** (Map 33) for hyper-local poetry.

TRAVEL

The city has some excellent travel book outlets, including the elegant **Complete Traveller Antiquarian Bookstore** (Map 9) and the wonderful **Idlewild Books** (Map 9, 29, 32), which curates its collection by country where guidebooks, fiction, and travel writing all happily commingle for a unique way of browsing. So if you can't afford to travel, a trip here is the next best thing.

ART

Printed Matter (Map 8) houses one of the best collections of artists' books in the world and is highly recommended. **The New Museum Store** (Map 6) also offers a brilliant selection of both artists' and art books. If you aren't on a budget and have a new coffee table to fill, try **Ursus** (Map 15). For handsome photography collections, check out **Dashwood Books** (Map 6) on super sleek Bond Street.

BOOKSTORES CONTINUED

NYC/GOVERNMENT

The City Store (Map 3) in the Municipal Building is small but carries a solid selection (and is still the only store we've seen that sells old taxicab medallions). **The Civil Service Bookstore** (Map 3) has all the study guides you'll need when you want to change careers and start driving a bus. **The United Nations Bookshop** (Map 13) has a great range of international and governmental titles. **The New York Transit Museum Gallery Annex & Store** (Map 13) at Grand Central also has an excellent range of books on NYC.

SPECIALTY

Books of Wonder (Map 9) in Chelsea has long been a downtown haven for children's books. For mysteries, **The Mysterious Bookshop** (Map 2) slakes the need for the whodunit. **The Drama Book Shop** (Map 12) is a great source for books on acting and the theater. **Bluestockings** (Map 4) is the epicenter for radical and feminist literature. Professional and amateur chefs turn to **Bonnie Slotnick** (Map 5) and **Kitchen Arts and Letters** (Map 17). **La Casa Azul Bookstore** (Map 17) adds much needed lit cred to East Harlem, offering adult and kids books in Spanish and English, an art gallery, and a lovely backyard.

BROOKLYN

Several neighborhoods in Brooklyn have great bookstores with lots of local (but well -known!) author readings, such as **Spoonbill & Sugartown** (Map 29) in Williamsburg, **Word** (Map 28) in Greenpoint, **Greenlight Bookstore** (Map 31) in Fort Greene, and **Book Court** (Map 32) in Cobble Hill. powerHouse Arena in DUMBO is a great destination for art books.

READINGS

Anyone can read great authors, but New Yorkers have ample opportunities to meet them as well. The four-story **Barnes & Noble** (Map 9) in Union Square regularly hosts major writers. **Housing Works Used Book Cafe** (Map 6) also draws some big names. And **McNally Jackson** (Map 6) in Nolita is another spot known for hosting great author events. Nearly all bookstores present readings, even if irregularly; check a store's Web page for listings. Even bars have taken a literary turn for the better: **KGB Bar** (Map 6) features fiction, poetry, and nonfiction readings each week. In Brooklyn, **Pete's Candy Store** (Map 29) and its weekly reading series are a good bet for your weekly dose of literature.

So long as there are adventurous artists putting on plays in abandoned storefronts and opportunistic real estate developers knocking down beautiful old theaters to put up hotels, the New York theater scene will always be adding a few venues here and deleting a few venues there. What remains constant is that on any given night there are at least dozens, and more often hundreds, of live theater performances to be seen. And the best ones are not always the most expensive.

Broadway (i.e., theaters in the Times Square vicinity that hold at least 500 people) still has the reputation of being the place to see American theater at its finest, but the peculiar fact of the matter is that there is much more money to be gained by appealing to the infrequent theater goer than there is by trying to please the connoisseur. As a result, shows that are looked down on, if not despised, by many lovers of the theater wind up selling out for years (Mamma Mia, anyone?), while more ambitious, artistically admired plays and musicals struggle to find an audience. Check out theater chat boards like BroadwayWorld.com and TalkinBroadway.com to see what the people who see everything have to say.

Nobody gets famous doing live theater anymore, so if you've never heard of the actor whose name is twinkling in lights chances are that person has the stage experience and acting chops to keep you enthralled for two and a half hours, unlike the big name celebrities who make their stage acting debuts in starring roles they're only sometimes somewhat prepared for. Of course, there are also the big-time actors with extensive stage credits who come back to Broadway regularly after becoming famous; you've got to admire anyone who willingly dives back into the grind of eight performances a week. Many great performers work Off-Broadway (Manhattan theaters seating 100–499 people) where the writing and directing are actually more important than spectacle and scores made up of classic pop songs. Off-Off Broadway (fewer than 100 seats) is a terrific grab bag of both beginners and seasoned pros doing material that is often unlikely to draw in masses. And tickets are pretty cheap, too.

TheaterMania.com keeps an extensive list of just about every show in New York, with direct links to the websites that sell tickets. Many shows offer a limited number of inexpensive standing room and/or same-day rush tickets. A detailed directory of such offers can be found at TalkinBroadway.com.

Thousands of same-day tickets for Broadway and Off-Broadway shows are sold for 20%–50% off at the TKTS booths in Times Square (long lines), at the South Street Seaport (shorter lines), and Downtown Brooklyn (which sells tickets to matinee performances a day in advance). They take cash, traveler's checks, and credit cards. Check for hours and to see what's been recently available at www.tdf.org. Don't expect to get a bargain for the top-selling hits, but most shows use this booth at some time or another. You can also download discount coupons at Playbill.com that you can use to get seats in advance.

The dirty little secret of New York theatre is that free tickets for high-quality shows are abundantly available through organizations that specialize in "dressing the house" for productions that depend more on word of mouth than expensive advertising costs. By giving a yearly membership fee to AudienceExtras.com or Play-By-Play.com, you can check your computer 24-hours a day to find free tickets (there's a small per-ticket service charge) for a dozen or so Off-, Off-Off-, and sometimes Broadway shows available at the last minute. That dinky little play in some church basement that you went to on a whim might wind up being the next great American classic.

Keep an eye out for shows by these lesser-known companies: The award-winning Classical Theatre of Harlem (www.classicaltheatreof-harlem.org) has earned a reputation for mounting exciting, edgy revivals of classics from Shakespeare and Brecht, as well as solid productions from more recent greats such as

August Wilson and Melvin Van Peebles. A multicultural company that frequently casts against racial type, they draw a youthful audience with imaginative interpretations.

The Mint Theatre Company (Map 11) (www.minttheater.org) specializes in reviving Broadway plays from the past they call "worthy, but neglected." In their tiny space you'll see interesting comedies and dramas from the likes of A. A. Milne, Edith Wharton, and Thomas Wolfe played traditionally with sets and costumes that really make you feel like you're watching a production from over 50 years ago.

Musicals Tonight! does the same kind of thing with forgotten musicals, only presenting them in low budgeted, but highly energized, staged readings. Nowadays most musicals revived on Broadway are revised and updated to the point where they lose their authenticity. But if you're in the mood to see what an Irving Berlin ragtime show from 1915 was really like, or if you want to see a Cole Porter tuner from the '30s with all of the dated topical references that confused audiences even back then, Musicals Tonight! serves up the past as it really was written. And check for their special concerts where Broadway understudies sing songs from the roles they are currently covering. Shows take place at the **Lion Theatre** (Map 11).

Broadway insiders know that Monday nights, when most shows are dark, is often the hottest night of the week for

entertainment. That's when performers use their night off to partake in benefits and special events. Consistently among the best are shows from Scott Siegel's Broadway By The Year series at Town Hall (Map 12) (www. thetownhall.org). Each one-night concert is packed with theater and cabaret stars singing hits and obscurities introduced on Broadway in one selected year. Siegel also produces Broadway Unplugged at Town Hall, a concert of theater performers singing showtunes without amplification. The atmosphere is like a sports event, with the audience wildly cheering each naturally voiced solo.

Elsewhere, *Pearl Theatre Company* (www.pearltheatre.org) (Map 11) has been mounting kick-ass productions of classics by Shakespeare, Moliere, Sheridan, Williams and the like since 1984. Horse Trade (www. horsetrade.info) produces a crazy assortment of readings, workshops, burlesque performances, and full - out productions in the East Village at venues like *The Kraine Theater* (Map 6). The multi-arts center *HERE* (Map 5) (www.here.org) not only houses two small theaters, but it also has an amazing gallery space and a cozy cafe/bar—perfect for pre- or post-show drinks.

Located in a former school on First Avenue and 9th Street in the East Village, *P.S. 122* (Map 7) (www. ps122.org) is a not-for-profit arts center serving New York City's dance and performance community. Shows rotate through on a regular basis, so check the website for the latest schedule. The outdoor *Delacorte Theater* (Map 15) in Central Park hosts performances only during the summer months. Tickets to the ridiculously popular and free Shakespeare in the Park performances are given away at noon at the Delacorte and also at the *Public Theater* (Map 6) on the day of each performance. Hopefully, you enjoy camping because people line up for days in their tents and sleeping bags just to secure a ticket!

Just on the other side of the Manhattan Bridge in Brooklyn is the world famous *Brooklyn Academy of Music* (Map 31). A thriving urban arts center, BAM brings domestic and international performing arts and film to Brooklyn. The center is home to multiple venues of various sizes, including the Harvey and Fisher Theaters, the Howard Gilman Opera House, the Bam Rose Cinemas, and the BAMcafe, a restaurant and live music venue. Our favorite season is the Next Wave, an annual three-month celebration of cutting-edge dance, theater, music, and opera. As an alternative to BAM, *St. Ann's Warehouse* (Map 30) in DUMBO also produces exciting cutting-edge work. Finally, there's this place called Lincoln Center you might have heard of...it's got a few things going on generally as well (see the Lincoln Center page in Parks & Places for a full description).

THE METROPOLITAN MUSEUM OF ART

GENERAL INFORMATION

NFT MAP: 15
ADDRESS: 1000 FIFTH AVE AT 82ND ST
PHONE: 212-535-7710
WEBSITE: WWW.METMUSEUM.ORG OR @METMUSEUM
HOURS: SUN-THURS: 10 AM–5:30 PM; FRI & SAT: 10 AM–9 PM; CLOSED
THANKSGIVING DAY, DECEMBER 25, JANUARY 1, AND FIRST MONDAY
IN MAY.
ADMISSION: A SUGGESTED $25 DONATION FOR ADULTS, $12 FOR
STUDENTS, AND $17 FOR SENIOR CITIZENS.

OVERVIEW

The Metropolitan Museum of Art is touted as the largest and most comprehensive museum in the Western hemisphere. Established by a group of American businessmen, artists, and thinkers back in 1870, the museum was created to preserve and stimulate appreciation for some of the greatest works of art in history.

In the first few years of its existence, the museum moved from its original location at 681 Fifth Avenue to the Douglas Mansion at 128 W 14th Street, and then finally to its current Central Park location in 1880. Calvert Vaux and Jacob Wrey Mould designed the museum's Gothic Revival red-brick facade, which was later remodeled in 1926 into the grand, white-columned front entrance that you see today. Part of the original facade was left intact and can still be seen from the Robert Lehman Wing looking toward the European Sculpture and Decorative Arts galleries.

The Met's annual attendance reaches over 4 million visitors who flock to see the more than 2 million works of art housed in the museum's permanent collection. You could visit the museum many times and not see more than a small portion of the permanent collection. The vast paintings anthology had a modest beginning in 1870 with a small donation of 174 European paintings and has now swelled to include works spanning 5,000 years of world culture, from the prehistoric to the present and from every corner of the globe.

The Met is broken down into a series of smaller museums within each building. For instance, the American Wing contains the most complete accumulation of American paintings, sculpture, and decorative arts, including period rooms offering a look at domestic life throughout the nation's history. The Egyptian collection is the finest in the world outside of Cairo, and the Islamic art exhibition remains unparalleled, as does the mass of 2,500 European paintings and Impressionist and Post-Impressionist works. The permanent gallery of Islamic art underwent renovations in 2008, following the 10-15 year renovation of the Greek & Roman collection. The redesigned galleries display works that have been in storage for decades, assuring even the most frequent visitor something fresh to check out including the museum's newly restored, world-famous, non-gas-guzzling Etruscan chariot.

Other major collections include the arms and armor, Asian art, costumes, European sculpture and decorative arts, medieval and Renaissance art, musical instruments, drawings, prints, ancient antiquities from around the world, photography, and modern art. Add to this the many special exhibits and performances the Met offers throughout the year, and you have a world-class museum with Central Park as its backyard.

This is a massive museum and seating can be difficult to find during busy weekends. When you need a break from all of the culture, sit down for a snack in the American Wing Café or lunch in the cafeteria. Do a triple-dollar-sign splurge and eat in the Members Dining Room overlooking the park. In the summer climb up to the Roof Garden Café for a glass of wine and the most beautiful view of Central Park that your lack of money can buy.

THE GREATEST HITS

You can, of course, spend countless hours at the Met. Pick any style of art and chances are you will find a piece here. But if you're rushed for time, check out the sublime space that houses the Temple of Dendur in the Sackler Wing, the elegant Frank Lloyd Wright Room in the American Wing, the fabulous Tiffany Glass and Tiffany Mosaics, also in the American Wing, the choir screen in the Medieval Sculpture Hall, the Caravaggios and Goyas in the Renaissance Rooms, the Picassos and Pollocks in Modern Art, and that huge canoe in Arts of Africa and Oceania. For a moment of tranquility, visit the beautiful Chinese Garden Court in the Asian galleries. When it's open, we highly recommend the Roof Garden, which has killer views of Central Park as a side dish to cocktails and conversation. When it's not, check out seasonal specials like the Christmas "Angel" Tree and Neapolitan Baroque Créche, an annual favorite set up in front of the medieval choir screen.

HOW TO GET THERE– MASS TRANSIT

Subway: Take the 4, 5, 6 to the 86th Street stop and walk three blocks west to Fifth Avenue and four blocks south to 82nd Street.

Bus: Take the bus along Fifth Avenue (from uptown locations) to 82nd Street or along Madison Avenue (from downtown locations) to 83rd Street.

THE MUSEUM OF MODERN ART (MOMA)

GENERAL INFORMATION

NFT MAP: 12
ADDRESS: 11 W 53RD ST
PHONE: 212-708-9400
WEBSITE: WWW.MOMA.ORG OR @MUSEUMMODERNART
HOURS: 10:30 AM–5:30 PM (FRI UNTIL 8 PM); CLOSED THANKSGIVING AND DECEMBER 25
ADMISSION: $25 FOR ADULTS, $18 FOR SENIORS, $14 FOR STUDENTS; FREE TO MEMBERS AND CHILDREN UNDER 16 ACCOMPANIED BY AN ADULT

OVERVIEW

The Museum of Modern Art opened in 1929, back when impressionism and surrealism were truly modern art. Originally in the Heckscher Building at 730 Fifth Avenue, MoMA moved to its current address on West 53rd Street in 1932. What started out as a townhouse eventually expanded into an enormous space, with new buildings and additions in 1939 (by Phillip L. Goodwin and Edward Durell Stone), 1953 (including a sculpture garden by Phillip Johnson), 1964 (another Johnson garden), and 1984 (by Cesar Pelli). During the summer of 2002, the museum closed its Manhattan location and moved temporarily to Sunnyside, Queens (MoMA's affiliate, MoMA PS1 remains a proud Queens institution). After a major expansion and renovation by Yoshio Taniguchi, MoMA reopened in September 2004.

After being re-Manhattanized, MoMA made waves when it became the first museum to break the $20 barrier–which sadly became all too common in the years since. If crowds on a typical Saturday afternoon are any indication, hefty entry fees are not keeping patrons away. Frequent flyers take note: If you plan to visit more than three times in a year, the yearly membership is the way to go. Plus, members get a 10% discount at MoMA stores, free tickets to all film screenings, and besides which, you're free to pop in whenever you want to see your favorite Picasso (or just use the restroom). For the best deal, visit the museum from 4–8 pm on Fridays when there is free admission–the crowds aren't as bad as you might think.

WHAT TO SEE

The fourth and fifth floors are where the big names reside–Johns, Pollock, Warhol (fourth floor), Braque, Cezanne, Dali, Duchamp, Ernst, Hopper, Kandinsky, Klee, Matisse, Miro, Monet, Picasso, Rosseau, Seurat, Van Gogh, and Wyeth (fifth floor). More recent works can be found in the contemporary gallery on the second floor. Special exhibitions are featured on the third and sixth floors. The surrealist collection is outstanding, but we've always suspected that MoMA has only a tiny fraction of its pop art on display. Well, you can't have everything...

Moving downstairs to the third floor, it's clear that the photography collection is, as always, one of the centerpieces of the museum and is highly recommended (although the Gursky pieces are actually dotted throughout the building). The architecture and design gallery showcases a range of cool consumer items, from chairs to cars to the first Mac computers, and is one of the most popular destinations in the museum.

BREAKDOWN OF THE SPACE

FLOOR ONE:
Lobby, Sculpture Garden, Museum Store, Restaurant

FLOOR TWO:
Contemporary Galleries, Media Gallery, Prints and Illustrated Books, Café

FLOOR THREE:
Architecture and Design, Drawing, Photography, Special Exhibitions

FLOOR FOUR:
Painting and Sculpture II

FLOOR FIVE:
Painting and Sculpture I, Café

FLOOR SIX:
Special Exhibitions

There are two theater levels below the first floor.

AMENITIES

Backpacks and large purses are not allowed in gallery spaces, and the free coat check can become messy when the check-in and check-out lines become intertwined. Leave large items (including laptops) at home. Bathrooms and water fountains are on all floors. We don't think that there are enough of them, and the bathrooms themselves are way too small to handle the crowds.

There are three places to get food in the museum, which has been elevated from the usual captive-audience fare by Danny Meyer's excellent Union Square Hospitality Group. Café 2, located on the second floor, offers a wide selection of small plates, sandwiches and panini, as well as above-average coffee drinks, beer and wine. Terrace 5 is a full -service overlooking the beautiful sculpture garden, has a la carte entrees and desserts, along with wine, cocktails, coffee, and tea. Both cafes open half an hour after the museum opens its doors and close half an hour before the museum closes.

The ultimate museum dining experience, The Modern (www.themodernnyc.com) boasts three New York Times stars and one Michelin star. It has two main rooms—the Dining Room overlooking the sculpture garden, and a more casual Bar Room. An outdoor terrace is also made available when the weather permits. The Modern serves French and New American food and hubba-hubba tasting menus. The Modern is open beyond museum hours, with the Dining Room serving dinner until 10:30 pm Monday–Saturday. The Bar Room is open continuously 11:30 am–10:30 pm daily (9:30 pm Sundays). There's a separate street entrance to allow diners access to The Modern after the museum closes.

THE AMERICAN MUSEUM OF NATURAL HISTORY

GENERAL INFORMATION

NFT MAP: 14
ADDRESS: CENTRAL PARK WEST AT 79TH ST
PHONE: 212-769-5100
WEBSITE: WWW.AMNH.ORG OR @AMNH
HOURS: DAILY, 10:00 AM–5:45 PM; CLOSED THANKSGIVING DAY & DECEMBER 25.
ADMISSION: SUGGESTED GENERAL ADMISSION IS $22 FOR ADULTS, $12.50 FOR CHILDREN (2–12), AND $17 FOR SENIOR CITIZENS AND STUDENTS. SPECIAL EXHIBITIONS, IMAX MOVIES, AND THE SPACE SHOW ARE EXTRA; PACKAGES ARE AVAILABLE. FREE TO MEMBERS.

OVERVIEW

Admit it. You secretly TiVo the Discovery Channel and the History Channel. You've even watched one—if not several—episodes of Star Trek. Something about African beetles, famous dead guys, and the unknown universe strokes your inner Einstein. Focus your microscope on this one, smarty-pants: the American Museum of Natural History, a paradise for geeks and aspiring geeks alike, not to mention good old nature lovers.

Decades before anyone knew what an atom was, and when relativity was just a twinkle in Einstein's eye, Albert Smith Bickmore established the AMNH. Completed in 1869, the museum held its first exhibition in the Central Park Arsenal a few years later, garnering enough respect to acquire space along classy Central Park West. Architects Calvert Vaux and J. Wrey Mould designed the new, posh building on limited Benjamins and opened it to the public in 1877. Key additions followed: The Hayden Planetarium in 1935, the Theodore Roosevelt Memorial Hall and Rotunda in 1936, and the Rose Center for Earth and Space in 2000.

As Saturday morning museum-going ritual dictates, it's going to be painfully crowded. On those days, you dodge out-of-towners, eyes wide, mouths gaping. It's much the same on weekdays with rowdy school kids on field trips. How to avoid the Excedrin-necessitating atmosphere? Two words: permanent collection. The amazing series of wildlife dioramas even inspired an entire Hollywood movie (albeit not a great one, by adult standards). Don't expect to see any PETA supporters in these halls though.

THE GREATEST HITS

Five floors of star-lovin', mammal -gazin', bird-watchin', fossil -fuelin' science await. Rain forest fever? Check out the Hall of Biodiversity. Didn't understand why that movie was called *The Squid and The Whale*? See the giant squid get his dimly lit comeuppance in the Milstein Hall of Ocean Life. Celebrity astrophysicist Neil deGrasse Tyson is the voice behind the *Dark Universe* space show. For more instant thrills, check out the gigantic meteorites at the Arthur Ross Hall of Meteorites, or the five-story-tall dinosaur display in the Theodore Roosevelt Rotunda; it's the largest freestanding beast in the world. The AMNH also produces spectacular IMAX features, a great alternative to the museum's amazing but creepy taxidermy. The Hall of Gems houses the Star of India, the largest star sapphire in the world. Finally, in the Butterfly Conservatory, tropical butterflies flit all around you from, you guessed it, all over the world. It's enough to put TiVo on pause.